CURRICULUM

ACTION

RESEARCH

A HANDBOOK OF METHODS
AND RESOURCES FOR THE
REFLECTIVE PRACTITIONER

JAMES McKERNAN

KOGAN
PAGE

For Mary and Ben: loving parents, great teachers

First published in 1991

Apart from any fair dealing for the purposes of research or private study, or criticism or review, as permitted under the Copyright, Designs and Patents Act, 1988, this publication may only be reproduced, stored or transmitted, in any form or by any means, with the prior permission in writing of the publishers, or in the case of reprographic reproduction in accordance with the terms of licences issued by the Copyright Licensing Agency. Enquiries concerning reproduction outside those terms should be sent to the publishers at the undermentioned address:

Kogan Page Limited
120 Pentonville Road
London N1 9JN

© James McKernan, 1991

British Library Cataloguing in Publication Data

A CIP record for this book is available from the British Library.

ISBN 0 74940 411 6

Typeset by The Castlefield Press Ltd, Wellingborough, Northants in Melior.
Printed and bound in Great Britain by Biddles Ltd, Guildford.

Contents

Acknowledgements   ix
Preface   xi
Introduction   xiii

**PART 1: CURRICULUM ACTION RESEARCH –
THE CONTEXT**   1

**Chapter 1: Action Research – Historical and Philosophical
Background**   3
Action research   3
Historical and philosophical foundations of action research   8
Typologies and models of action research   15
Conclusions   33

Chapter 2: The Teacher as Researcher and Professional   35
The school as a centre for inquiry: towards a new
professionalism   36
The teacher as researcher: the autonomy of inquiry   38
Constraints on curriculum action research   44
The teacher as a reflective practitioner   46
The teacher as a reflective professional   47
Promoting teacher professionalism   48
Education and teaching as a profession   50
Action research and the reflective-teacher professional   53
Conclusions   55

PART 2: ACTION RESEARCH METHODOLOGY   57

Chapter 3: Observational and Narrative Research Methods   59
Narrative data   59
Participant observation   63
School and classroom observation: aide-mémoire   65
Anecdotal records   67
Short action research case reports   70
Analytic memos   72
The case study   74
Case records/case data   82
Diary/journal   84

Contents

Dialogue journals   89
Field notes   93
Stream of behaviour chronicles: the specimen record or
shadow study   97
Photography   100
Videotape recording   102
Audio/tape-slide recording   106
Checklists   108
Personal action logs   111
Interaction analysis protocols   115
Rating scales   119

**Chapter 4: Non-Observational, Survey and Self-Report
          Techniques**   **124**
Attitude scales   124
Questionnaires   126
The interview   129
Key informant interview technique   132
Projective techniques   134
Life/career history technique   136
Physical traces   140

Chapter 5: Discourse Analysis and Problem-Solving Methods   142
Dilemma analysis   142
Constraints analysis   146
Content analysis   148
Document analysis   150
Personal time analysis   153
Sociometric analysis   156
Episode analysis   162
Action inquiry seminar   165
Brainstorming   168
Group discussion   171
The problem survey   175
Small groups: the deliberative working party   179
Neutral chairperson   183

**Chapter 6: Critical-Reflective and Evaluative Research
          Methods**   **189**
Triangulation   189
Quadrangulation   192
Collegial review   196
Lecture feedback   199
Lesson profiles   200
Student course/teacher evaluation form   202

Curriculum criticism   206
Discourse evaluation   210
Critical trialling   216

PART 3: ANALYSIS AND ISSUES IN ACTION RESEARCH   **221**

Chapter 7: Analysing Action Research Data   **223**
Cycles of inquiry   223
Getting started   225
Stages of data analysis   226
Conducting data analysis: some guidelines   227
Analytic induction   232
Constant comparative method   233
Concluding comments   234

Chapter 8: Towards Critical Communities: Networks,
      Dissemination and the Ethics of Action Research **235**
Collaborative networks   235
Towards a critical community of discourse   239
Supporting and maintaining a project   242
Dissemination: the written report   244
Ethical issues and action research   249

Epilogue   **251**

References   **254**
Author Index   **267**
Subject Index   **271**

Acknowledgements

Action research is research by practitioners to solve their own problems and to improve practice. It is a growing form of professional development for the reflective practitioner. As a social activity it is necessarily collaborative: involving many individuals. Thus a book about action research owes an enormous debt to those individuals. This work has emerged from a dialogue with students, teachers, academics and others in several countries, and through experimentation in schools, universities and other educational settings over a number of years. Action research changed dramatically during that time, particularly in the continuing development of the 'practical' and emerging 'critical' conceptions, and the almost complete abandonment of 'scientific' action research.

My early introductions to curriculum and action research were presented by Malcolm Skilbeck, Hugh Sockett, and David Jenkins, all colleagues at the Ulster University, Northern Ireland in the 1970s, where we applied curriculum action research to the problems of intergroup education for tolerance and mutual understanding, through the Schools Cultural Studies Project. I owe an enormous debt to the SCSP teachers who tolerated my ideas and responded generously in kind. The curriculum can be a humanizing influence and an intelligent response to intergroup conflict. It was this relationship between social research, the curriculum and cultural conflict which attracted me to action research, just as it was for Kurt Lewin with his *Resolving Social Conflicts.*

The work of the late Lawrence Stenhouse, and his colleagues at the Centre for Applied Research in Education, University of East Anglia, particularly John Elliott, has been inspirational. I owe an incalculable personal and intellectual debt to John Elliott for his continuing encouragement, collegiality and support: he has done more than anyone to champion the 'teacher-as-researcher' movement.

Colleagues in the USA and Australia have been helpful. Edmund C. Short encouraged my writing and suggested that I should organize the International Symposium on Teacher As Researcher at the 1989 American Educational Research Association (AERA) Meeting, and Ortrun Zuber-Skerritt organized the First World Congress on Action Research at Griffith University, Brisbane, Australia, where I was invited to speak in July 1990.

A sabbatical year as a Fulbright Scholar in the United States in

Acknowledgements

1985 signalled the serious beginning of this book. Thanks are owed to University College Dublin, particularly to Desmond Swan and Joseph McHale and to the Department of Foreign Affairs, Ireland, for facilitating that visit. Courtney Cazden of the Graduate School of Education, Harvard University; James Block of the Graduate School of Education, University of California, at Santa Barbara; and Allan A. Glatthorn, then at the Graduate School of Education, University of Pennsylvania, were outstanding hosts in providing access to resources, and for their encouragement to move this project forward.

I am especially grateful to Allan Glatthorn who has remained a loyal and critical colleague and mentor; the best sort to have. Postgraduate students in University College Dublin, particularly Shirley Brook, have acted as a critical group for the testing of many of the ideas contained herein.

Gerald McConeghy and John Connelly of Philadelphia remain inspirational as friends and teachers. In Ireland, Rev. Eustas Ó hÉideáin, O.P., and James Russell taught me much about educational research. Luke Murtagh provided a school base for research and development work in Tipperary. Colleagues in the Educational Studies Association of Ireland, in particular John Coolahan, Donal Mulcahy and Don Herron have been a well of support.

I wish to thank Margaret Wilsman, Susan Florio-Ruane, Alan Robinson and John Elliott for help with the international survey of constraints on action research.

For permission to reproduce material I thank John Elliott, Ned Flanders, David Ebbutt, Richard Brandt, Don Herron, Allan Glatthorn, Michael Foster of the Tavistock Institute, Plenum Press and Deakin University Press. For critical comment I am grateful to Joy Peyton, John Elliott and Richard Winter.

Finally, I wish to acknowledge the sacrifices, understanding and love I have received from my wife, Valerie, and my son, Ross, aged nine, who has been my constant companion and teacher. My parents, Mary and Bernard, and my brothers and sisters, have never faltered in their love, interest and encouragement.

Preface

In recent years there have been repeated calls for educators to become researchers and self-reflective practitioners. Despite a growing international movement, few have identified a coherent and comprehensive research methodology for 'doing' action research. This book has been written chiefly as a guide for practitioners to research their own settings in a manner in which they can not only solve practical curriculum problems but also learn from their experience of research. I have tried to make both the theory and the principles of procedure for conducting action research available as a support for the practitioner by providing extensive coverage of the nature and dynamics of action research and by offering an adequate set of references to guide further reading. Additionally, it demands experimentation and mature reflection if it is to be understood. The ability to both produce and understand research is of singular importance to a profession. I believe that action research is a good horse to back in the in-service education of teachers.

There are also personal reasons for writing this book. I have been close to conflict most of my life: growing up in the North Philadelphia terraces where racism and prejudice were rife; doing military service in Vietnam; researching the Irish 'Travellers', a nomadic gypsy-like race much discriminated against by the majority population; working on peace education for mutual understanding across the sectarian divide as a curriculum development officer in Northern Ireland; working as a prison teacher of the young men whose lives have been destroyed by Ireland's 'Troubles'; and with my meagre attempts to involve teachers in action research and curriculum development. A new project for West Bank Palestinian schools beckons at this moment.

Since 1980 I have been involved in teacher education in University College Dublin, where I give courses in curriculum studies and a practicum in educational action research. It has been from this life history of teaching, curriculum development for cultural reconstruction and my work with postgraduate teachers and administrators that my interest in action research derived.

This book is not a blueprint for success: it invites a critical response, and it is offered as a unique contribution to the profession.

James McKernan
University College Dublin
March 1991

Introduction

This book is intended as a practical guide for teachers, administrators and others interested in the conduct of action research to improve curriculum in classrooms and other educational settings. It is thus a book concerned with how to do action research. It addresses issues and questions concerned with the evolution and status of curriculum action research, data collection strategies, modes of organizing and analysing data, presenting and disseminating results, and the ethics of action researchers. The main body of the text outlines 48 research techniques and resources; while some traditional methods are included, such as diaries and interviews, the work introduces a number of novel and experimental techniques for doing action research: *short action research reports, episode analysis, constraints analysis, personal time analysis, problem surveys, quadrangulation, curriculum criticism, discourse evaluation,* and *critical trialling.* These techniques are described here for the first time; they invite the critical response of practitioners and are offered in the spirit of pushing forward the methodological boundaries of the action research community.

The central thesis is that curriculum research and development belong essentially to the practitioner as part of an emerging extended professional role. The book is aimed at several audiences: practising teachers and administrators, participants engaged in inservice programmes and curriculum development projects, graduate students of curriculum, scholars, and external educational researchers. As such, the work attempts to bridge the theory-practice divide by demonstrating how inquiry can inform theory and improve practice. The book can serve as a resource handbook for the practitioner, or as a textbook for the student of curriculum studies.

There is an urgent need for a handbook due to the current upsurge of interest in curriculum action research — a phase that may be interpreted as a logical outcome of the curriculum development and research movement which began with a concern for the production of materials and has now settled upon teacher development and professional behaviour.

The work has developed due to a lack of appropriate resources for teaching the methodology of action research. There is a major gap in the literature of curriculum research techniques which is only now beginning to be filled (see Nixon, 1981; Hopkins, 1985; Walker, 1985; Hustler, Cassidy and Cuff, 1986; Goswami and Stillman, 1987; Mohr and Maclean, 1987; Winter, 1987 and 1989; Gregory, 1988;

Lomax, 1989), yet these works are not comprehensive of the range of research techniques available to the practitioner. Texts related to research methods (McCall and Simmons, 1969; Schatzman and Strauss, 1973; Goetz and LeCompte, 1984) presume a thorough grounding in social science literature, particularly qualitative traditions of ethnography which are often perceived as alien and exotic for curriculum practitioners. The research concerns of those engaged in school-based curriculum development have tended to develop parallel to those of social scientists and are more centrally addressed to issues concerning pupil, programme and teacher self-evaluation. The present work attempts to describe how practitioners can inquire into pressing day-to-day practical problems in their attempts to solve these difficulties, and thus improve the curriculum in a professional way.

This book is an attempt to fuse styles and techniques now confined to various research camps, and thus to weld together work from qualitative social science inquiry, standard social survey type research, with that usually undertaken in curriculum evaluation and classroom action research.

The book is in three parts. Part 1 contains two chapters and sets the context and background to the development of the 'teacher as researcher' tradition, taking account of historical developments in curriculum research and examining the underlying philosophical traditions and ideologies associated with action research as a discernible paradigm, while contributing to the theory-building process. Chapter 1 provides a rationale for, and a broad overview of, the origins and types of action research. Chapter 2 contributes to the discussion of the teacher as a researcher and reflective practitioner, and offers a code of practice or set of criteria to ensure professionalism.

Part 2 consists of four chapters dealing with reactive (obtrusive) and non-reactive (unobtrusive) research methods. Thus, Chapters 3 to 6 deal with the central methodological questions of research procedures and describe the variety of techniques and methods of doing action research in educational settings. This is the heart and main thrust of the book: the aim is modest — to provide practitioners and students of curriculum with access to techniques for researching their own behavioural settings so that they can solve practical problems and improve their professional practice.

Chapter 3 examines observational research methods, including narrative approaches and more structured category observational systems. Chapter 4 explores some non-observational styles of inquiry, including surveys, attitude scales, interviews, etc. Chapter 5 focuses on modes of analysing discourse and text data, e.g. document analysis, content analysis and episode-narrative discourse, and on the use of instructional-pedagogical techniques to elicit data in action research, such as 'neutral chairman', discussion and other methods. Chapter 6 concludes the methodological section with a discussion of research techniques that focus upon the critical, reflective and evaluative aspects of action inquiry, and offers strategic suggestions for the use of 'triangulation', 'curriculum criticism', 'collegial review' and other techniques that can be used so that practitioners may learn from reflection on action.

Part 3 contains two chapters dealing with problems and issues in the conduct of action research. Chapter 7 discusses the processing and analysis of action research data. Conceptual schemes for the analysis of qualitative data are presented and practical guidelines are offered for the treatment and interpretation of action research data.

Chapter 8 addresses the issue of dissemination of research findings within the critical community of action researchers. Special attention is devoted to the idea of 'collaborative networks' and 'critical communities of discourse' in action inquiry. Strategic suggestions are made concerning the maintenance and sustenance of project communities and the ultimate dissemination of action research findings. Finally, attention is given to the ethics of action research and a number of ethical criteria for the conduct of inquiry are discussed.

The book offers: a history of action research; a rationale for the teacher as researcher; a set of criteria to ensure professionalism in teaching; a variety of reactive and non-reactive action research methods and resources; a note on data analysis; and advice on the maintenance of a community of discourse. It is essentially an 'operator's manual' for educators and other practitioners who wish to learn from their inquiries and improve their practice through research. I hope that the book will be useful to all reflective practitioners.

PART 1

Curriculum Action Research — The Context

The central thesis of this work is that the curriculum can be improved through action research and that teachers and other practitioners are best placed to conduct such inquiry. The main thrust of the book is devoted to the development of the *research methodology* by which this task can be sustained.

Part 1 sets the context for the development of action research and, more precisely, the impact of the reflective professional in educational action research. Chapter 1 explores the historical and philosophical foundations of the action research movement — suggesting sustained scientific problem solving as a major feature of action research that extends from the influence of the nineteenth-century Science in Education movement up to the present time, and noting shifts in emphasis and philosophy, including scientific, practical-deliberative initiatives, and the more recent impact of critical-emancipatory action research. Second, it outlines various attempts at theorizing about action research and offers a new model to guide inquiry. Finally, it offers up a portrait of the countenance of action research by defining a number of concepts. Chapter 2 discusses the teacher as a researcher and a professional, and offers criteria for a professional code of ethics to govern practice.

1 Action Research — Historical and Philosophical Background

Research that produces nothing but books will not suffice.
Kurt Lewin (1948) *Resolving Social Conflicts*

The action research movement offers practitioners a research stance towards their work and is now enjoying a resurgence of interest as practitioners continue to expand their notion of what counts as good curriculum research. Action research offers exciting new beginnings for the development of the curriculum, the profession and the person. The importance of the *practical* contributions that can be made through this form of inquiry, and the methodology of research and logic in pre-service training and inservice education of practitioners, should never be underestimated. Action research, as a teacher-researcher movement, is at once an ideology which instructs us that practitioners can be producers as well as consumers of curriculum inquiry; it is a practice in which no distinction is made between the practice being researched and the process of researching it. That is, teaching is not one activity and inquiring into it another. The ultimate aim of inquiry is understanding; and understanding is the basis of action for improvement.

This chapter has three aims: first, to define and offer a rationale for action research; second, to examine and explore the evolution of separate conceptions of action research; and finally, to review theories, models and concepts that disclose the 'countenance' or character of contemporary curriculum action.

ACTION RESEARCH

Action research has attempted to render the problematic social world understandable as well as to improve the quality of life in social settings. Action research has been used in industrial, health, educational, and community behavioural settings (Clark, 1976; Marsh et al., 1984; McKernan, 1988a; Selander, 1987; Wallace, 1987). Curriculum has no monopoly on action research.

The aim of action research, as opposed to much traditional or fundamental research, is to solve the immediate and pressing day-to-day problems of practitioners. Elliott (1981) has defined action research as 'the study of a social situation with a view to improving the quality of action within it'. Action research is carried out by practitioners seeking to improve their understanding of events, situations and problems so as to increase the effectiveness of their practice. Such research does not have the writing of research reports and other publications as a primary goal.

Action research aims at feeding the practical judgement of actors in problematic situations. The validity of the concepts, models and results it generates depends not so much on scientific tests of truth as on their utility in helping practitioners to act more effectively, skilfully and intelligently. Theories are not validated independently of practice and then applied to curriculum; rather they are validated through practice. Action research is thus grounded curriculum theory.

One of the most cited definitions is that of Rapoport (Rapoport, 1970:499): 'action research aims to contribute both to the practical concerns of people in an immediate problematic situation and to the goals of social science by joint collaboration within a mutually acceptable ethical framework.' Rapoport sees action research as a special type of applied research which involves participants experiencing problems directly in the search for a solution and also feeds social science with some theoretical pay-off.

Halsey (1972) defined action research as a 'small-scale intervention in the functioning of the real world . . . and the close examination of the effects of such interventions'.

Action inquiry is often undertaken to improve social settings, as is evident in Bogdan and Biklen's (1982:215) definition: 'Action research is the systematic collection of information that is designed to bring about social change.'

Carr and Kemmis (1986:162) postulate a definition rooted in critical-emancipatory terms: 'Action research is simply a form of self-reflective enquiry undertaken by participants in social situations in order to improve the rationality and justice of their own practices, their understanding of these practices, and the situations in which the practices are carried out.'

A curriculum is at base an educational proposal, or hypothesis, which invites a critical response from those who implement it. A curriculum then invites teachers and others to adopt a research stance towards their work, suggesting rigorous reflection on practice as the basis of further professional development. Stenhouse defined research as 'systematic and sustained inquiry, planned and self-critical, which is subjected to public criticism and to empirical tests where these are appropriate' (Stenhouse, 1981:113). The key idea is that each classroom or work space becomes a laboratory for testing, empirically, hypotheses and proposals that are the planned and implemented curriculum. Every practitioner is thus a member of a critical community of educational scientists.

A minimal definition of action research would be:

action research is the reflective process whereby in a given problem area, where one wishes to improve practice or personal understanding, inquiry is carried out by the practitioner — first, to clearly define the problem; secondly, to specify a plan of action — including the testing of hypotheses by application of action to the problem. Evaluation is then undertaken to monitor and establish the effectivness of the action taken. Finally , participants reflect upon, explain developments, and communicate these results to the community of action researchers. Action research is systematic self-reflective scientific inquiry by practitioners to improve practice.

This definition stresses two essential points: first, action research is rigorous, systematic inquiry through scientific procedures; and second, participants have critical-reflective ownership of the process and the results.

A rationale for action research

The rationale for action research rests, initially, on three pillars: first, that naturalistic settings are best studied and researched by those participants experiencing the problem; second, that behaviour is highly influenced by the naturalistic surroundings in which it occurs: and third, that qualitative methodologies are perhaps best suited for researching naturalistic settings. Taken as a triad, these hypotheses suggest a rationale in the form of a critical-participant observation mode of practitioner inquiry.

1. Teacher as researcher
Leading on from the belief that the participant is best placed to conduct inquiry into pressing professional problems, then it follows that practitioners must engage in curriculum inquiry to improve their art and practice. Research on this view is a form of self-critical inquiry.

It was not always considered so. Teachers and administrators with questions most often turn to outside professionally trained researchers skilled in social science discourse and methodology for answers. Some turn to philosophers and theologians for answers through the belief in *divine revelation* and *traditional authority*.

The most recent conception of teacher as researcher is that deriving from the naturalistic, 'field', or case study paradigm of research. It has arisen largely due to the failure of positivistic 'basic research' and conventional disciplines within the 'foundations of education', such as psychology, sociology, history and philosophy, to contribute meaningfully to questions concerning problems of practice in teaching and learning. Now, teacher education programmes are still highly dominated by the foundations of education but since the early 1970s this field has been on the decline, in Europe at least.

John Elliott (1987) reminds us that the ultimate test of the usefulness of the disciplines as sources of ideas is whether teachers can indeed use them to construct a workable theory of the case in question. The notion of 'workability' is instructive in the sense that not only is curriculum theory a goal, but because practical reflection should lead to an improved form of *human action*.

The present status of curriculum action research has arisen out of the problems met by teachers and curriculum collaborator-developers in trying to improve practice. It is more centrally focused upon improving the quality of human action and response than it is with formulating theories for action. One of the most interesting developments in the teacher-researcher movement is that it has been turned into a vehicle for the effective inservice education and training of practitioners and pre-service teachers. The disciplines have had to give way to a new field which is loosely held together as 'Curriculum Studies'. It would be a danger if it is only seen as another contributing 'discipline' taking a place alongside traditional foundation disciplines in education. The movement towards the 'practical' is now well under way with the seminal work of Schwab and Reid in curriculum philosophy; work at the Centre for Applied Research in Education at the University of East Anglia by Stenhouse, Elliott and MacDonald, most notably the Humanities and Ford Teaching Projects; the emerging 'critical' emancipatory style of teacher research advocated by Wilfred Carr in the UK and his co-author Stephen Kemmis in Australia; and the case study tradition of curriculum evaluation of folk like Lawrence Stenhouse at East Anglia, Robert Stake of the University of Illinois, and Elliot Eisner of Stanford.

The teacher as researcher has shifted in the past few decades from problem solving, using quantitative measurement tools, to naturalistic research, using descriptive-illuminative designs based on case study and social anthropological designs. More recently, the movement towards a practical theory has shifted to favour European critical theory as espoused by the 'Frankfurt School' of philosophy, most notably Hans Gadamer and Jurgen Habermas, thus lending a philosophical interpretive-reflective note to our text. This has appeared the natural direction to take given the emphasis on personal *understanding*. The search seems to be for the best models and theories of understanding, and hermeneutics and critical theory were likely candidates.

2. The naturalistic and practical perspective
We begin with the idea that human behaviour is highly influenced

by the surroundings in which it occurs. One must ask, 'How does the setting influence the actors? What roles, traditions and norms dictate regularities in behaviour?' Participants are aware of these norms and role expectations (Sarason, 1971) in the culture of the school. External researchers affect behaviour and interfere with the research setting. To counteract these effects unobtrusive methods have been advocated (Webb et al., 1966). A key premise therefore in the rationale is that *behaviour must be studied in the field* or, as they say, *in situ*, by the practitioner, who may be helped by a collaborating team.

3. The primacy of field study and qualitative methodology

Naturalistic field research seeks understanding and description while sacrificing some measurement and prediction. The emphasis is therefore on heuristics, realism and relevance. This type of work is known as '*ex post facto*' research. Some researchers of the symbolic inter-actionist and phenomenological persuasion would argue that one cannot understand human behaviour unless one understands the framework within which the actors construct their thoughts, beliefs and actions.

Naturalistic research refers to investigations of phenomena within and in relation to their naturally occuring contexts. The assumption is that there is some driving natural theory in the research setting which creates the order that we observe and which is independent from our theorizing. Barker (1965) has suggested that nature is the inducer and the researcher the transducer in this phenomenon. A major issue in field study work is the objectivity-subjectivity issue. Researchers need to find ways of reducing the role of bias and subjectivity — in devising a scheme for coding verbal behaviour in the classroom, for example. Yet it should be pointed out that coding schemes are arbitrary — any number could be adopted.

Traditional quantitative-empiricists would trust their senses as opposed to those of their subjects; while the qualitative participant observer would give primacy to the feelings, narrative and values of the subjects in the setting. It is not enough to collect facts and feelings — the researcher must come to see these through the eyes, and from standing in the shoes, of the subjects. The qualitative participant field study researcher allows the data to emerge on their own, without any preconceived theories or forced structures imposed on the study, and looks for meaning in the events.

Research is action research to the extent that it can solve practical problems. But one point seems crystal clear: practitioners must be engaged in curriculum research and have control over the process and results of such inquiry. The practitioner[1] is a participant

1. In this book the terms 'teacher' and 'practitioner' as researcher are used interchangeably — recognizing also that other 'practitioners' of curriculum have an action research remit, e.g. administrators, supervisors, etc.

observer and it ought to be difficult to deny the teacher research possibilities.

HISTORICAL AND PHILOSOPHICAL FOUNDATIONS OF ACTION RESEARCH

Action research has developed from a complex web of scientific and social enterprise. A number of writers (Chein, Cook and Harding, 1948) argue that Kurt Lewin was the 'founding father' of action research through his work in the Group Dynamics movement of the post-war reconstructionist period. Careful study of the literature (McKernan, 1988a) shows quite clearly and convincingly that action research is a root derivative of the 'scientific method' reaching back to the Science in Education movement of the late nineteenth century. There is some evidence of the use of action research by a host of social reformist initiatives prior to the Lewinian conceptualization (Collier, 1945; Corey, 1953; Lippitt and Radke, 1946). Collier used the idea and terminology prior to Lewin, and as US Commissioner on Indian Affairs (1933–1945) wrote:

> Since the findings of research must be carried into effect by the administrator and the layman, and must be criticized by them through their experience, the administrator and the layman must themselves participate creatively in the research impelled as it is from their own area of need. (Collier, 1945:276)

It is important to recognize these diverse strands in the evolution of action research and to appreciate fully that various principles and procedures have been employed throughout its long history. Action research is in a transient stage of redevelopment.

Action research originated in the USA and from the early years of the twentieth century recruited a large following (Wallace, 1987). Action research has been influenced by the historical and philosophical flavour of the following:

1. *The Science in Education movement* of the nineteenth and early twentieth century. Included here would be a whole cavalcade of books dealing with the scientfic method applied to education by Alexander Bain (Bain, 1879); Richard G. Boone, (Boone, 1904); and, notably, Burdette Ross Buckingham's *Research for Teachers* (Buckingham, 1926).
2. *Experimentalist* and *progressive* educational thought, partic- ularly the work of John Dewey (Dewey, 1910; 1929; 1938) who applied the inductive scientific method of problem solving as a logic for the solution of problems in such fields as aesthetics, philosophy, psychology and education. Indeed, his *stages of*

reflective thinking contain all the features of the scientific action research of the post-war reconstructionists like Hilda Taba and Stephen Corey. Teacher involvement in both curriculum research and development became more direct after 1930 as a result of two famous American projects: The Eight Year Study (Aiken, 1942) and The Southern Study (Jenkins et al., 1946). The latter project adopted an action research programme by having practitioners identify and solve problems of curriculum design and materials production through curriculum teams and workshops where the scientific method was rigorously employed as the work ethic.

3. *The Group Dynamics movement* in social psychology and human relations training. Just as social problems of poverty, housing and urban life gave rise to qualitative social inquiry in the nineteenth century (Webb and Webb, 1932), so did the swing come full circle again in the 1940s with the onslaught of war, problems of intergroup relations, social reconstruction, prejudice, and various other social problems which demanded a social science response. Out of this need to understand and solve social problems, practitioner inquiry was once again rediscovered and action research was seen as a credible response.

In the mid-1940s, Kurt Lewin discussed action research as a form of experimental inquiry based upon the study of groups experiencing problems (Lewin, 1946; 1948). Lewin argued that social problems should serve as the locus of social science research. Basic to Lewin's model is a view of research composed of action cycles including analysis, fact-finding, conceptualization, planning, implementation and evaluation of action (Lewin, 1947a; 1947b). Lazarsfeld and Reitz (1975) point out that Lewin used his social scientific expertise to help one of his students, Alfred Marrow, whose family owned a factory with morale problems. Lewin helped not only out of personal interest, but because of his belief in his theories and his desire to apply them to work situations — for Lewin it was the study of individual attitudes and the decisions made in small groups, which in turn could later be manipulated, which attracted his interest. In fact, Marrow later wrote a definitive biography of Kurt Lewin (Marrow, 1969) in which he described him as a 'practical theorist'. Lewin was interested above all else in group dynamics and the concept of action in group settings. In his native Germany, the concept of action (*handlung*) had been pivotal in the social sciences, but this was not the case in the USA before the war.

Lewin's contribution is important because, although not the first to use and write about action research, he did construct an elaborate theory and made action research 'respectable' inquiry for social scientists. Action research began to be hailed as an innovation in social inquiry. Lewin believed that science should have this social-help function and he stated, 'research that produces nothing but books will not suffice.' (Lewin, 1948:203).

Action research was used in the study of industry (Jaques, 1952; Whyte and Hamilton, 1964) and developed a committed following in the USA at the Massachusetts Institute of Technology and its Research Center for Group Dynamics, and through links with the Tavistock Insitute of Human Relations in London. Many action research projects have been described in the journal of the Tavistock Institute, *Human Relations.* Wallace (Wallace, 1987) argues that action research as promoted by the Tavistock approach paved the way for the 'external intervention' style of collaborative action research currently enjoying widespread usage; a style that highlights the concerns of the target group rather than the professional researchers. It is vital to acknowledge Lewin's idea that in order to understand and change certain social practices, social scientists have to include practitioners from the real social world in all phases of inquiry. The Commission on Community Interrelations sponsored many action research projects during the 1940s and 1950s (Marrow, 1969).

4. *Post-war 'Corey-era' reconstructionist curriculum development activity* in the USA. A number of post-war social reconstructionist writers promoted and championed the use of action research in education. Stephen Corey (Corey, 1953) was foremost in leading this movement, and he believed that action research could significantly change and improve curriculum practice principally because practitioners would use the results of their own research investigations.

Interest was very high during the 1950s in using action research as a general strategy for designing curricula and attacking complex problems, such as intergroup relations and prejudice, through large curriculum development projects (Taba, et al., 1949; Taba, Brady and Robinson, 1952).This period is referred to as the era of 'cooperative action research' (Verduin, 1967) in that teachers and schools 'cooperated' with outside researchers by becoming clients and making their pupils and teachers available for research.

Towards the end of the 1950s action research was in decline and was the subject of increased attack (Hodgkinson, 1957). In a telling title, 'Whatever happened to action research?', Sanford (Sanford, 1970) suggested that the decline was directly related to the split between science and practice which was supported by the movement, and to the shift towards the establishment of expert educational research and development laboratories. This highlighted the separation of theory and practice, and was manifested through the top-down development strategy of the research, development, and dissemination (RD&D) model which insulated professional researchers from the teaching ranks. This separation has had the negative consequence of preventing researchers from studying problems in the field, particularly innovative practices.

5. The *teacher-researcher movement* including new modes of evaluation, and qualitative research methodology in social science (McKernan, 1988a). The teacher-researcher movement marks a radical departure from the conventional view of curriculum research as a specialist occupation. In Britain, the call came initially from the late Lawrence Stenhouse (Stenhouse, 1971;1975) and his pedagogical concerns, based upon the Humanities Curriculum Project (1967–1972) in which he linked teacher-research to his 'Neutral Chairperson' strategy for handling controversial issues. Stenhouse's influential *An Introduction to Curriculum Research and Development*, published in 1975, offered a chapter titled 'The teacher as researcher' in which he stated his major thesis: that all teaching ought to be based on research and that research and curriculum development are the preserve of teachers; the curriculum then becomes a means of studying the problems and effects of implementing any defined line of teaching. The practitioner gains increased understanding of his or her work and thus teaching is improved.

Other significant teacher-researcher developments include the Ford Teaching Project, directed by John Elliott and Clem Adelman, which gave teachers an action research remit; and the dissemination work of the Classroom Action Research Network (CARN) and the National Association for Race Relations Teaching and Action Research (NARTAR). Works by Nixon (1981), Hopkins (1985), Carr and Kemmis (1986), Walker (1985) and Winter (1989) have advocated a critical stance. In 1990 the First World Congress on Action Research was held in Australia (Zuber-Skerritt, 1991).

Collaborative action research for professional development

Action research has been promoted in US circles mainly through the collaborative or interactive style of research, through development and through dissemination teams — usually involving participants from internal and external organizations. Lieberman and Miller (1984) posit that in the 1970s action research was rediscovered and renamed 'interactive research and development'. This interactive, or collaborative, research and development perspective has been widely endorsed. Previous interventions have included: the Interactive Research and Development on Teaching Study (IR&DT) of Tikunoff, Ward and Griffin (1979); the Interactive Research and

Development Study of Schooling (IR&DS) of Griffin, Lieberman and Jacullo-Noto (1983); the IR&D projects by Huling et al. (1981); and the National Institute of Education sponsored project, Action Research on Change in Schools (ARCS) (Oja, 1983). A good example of the genre is the recent work by Oja and Smulyan (1989). In Canada, the North American tradition of 'collaborative action research' is endorsed by the Alberta Teachers' Association and a recent collection of project papers is now available (Carson and Coutre, 1987); though practice there more closely resembles the 'practical' model of the British tradition of John Elliott's self-monitoring teacher-researcher, than the interactive research, development and dissemination model of the USA.

Collaboration suggests that each team shares in the planning, implementation, analysis and reporting of the research and that team members contribute unique skills and expertise in a collective process (Connelly and Ben-Peretz, 1980). Often teams are made up of university faculty, district teachers, administrators, educational laboratory research and development personnel, and funding body staff. This interactive team perspective seems to be the major mode of conducting action research in the USA at present, and continues the scientific-positivistic mode of US action research.

Contemporary approaches have stressed the development of teachers' research skills (Rudduck and Hopkins, 1985). In addition to helping practitioners acquire research skills, collaborative-interactive action research will probably increase the likelihood that teachers will use their own, and learn from others', researches in their work, while enabling practitioners to develop a more personal conception of what counts as legitimate 'research' (Ross, 1984). In the USA, the National Science Teachers' Association has sent out the call 'every teacher a researcher' (Butzow and Gabel, 1986). The contemporary status of the action research movement is closely linked with the growing belief in school-based curriculum and staff development, inservice education and training, and qualitative styles of curriculum evaluation — especially teacher self-evaluation.

Coming from the new 'professional development schools' or academic alliances with school staff, Ric Hovda and Diane Kyle advocate a genuine partnership-collaborative approach to action research. Action research has been perceived by Hovda and Kyle (1984) as a realistic professional development strategy over and beyond the tangible results for a practical concern. Hovda and Kyle (1984:23) argue that first, teachers must perceive their own role as including a research remit. Second, they may secure the support of a research group who serve as peer-critics. They offer the following plan:

1. Identify interested participants. For example, teachers from one or a number of schools who are willing to join in the action research.
2. Provide a context for action by discussing questions such as:
    *   What is action research?
    *   What are some possible benefits and functions of research?
    *   What methods seem appropriate for teachers doing this research?
    *   What topics have others studied and written about?
    *   What methodological and ethical issues need to be addressed?
    *   What constraints and limitations need to be acknowledged?
3. Complete 'trial runs' of topics to provide experience in research and analysis and to help teachers gain confidence. For example, everyone in the group might tape record a 20-minute lesson in their classroom — then analyse the type of questions they pose for pupils.
4. Participants are asked to share several possible study topics which they might employ in their classroom. Through small and large group discussion, each teacher-researcher selects one problem to research.
5. Each participant identifies an appropriate research method for gaining a handle on the specific research issue. These might include diary-writing, interviews, logs, etc.
6. As each researcher writes a descriptive proposal about the research problem and its methodology, time is needed for the peer-critcis to offer advice about where further elaboration or clarification is required.
7. As teacher-researchers develop their studies, time is allocated to the discussion of results, problems, idiosyncratic asides, etc.
8. Time is given over to discussion of how best to write the studies up. Researchers then share the study with peer-critics before a final report is written.
9. Focus final questions on:
    *   What issues are thrown up by the study?
    *   What do the studies let one know about the curriculum?
    *   What impact might the study have on future practice?
    *   What have we learned about action research as a tool for professional development?
10. Explore the possibility of having the teachers' studies published, presented or shared in some way with other teachers.

Curriculum research: shifts in emphasis 1970–1991

One of the more obvious features of contemporary curriculum research is the proliferation of studies and the styles of curriculum inquiry (Short, 1991). The general tendency has been away from law-establishing nomothetic-type studies and towards thick description-type qualitative, interpretive and microethnographic studies. The urgency of the reform for 'excellence' in the education movement has pushed curriculum researchers to address practitioners' agendas, with self-monitoring, accountability and action research becoming household words in the staffrooms of many schools. The shift has been decidedly away from rational-managerial ends-means models and towards a more moral and practical conception — a humanistic model, if you like — which embraces concepts of deliberation, values, power, autonomy and emancipation. Short (1987) makes the point that 'the critical form of inquiry associated with these kinds of studies could not proceed under a highly rationalistic or technical conception of curriculum.'

Critical theory and action research
A radical alternative approach to educational action research has been posited by Carr and Kemmis (1986) in both philosophical and methodological terms, with the publication of *Becoming Critical: Education, Knowledge and Action Research.* Carr and Kemmis eschew a positivist-empirical approach in favour of a critical-interpretive-activist philosophy, which has much in common with the new critical theory in philosophy and the social sciences informed by Habermas and members of the 'Frankfurt School', with aspects of Friere's 'liberation pedagogy' and Marxist conceptions added.

Carr and Kemmis have sketched this critical-emancipatory mode of research and describe its relationship with educational science and theory. This 'critical' action research is akin to the new interpretive sociology, with the added dimension of action accompanying the sister concepts of interpretation and explanation of social reality.

Developments in evaluation and qualitative methodology

Demands for school accountability, curriculum programme evaluation and teacher self-evaluation have developed simultaneously with the explosion of interest in qualitative field methodology — all moving away from strict measurement, prediction and control and towards increased description, narrative and explanation rooted in understanding as the principal concerns of investigators. Illuminative evaluation (Parlett and Hamilton, 1972) was an initial starting point in evaluation, and Short (1987) has noted the major trends in curriculum research from the mid-1970s, which includes increasing work using historical, ethnographic, artistic, interpretive, critical and other forms of inquiry.

Alternatively, there has been the growing number of teacher-researchers doing research in response to the demands of accountability. These practitioners often reject psychometric forms of educational research, preferring a discourse rooted in the lingustic framework of classroom language. This alternative community of teacher-researchers has also continued to expand, largely due to the inability of more traditional styles of research to address the pressing problems faced by practitioners. Even when outside experts have studied these problems, they have tended to define them in their own terms, employing social-scientific conceptual frameworks and using research methods and report language that are alien to the practitioner.

Curriculum research, and much educational research, still remains a specialist activity engaged in by professionally trained social scientists who operate *outside* the curriculum and classroom chiefly for the benefit of those *outside* the school and classroom. A major theme of contemporary curriculum research has been the *equality* of both *insiders* and *outsiders* in the inquiry process and in working from problem definition to data collection, analysis and solution. This dynamic partnership of insiders and outside facilitators has mutual benefit for all participants, but especially for those *inside* the classroom.

Qualitative field researchers have made major contributions to the study of curriculum. In 1954, the US Congress passed the Cooperative Research Act which gave funds for educational research for the very first time. The work of anthropologists like Jules Henry in *Culture Against Man* (1963) demonstrated how field research could illuminate educational settings. Since the late 1960s naturalistic and ethnographic inquiry has flourished (Smith and Geoffrey, 1968; Wolcott, 1973; Bogdan and Biklen, 1982; Goetz and LeCompte, 1984; Woods, 1986), bringing the use of anthropology to bear on school rituals, curriculum evaluation and school culture in a compelling manner through qualitative educational research. Such a tradition requires substantial time in the field setting, normally through the role of participant observer but also through interviewing, journal-keeping etc.

TYPOLOGIES AND MODELS OF ACTION RESEARCH

The purpose of this section is to review theoretical models of the action research process. The models are divided into three camps or types: Type 1 theories are referred to as *scientific action research;* Type 2 are referred to as *practical-deliberative action research;* and Type 3 models are referred to as *critical-emancipatory action research.* Finally, the chapter presents a new, practical model of action research as a rational-interactive dynamic. Hopkins (1985) offers a brief overview of models of action research.

The question that must be asked is 'What is involved in doing action research?' The answer will seek to describe principles of procedure for conducting such research. The chief concern here is with the manner, or conduct, rather than the matter, or content, of the research. These categories may be contestable and rough-hewn, yet they do demarcate in a crude manner work on the action research scene. Schubert (1986) applies a similar set of categories to explain shifts in curriculum theory.

Type 1: The scientific-technical view of problem-solving

Early advocates (Lippitt and Radke, 1946; Lewin, 1947b; Corey, 1953; Taba and Noel, 1957) put forward the scientific method of problem solving: 'The development of action research projects needs to proceed by certain steps which are indicated in part by the requirements of an orderly research process, in part by the fact that the 'researchers' are learning while they go on, and in part because essentially an *inductive procedure* is indicated.' (Taba and Noel, 1957:12; see also Gregory, 1988.)

The implicit theory of inquiry and reflective action developed by Dewey (1910) was to be applied by a number of social problem solvers. We must bear in mind that the penchant for theorizing and conceptual-graphical model-building is a modern-day phenomenon in education, though it no doubt owes much to its scientific origins.

Lewin and his group of researchers contributed enormously to a specific action research model which he prepared for publication (Lewin, 1947a; 1947b) shortly before his death. It was clear at this stage that various behaviouralist researchers had employed a scientific approach to the study of perplexing curriculum problems — e.g. the progressive *Eight Year Study* and the *Southern Study*. Yet no one had illustrated this process graphically until Lewin in 1947. It should be remembered that Lewin had embarked on a wide range of experimental projects and activities involving social and practical problems such as prejudice, group relations, eating habits and industrial unrest (Marrow, 1969). It should also be remembered that a principal factor accounting for much of Lewin's testing of theory in action was America's entry into the Second World War. The military machine demanded research expertise from many behavioural scientists and Lewin was recruited. Of importance were questions such as: What techniques of psychological warfare would weaken the enemy's will to resist? How could leaders be found and trained? What was the state of morale on the home front and in enemy territories? During this period Lewin contributed to the programmes of the Office of Naval Research (ONR), along with such notables as Margaret Mead, Paul Lazarsfeld, Rensis Likert and others. In Britain, techniques of officer selection and training and the resettlement of prisoners of war drew upon action research (Brown, 1967).

Of paramount concern to Lewin was the problem of group decision-making about social action, so that decisions could be taken which would not allow practice to drift back to old levels of habit and action. Lewin therefore, quite correctly, focused on *group decisions as a means of effecting social and cultural change.*

Lewin's model of action research: planning, fact-finding and execution

Figure 1.1 describes Lewin's model of the action research process as a series of spiralling decisions, taken on the basis of repeated cycles of analysis, reconnaissance, problem reconceptualization, planning, implementation of social action, and evaluation regarding the effectiveness of action. The key idea for Lewin was that a social process can be studied by introducing changes and observing scientifically the effects of these changes on it. This procedure may have caused Michael Scriven to coin the phrase 'formative evaluation' which consists of examining how well practice functions and refreezing the practice at its higher level of effectiveness. The idea is that evaluation is continuous and always undertaken with a view to improving the quality of the action.

Lewin can be truly called the 'practical theorist' for his belief that a mere piling up of facts and data was not enough — this he believed to be antithetical to theory construction. A science without theory was blind, he argued, because it would not provide answers to the key questions, which for him evolved around practical purposes — namely, what can be done to improve this situation? To answer such practical concerns Lewin argued for empirical evidence rather than speculation in theory building. That is, there must be an interplay between theory and facts.

Action research for Lewin (1947b) is composed of a series of action steps including *planning, fact-finding, execution* and *analysis.* Lewin believed that social science could effect general laws of social life. Knowledge of laws, was, however, insufficient for action; only through field experiments could individuals gain the situational practical knowledge to effect social improvements. Planning, on Lewin's account, begins with a general idea or a difficult problem requiring resolution. This is followed by further fact-finding, or 'reconnaissance', resulting in an 'overall plan' of how to solve the problem (see Figure 1.1). This planned action is implemented, and monitored in an attempt to evaluate the effectiveness of the first action step, to plan the next step and to modify the 'overall plan'. More concretely, the reconnaissance shows if the plan and resultant action achieved above or below its expectations while allowing the researchers to learn from the experiment. These action steps constitute a field change experiment focusing upon the plan, the action, and research into the effects of the action. The researcher then spirals into developing a second and possibly further action steps leading to further planning, implementation, evaluation and decision-making. For Lewin, action research was a form of rational management, or social engineering (Lewin, 1946:38), a sort of comparative inquiry into social action and its effects in producing improved action; not the production of books alone.

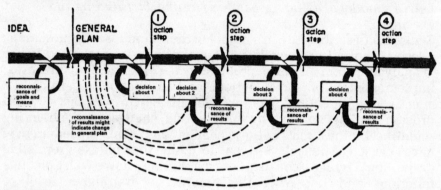

Source: Lewin, 1947b.

Figure 1.1   *Lewin's action research model: planning, fact-finding and execution*

Lewin argued that action research required *group participation* through democratic processes based on careful planning, analysis, fact-finding and evaluation — the grounding was therefore in systemic scientific rational methodology. It is crucial to recognize Lewin as the empirical-rational scientist that he was. It has become trendy of late to latch on to concepts such as *collaboration, group dynamics* and *spiral of reflective cycles of action,* especially by those advocating 'critical action research'; this is somewhat ironic as these terms were first used by positivistic-minded educational and social scientists.

Taba's model of the action research procedure
At about the same time that Lewin was establishing his group dynamics experiments at the Massachusetts Institute of Technology, Hilda Taba, the curriculum writer, was directing large-scale curriculum action research aimed at the problems posed by intergroup relations in American society (Taba et al., 1952; Taba and Noel, 1957).

Taba's idea for an exploratory project in intergroup education was hatched in 1944 and the results were published some years later as *Intergroup Education in Public Schools* (Taba et al., 1952). The project, which ran from 1945 to 1948, was sponsored by the American Council on Education principally to improve relations between majority-minority groups through curriculum development. This continued the theme of action research and intergroup relations first noted by Lewin's group of researchers (Marrow, 1969). Yet what is of importance for curriculum theorists is not the new materials produced by the project but the emphasis on a scientific approach to curriculum action research. In fact, Taba used action research as an indispensable tool for curriculum workers (Taba and Noel, 1957; Taba, 1962). The project departed from traditional curriculum building in that it requested schools to line up problems worthy of attacking; to decide what sort of programmes to develop; and to develop project-specific methods of evaluating work accomplished.

Taba-Noel procedure
Hilda Taba was one of the most prolific of American curriculum theorists working and writing in mid-century (Taba and Noel, 1957; Taba, 1962). Taba applied Dewey's five stages of scientific reflective thinking — the scientific method — to problems of curriculum. The process she outlined has a number of stages: *identifying problems*; *analysis of problems*; *formulating ideas or hypotheses*; *gathering and interpreting data*; *implementation-action*; *evaluating the results of action.*

   Taba and Noel warn that there is not a lock-step commitment to these stages of work, nothing is sacrosanct and that problems may even change as the research proceeds. Generally they regard this as a sequence which 'it is not wise to reverse' (Taba and Noel, 1957:12).

Lippitt-Radke action research procedure
In their work on social prejudice, Lippitt and Radke (1946) developed a number of principles of procedure for doing action research:

1. *Initially a group needs to discover some facts that exist, or are created.* Usually the group takes on the task of finding out about the facts of a problem, and the process of finding out itself will be educational.
2. *The group, or representatives of it, share in deciding 'what do we need to know?'* The research technician realizes that internal participants have some hunches or ideas about worthy questions and where answers might be found. It is within this principle that the basis of interactive, or joint/collaborative, participatory research was born. This insider-outsider involvement is crucial if the facts which are discovered are to be seen as valid, authentic and reliable by the group.
3. *Scientific research instruments are constructed.* Early studies concentrated on sound instrument development, albeit using a limited number of methods: questionnaires, interviews, rating scales and checklists are mentioned. The emphasis seemed to be

upon researchers developing the instrumentation after joint planning sessions — a practice still evidenced today in certain joint projects.

4. *Further achieving of the 'objectivity' role occurs in making decisions about sampling and learning to use the research tools reliably.* Great emphasis was laid upon training researchers to use instruments, adequate sampling in research design, etc. The emphasis is on technical specifications, measurement, and the aping of quantitative social science.

5. *Supervision of data collection must help to ensure success and deal sympathetically with discouragement problems.* Using untrained staff to collect data often led to problems in so far as lay persons became discouraged through unsuccessul interviewing. Training of data collectors helped enormously.

6. *Evidence of attitude change often appears during this phase of participation in fact-gathering.* The research process had enormous social psychological effects on the participating researchers — e.g. one administrator remarked, 'you certainly see things differently when you are looking for facts.'

7. *Collaboration in putting the facts together and interpreting them requires special skill of the research technician.* The professionally trained researcher should not take the data away for analysis or only assign boring tasks to the lay workers — the most successful projects shared the workload between researchers and lay persons.

8. *Sometimes more is needed than a change in the values and social perception of the individual or group.* The argument here is that often new knowledge is not enough to get individuals to change their behaviour — in most cases the changed outlook which results from the ability to see the facts will lead to changed behaviour. When it does not, the situation can be helped by group exploration of ideas and feelings through simulations such as role-playing.

9. *Spreading the facts to other groups by oral and written reports can be a final step — and a new first step.* Lippit and Radke argue for the dissemination of reports of projects, not because they will change behaviour themselves but because they may trigger responses for action research projects in readers.

Type 2: Practical-deliberative action research

The *practical* model of action research trades off some measurement and control for human interpretation, interactive communication, deliberation, negotiation and detailed description. The goal of practical action researchers is understanding practice and solving immediate problems. Practical deliberation responds to the immediate situation which is deemed problematic from a moral perspective — there is a sense in which curriculum action must be taken to put things right. The practical is also connected with the *process* rather than the end *products* of inquiry. This crucial point was first made by Aristotle in his *Ethics,* and more recently picked out by R.S. Peters (Peters, 1966:37) in his *Ethics and Education,* where he argues against some technical-scientific model of education in favour of a procedural approach which characterizes the 'tasks of education rather than the achievements'. Peters suggests that for something to count as educational it will have principles or procedures immanent in the process itself which are worth pursuing. Another point is that such procedures have the in-built feature of understanding and of some cognitive perspective.

Curriculum is a practical and highly moral matter which views itself as a changeable process, capable of transforming human action and, indeed, culture. As a theory of *practice*, action research attempts to make some difference to how people behave or live their lives; to how they feel and think. This notion was neatly captured by Michael Oakeshott (1962) some years before the current concern for the practical argued for by Schwab, Reid and Stenhouse. Oakeshott suggests that, at the personal level, there is a relationship between practice and the human desire for improvement:

> In practical activity, then, every image is the reflection of a desiring self engaged in constructing its world and in continuing to reconstruct it in such a manner as to afford it pleasure. The world here consists of what is good to eat and what is poisonous, what is friendly and what is hostile, what is amenable to control and what resists it. And each image is recognized as something to be made use of or exploited.
>
> (Oakeshott, 1962:207)

Practical action research is tied up closely with human deliberation in curriculum matters; in this area much is owed to Joseph Schwab (Schwab, 1969; 1971; 1973; 1983) in the USA, and in the UK to Lawrence Stenhouse (Stenhouse, 1967; 1975) who grounded his *process model* in the practical in *Culture and Education*, prior to William Reid's lucid discussion of the curriculum as a practical-deliberative activity (Reid, 1978). Malcolm Skilbeck (Skilbeck, 1984) should also be included with these practical pioneers for his focus on the practical and on the school-based nature of curriculum development. In this influential sphere I would also locate the pioneering work of John Elliott (Elliott, 1977; 1985a; 1987), who laid emphasis on the hermeneutic nature of inquiry for understanding. While Stenhouse might have produced the bare bones of a number of seminal ideas, such as the 'neutral chairman-researcher', it was John Elliott who put the curriculum flesh on these skeletons, and who developed the pedagogy by which they could be implemented. Elliott worked these ideas out in the Humanities Curriculum Project, and later with Clem Adelman in the Ford Teaching Project and through their work in establishing the Classroom Action Research Network.

However, it should not be understood from this discussion that action research lies within an Aristotelian or scientific model. Simply because one can locate theoretical aspects within one or another of these intellectual traditions does not mean that these separate traditions encapsulate discrete and different models — it is more likely that there has been a gigantic 'knock-on' effect in which much overlap has occurred.

Action researchers argue that practice and research ought to be fused. The importance of *practical deliberation* as procedure has been receiving increasing attention in the curriculum literature since the publication of Schwab's thesis (Schwab, 1969) some 20 years ago (Walker, 1971; Reid, 1978; Roby, 1985; Schubert, 1986). The deliberative group must uncover the spiralling meanings which present themselves in each cycle of the action research process. This suggests that a single research cycle or loop would only serve to throw up some preliminary meanings and that further evaluation and experimentation are required to exploit the deliberative process fully. Thus the reflective-deliberative action is as important, or more so, than other aspects of the inquiry process; it must not be controlled rigidly but rather allowed to unfold naturally — free of constraints. Here it is important to acknowledge the work of Professor Don Schon of MIT (Schon, 1983; 1987) on the concept of the 'reflective practitioner', which is itself generating a whole new specialism within the teacher-researcher camp. Several researchers in Australia (Bonser and Grundy, 1988) have reported on the use of reflective deliberation as a mode of developing a school-sited curriculum policy evolved from deliberations by the individual, the small support group, the whole group or staff and finally in collaboration with external researchers and other personnel in search of an agreement and final documentation of the written policy, which would, of course, be a joint-authored statement.

Elliott's model

John Elliott, the British curricularist, has probably done more to advance the cause of curriculum action research than anyone. In 1978, he published the first complete analytic account of the action research concept (Elliott, 1978a) in the UK under the title 'What is action research in schools?'. Professor Elliott's paper signalled the arrival of a powerful idea whose time had come — given that curriculum research was dominated by the positivist tradition in the UK. What made Elliott's analysis so compelling was his insistence that teaching *is inescapably a theoretical activity;* the task for practitioners was to interpret their everyday practice in the pursuit of reflective self-development. What was on offer through Elliott's analysis was nothing less than the reunification of theory and practice. John Elliott began his career as a science teacher and later joined Lawrence Stenhouse's central team of workers with the Humanities Curriculum Project, working out of the Centre for Applied Research in Education 1970–1976; then moving to the Cambridge Institute of Education (1976–1984) where he refined many of his teacher-researcher ideas; and then returning to the University of East Anglia, CARE (1984–present) where he holds a Chair of Education.

Elliott (1980; 1987; 1988) has argued that the revival of action research has been largely associated with the curriculum development reform movement of the 1970s. For Elliott, action research attempts to improve the quality of life in a social situation (Elliott, 1981:2). Elliott's model of the action research process is outlined in Figure 1.2. Central to Elliott's analysis is the idea that the action researcher develops a personal interpretive understanding from working on practical problems, and that theoretical understanding is constitutive of practical action and discourse (Elliott, 1987:157).

For John Elliott, educational research is a moral endeavour in that it seeks to realize values in practice. Elliott (1985a) argues that educational research ought to become a reconstructed form of action research; a moral science paradigm to which teacher-researchers would be the main contributors, rather than those in academic disciplines.

John Elliott and Clem Adelman (Elliott and Adelman, 1973) reconceptualized teacher action research through the Ford Teaching Project (1972–1974), which attempted to support a small band of teachers to research their working practice in implementing and developing a pedagogy of inquiry learning. It was during this project that Elliott and Adelman worked out procedures such as 'triangulation'. Crucial for Elliott is the idea that curriculum and teaching are highly theoretical enterprises and that research itself is a self-reflective process in which practitioners are enabled to examine their theoretical world of practice, which they perceive in fundamentally very different terms from outside 'professional educational researchers'. Elliott would claim that he is simply reconstructing a tradition of inquiry begun by Aristotle.

Ebbutt's model
David Ebbutt, a colleague of John Elliott, has claimed (Ebbutt, 1983a) that the spiral is not the most useful metaphor or image to use to think about the action research process. Ebbutt argued that the best way of thinking about the process was as a series of successive cycles, each incorporating the possibility of providing evaluative feedback within and between the cycles of action. Ebbutt's notion would be much closer to that of the model offered by the present writer in this work.

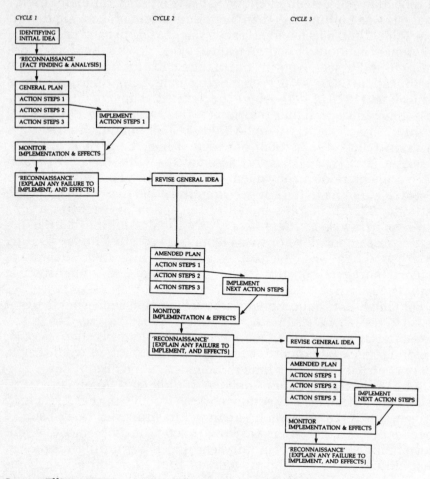

Source: Elliott, 1981.

Figure 1.2   *Elliott's model of action research process*

Type 3: Critical-emancipatory educational action research

Deakin model of the action research process
In Australia, Stephen Kemmis and his colleagues at Deakin University have postulated a model of critical educational action research (McTaggart et al., 1982; Kemmis, 1983; Carr and Kemmis, 1986; Kemmis and McTaggart, 1988). This model is outlined in Figure 1.4. At a substantive level, critical educational action research rejects the positivist belief in the instrumental role of knowledge in problem-solving, arguing that critical inquiry enables practitioners not only to search out the interpretive meanings that educational actions have for them but to organize action to overcome constraints. It is a critical theory linked with reconstructive action

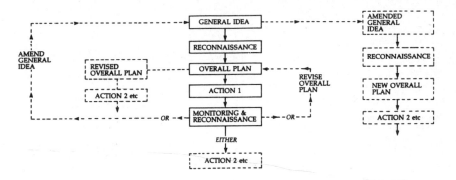

Source: Ebbutt, 1983a in Hopkins, 1985.

Figure 1.3 *Ebbutt's action research model*

and is critical of both positivist and critical-interpretive theories in so far as they are passive — seeking to explain and not linked with human action.

Critical educational action research is supposedly grounded in the interpretive categories of practitioners. Like other critical theories, the Carr and Kemmis account gives priority to a critique of practices which thwart rational goal achievement. It also deviates from more conventional action research in terms of its fieldwork methodology; it stresses equipping practitioners with discursive, analytical and conceptual skills so that they may be free of the control of positivism and interpretive theory through their communities of self-reflective group understanding. The heightening of understanding through hard critique is the *modus operandi*.

In Australia, significant action research work of the critical-emancipatory type has been developed at Deakin University and reported by Kemmis et al. (1982) in *The Action Research Reader* and Kemmis and McTaggart (1988) in *The Action Research Planner*.

Critical-emancipatory action research perceives curriculum problems as value-laden and moral concerns rather than as purely technical, and they combine what Habermas (1972) refers to as two knowledge-constitutive interests: 'practical' and 'emancipatory'. Science then becomes hermeneutical, or critical, based as it is on a series of self-reflective spirals of human action playing off past retrospection against possible future action. Critical theorists argue that positivism has made scientific thinking technical, thus placing constraints on reason. Critical action research is seen to be a flight from this 'technologization of reason'.

Kemmis' thinking conceives of the process as a series of reflective spirals in which a general plan, action, observation of action, and reflection on action (Kemmis and McTaggart, 1988) is developed

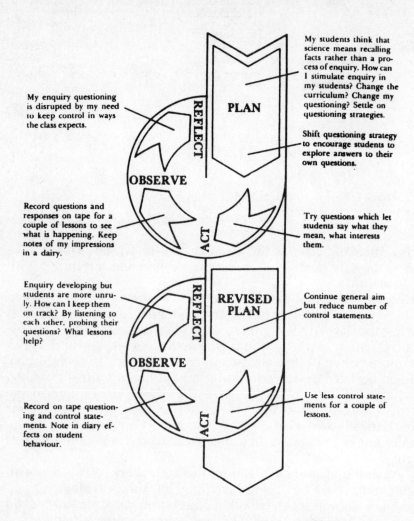

My students think that science means recalling facts rather than a process of enquiry. How can I stimulate enquiry in my students? Change the curriculum? Change my questioning? Settle on questioning strategies.

My enquiry questioning is disrupted by my need to keep control in ways the class expects.

Shift questioning strategy to encourage students to explore answers to their own questions.

Record questions and responses on tape for a couple of lessons to see what is happening. Keep notes of my impressions in a dairy.

Try questions which let students say what they mean, what interests them.

Enquiry developing but students are more unruly. How can I keep them on track? By listening to each other, probing their questions? What lessons help?

Continue general aim but reduce number of control statements.

Record on tape questioning and control statements. Note in diary effects on student behaviour.

Use less control statements for a couple of lessons.

Source: McTaggart et al., 1982. Copyright Deakin University Press.

Figure 1.4   *Deakin action research model*

and then moved to a new and revised plan with action, observation and further reflection (Carr and Kemmis, 1986). This trading off between retrospective understanding and future action is drawn directly from the Lewin theory of action research as an attempt at curriculum reform and renewal. What Carr and Kemmis offer is a return to the self-reflective spiral or loop coined by Lewin, each loop with four elements: the general plan, the action implemented, the action observed, and the reflective critical evaluational element necessary to revise the plan or problem.

	Reconstructive	**Constructive**
Discourse (among participants)	**4 Reflect** Retrospective on observation (reconnaissance and evaluation)	**1 Plan** Prospective to action (constructed action)
Practice (in the social context)	**3 Observe** Prospective for reflection (documentation)	**2 Act** Retrospective guidance from planning (deliberate and controlled strategic action)

Source: McTaggart et al., 1982. Copyright Deakin University Press.

Figure 1.5 *The moments of action research*

Kemmis is concerned with *focusing* the problem. To achieve this he poses three questions: What is happening now? In what sense is it problematic? What can I do about it?

Critical action research is seen as a politically empowering process for participants; the struggle is for more rational, just and democratic forms of education. Thus the creation of theory is the business of all practitioners on this model; not the expert few who research education from outside. As a theoretical activity it invites teachers and other practitioners to consider not only the curriculum and other educational domains, but the totality of relationships with the social system and structure of the society in which they live and work. Thus teachers are cast as social reformers of education within the wider society. The theory of critical action research is bound up with issues of control of education and the avenues by which political action can be taken.

The practitioner and the action research time-process cycle

The curriculum contains elements of practical as well as technical and critical endeavour, in which means and ends are negotiated through complex human interaction and decision-making is shared by a wide range of participants: teachers, administrators, parents, policy makers and others. In such a system the practitioner needs technical skills (e.g. how to define instructional objectives) as well as practical skills (e.g. making judgements, self-reflective monitoring, skills in small group work), but most especially *curriculum development and research skills.*

The model in Figure 1.6 presupposes scope for total curriculum planning, not *ad hoc* or piecemeal reform. As a change agent, the practitioner has a problematic situation to consider. What is proposed here is that action research be considered as a practical, technical and critically reflective process. Moreover, all those with an educational stake in the process need to be involved: parents, practitioners and pupils.

The first cycle of action

A time-process model of the action research process is illustrated in Figure 1.6. The model may be interpreted in the following way: at some particular point in time (T1) an indeterminate or unacceptable situation or problem is identified as requiring improvement. The first cycle of action is triggered off by attempts to define the situation or problem more clearly. A careful statement of the problem next leads to a 'needs assessment'. At this stage the internal (school-situated) and external (community) constraints that impede progress are established and ranked in order of priority. The review of the situation should suggest hunches, or hypotheses, which will function as strategic ideas deemed worthy of testing in practice. The hypotheses proposed for solving the action research problem merely claim to count as 'intelligent' ideas rather than as 'correct' solutions.

The next stage is devoted to developing an overall plan of action which will serve as an operational blueprint for the project. The plan will detail who reports to whom and when; specification of roles and goals; schedule of meetings, etc. Implementation of the plan follows; this is the stage of installing the plan in the setting and taking action. Evaluation of the action steps taken follows. At this stage the critical research group seeks to understand what the effects have been and what has been learned as a result of action. By carefully reflecting on the action the practitioner becomes a 'self-monitoring' teacher-researcher. The data and conclusions are then shared within the group which will make decisions about the acceptability of the steps.

The second cycle (and subsequent cycles) of action

The project now moves on to a second cycle, or action loop, of events in which the experience and steps of the first action cycle are employed to produce a 'revised definition of the situation' commencing at a timeframe depicted by T2 in the model. The important thing about the second action cycle (T2) is that the original research problem is allowed to redefine itself as the result of the action taken in time period T1. Too often action researchers seem

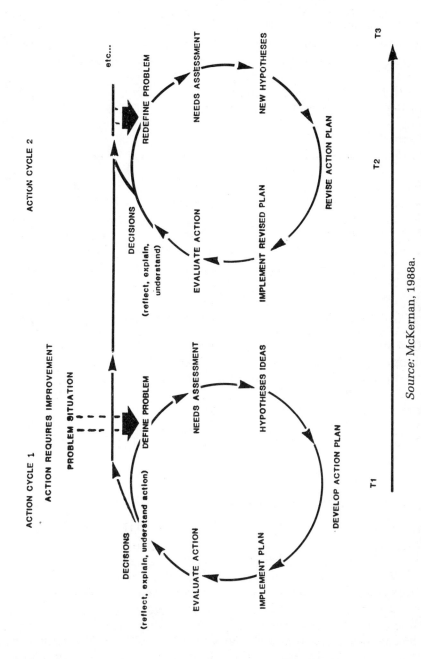

Source: McKernan, 1988a.

Figure 1.6 *McKernan's model of action research: a time process model*

to allow a problem to become rigidly fixed and adhered to. In T2 the problem is recast and a review of the situation is conducted. The collaborative group may have various ideas or hypotheses for improving the situation. These are then written into the revised action plan which is tested and observed empirically in the setting. On the basis of evaluation and group critique the action initiatives in T2 are further subjected to scrutiny and decisions are reached. It may be that further testing and experimentation is deemed necessary and this would then form the basis of a third (T3) action cycle and a wholly reconstructed action plan.

The essential features of this model are its scientific-rational method of problem solving and its democratic, or collegial, ownership by the self-critical community of researchers. The focus is on improving curriculum through moral problem solving using practitioners as research and development workers. The relationship between action and theory is acutely dialectical in that action cannot be set apart from the entity it explains. This practical perspective takes precedence over theoretical model-building and research report writing since it is concerned with an answer to the question 'What ought to be done?' It is therefore highly normative in thrust: a moral and intensely practical pursuit.

Formal, traditional research, no matter how rigorous and thorough, is seldom read, let alone conducted by practitioners. There are a number of reasons why this is the case but the main one is lack of *time* — time to do research, which would also include looking for reports, reading them, and above all *understanding* them. More fundamentally, formal research often has no immediate impact or application to curriculum and specific school situations. Given that some teachers do get involved in research, e.g. thesis and dissertation work, there is the problem of disseminating the results of findings to practitioners. The model argues that the practical can never be truly separated from the critical or the technical in curriculum.

Characteristics of the action research process

Curriculum action research has implications of three kinds. First, it can serve to improve problematic social situations. Second, it can enhance the personal understanding of the researcher. Third, it can serve to illuminate the researcher's social surroundings, or the environment and conditions in which he or she works. In recent years action research has been applied to problems involving curriculum development, professional staff development and inservice education, particularly within the field of self-evaluation. Elliott (1978a) outlines the following ten distinguishing characteristics of the process:

1. It examines problems which are deemed problematic by practitioners.
2. These problems are deemed solvable.
3. Such problems require a practical response.
4. Action research suspends a full definition of the situation until exploratory research is undertaken.
5. The goal is to deepen the researcher's understanding of the problem.
6. Action research uses case study methodology in an attempt to 'tell a story' about what is going on and how events hang together.
7. The case study is reported in terms of the perceptions and beliefs of those in the setting — teachers, children, etc.
8. Action research uses the language of everyday discourse employed by the participants.
9. Action research can only be validated in unconstrained dialogue by the participants.
10. There must be a free flow of information within support groups and between actors in the project.

The countenance of action research: principles and key concepts

The purpose of this section is to offer a sketch of the major concepts which illuminate the character and 'countenance' of action research. This portrait, of some 16 key concepts, is derived from what the author understands about action research as a whole, fully realizing that these features have precedence in other types and traditions of action research. Accordingly, it borrows concepts from the Type 1 action research tradition (Dewey, Corey, Lewin, Taba, and recent IR&D proponents), which might be labelled 'scientific'; Type 2 tradition may be called 'practical' (Stenhouse, Elliott); and Type 3 action research may be called 'critical' in that it leans heavily upon the critical theory of the Frankfurt School of philosophy (Carr, Kemmis, Freire, Habermas). It is thus eclectic and synthesizing, choosing to select profound ideas from diverse strands of theoretical and practical interventions in the field, rather than to dismiss whole paradigms and traditions. The unifying theme is that all action research is a form of *reflective inquiry* governed by rigorous principles, or canons of procedure. It is the scientific method which provides a unity of commonsense thought and science. This was the case made by both Lewin and Corey. McKernan (1988a) and Carr (1989) have both argued that action research needs to recognize the linkage and similarities with scientific positivism — the latter being the precursor of modern action research; and 'that action research may yet become a twentieth-century re-enactment of nineteenth-century positivism' (Carr, 1989). This is just a rough portrait, yet it aspires to portray the idiom of the activity.

1. *Increase human understanding.* As a form of hermeneutical, or critical inquiry, action research focuses upon understanding one's own and others' understanding of curriculum problems. Reflective thinking and reflexivity or the key notions here. Gadamer (1984) argues that interpretive understanding is the most central act of being human, and that by engaging in such acts we enhance our humaness.
2. *Concern to improve quality of human action and practice.* Action research seeks to make human performance more intelligent and effective, skilfully and reflectively.
3. *Focus is on problems of immediate concern to practitioners.* Problems are defined by those experiencing them since practitioners are best placed to identify, analyse and inquire into these problems.
4. *Collaborative.* All those with a stake in the problem have a right to be included in the search for a solution. This also implies a shared 'community of discourse' between insiders and outsiders; and that practitioners are not merely treated as 'clients' but as co-investigators.
5. *Conducted in-situ.* Research is undertaken in the setting where the problem is encountered.
6. *Participatory nature.* Those affected participate in the research and implementation of preferred solutions. There is a demand that participants share their understanding of events and actions so that they appreciate the social construction of their practice.
7. *Focus on the case or single unit.* Action research examines a single case and not a sample population. Whole populations are studied: the classroom or school. Generalizations are problematic, though not impossible (Stenhouse, 1981) and case study methodology is a preferred form of research.
8. *No attempt to control setting variables.* Key variables are not isolated and manipulated as in experimental research. To place controls on subjects and parameters is to interfere artificially with a naturalistic setting.
9. *The problem, aims and methodology may shift as inquiry proceeds.* Action research does not consider problems to be 'fixed'. As research proceeds the problem may be seen in a new light and a new definition of the situation may be required.
10. *Evaluative-reflective.* It is crucial to stand back and reflect, particularly at the end of a cycle of action, and to describe, interpret and explain 'what is going on'. Researchers need to judge actions and results as a critical group.
11. *Methodologically eclectic-innovative.* Researchers may have to design new instruments and techniques to gather data, as dictated by the novelty of the problem. There is no single

preferred method — indeed, 'triangulation' of methods, perspectives and theories is desirable.

12. *Scientific.* By stating problems; formulating action hypotheses; planning data collection; analysing results; and reformulating hypotheses the action researcher exercises rigorous scientific principles of procedure.

13. *Shareability and utility.* Of fundamental concern is the application of results — their usefulness, or utility value, should be shared among the participants.

14. *Dialogue/discourse-based nature.* Discourse is the central data of action research. Understanding can only be achieved through unconstrained dialogue with project participants. Discussion and reflection on discussion appear axiomatic.

15. *Critical.* Action researchers seek reasoned critique grounded in social practice. Critique is a pivotal aspect of the process and an important step towards understanding, interpretation and emancipation.

16. *Emancipatory.* Some action research seeks to liberate those who suffer repressive and unjust practices. It attempts to free participants and give them greater autonomy through collective reflection. Empowerment of the research group through their taking responsiblity for decision-making, is a central goal.

CONCLUSIONS

Not only has there been a shifting conception of what counts as 'science', but the definition of action research has changed, according to one's orientation — from statistical tests of hypotheses within 'scientific' formalistic models, to empirical observations, case studies, and critical-interpretative accounts of the emerging critical theory of action research. In understanding the countenance of action research, one must understand the historical traditions of the movement and the diversity of approaches for doing action research. Some quantitative renditions and some qualitative approaches can be found between different time periods, as well as within the same timeframe and generation.

Contemporary action research does not fit neatly into any one stable, but recognizes diverse styles of curriculum inquiry: from commonsense-type case study work; to the 'teacher-researcher' working within the interactive research and development partnership team; to the self-monitoring teacher from the 'practical' Elliott-Stenhouse camp; to the critical-emancipatory researcher. All seek understanding but they employ different research methods and praxis. Such diversity has significant implications for required, or needed, research skills as noted by the teacher-researcher movement. Whether one assigns meaning to events through numbers or narrative, both styles of quantitative and qualitative inquiry can be rigorously empirical and scientific.

Some final observations. Research is a method. Research is a mode of looking at the world; a point of view. Practitioners, it may be argued, are not only distributors of curriculum knowledge, but also producers of knowledge. A research stance by practitioners will provide what Schon (1983) has referred to as 'reflection-in-action', or schools that learn for themselves. Action research engages both teacher and student in a shared search for knowledge — as such, it is an educative experience for both. It thus sets up knowledge as 'provisional' and open to question. The practitioner is not cast as an expert but as an inquirer and co-learner treating his or her practice as provisional and improvable. Action research thus becomes the basis for personal and professional development and autonomy. The exciting thing is that the present fermentation in styles and strategies for doing action research permits the possibility of understanding curriculum problems, not the continuance of ignorance.

2 The Teacher as Researcher and Professional

> To call for research-based teaching is, I suggest, to ask us as teachers to share with our pupils or students the process of our learning the wisdom which we do not possess so that they can get into critical perspective the learning which we trust is ours.[1]
>
> Lawrence Stenhouse

Calling upon teachers to conduct research will require two essential conditions. The first condition is that practitioners should understand and possess *research skills*, which generate curriculum data; and the second is that the findings should inform teachers in such a manner as to compel them to take action. Teacher research must be seen to count as a significant part of behaving in a professional way.

This chapter has three objectives: first, to discuss the school as the centre for curriculum inquiry; second, to offer a rationale which places the practitioner in the centre of this new research role; and finally, to extend the debate about the criteria for a new conception of teaching as a profession.

A major premiss of this book is that the teacher has opportunities, that are often unappreciated, to conduct action research and to begin to build upon his or her pedagogical-practical knowledge and to establish solid school-based curriculum theory. At the heart of this thesis is the idea that a partnership be created linking teachers with research in a new conception of the profession so that some relief is found for the problems of teaching and learning. The creation of this new extended professionalism will require that a new *work ethic* or *attitude* is prevalent which treats ideas as ideas, that is, as hunches that are worthy of testing. There is nothing wrong with educational innovative practices and proposals — e.g. a core curriculum, individualized instruction and so forth — if they are treated as worthy ideas and not as some 'New Jerusalem'.

Given that research is more in keeping with a conception of teaching as a profession, the second premiss is that *curriculum development and curriculum knowledge ought to be based upon the actual study of classrooms and other educational settings.*

1. Lawrence Stenhouse. 'Research as a basis for teaching'. Inaugural Lecture, University of East Anglia, February 1979. In L. Stenhouse (1983) *Authority, Education and Emancipation.* (London: Heinemann Educational Books) p. 178.

Curriculum knowledge must be based on the work of practitioners. It is not enough that the curriculum be studied; it needs to be studied by practitioners. Too often practitioners are treated as the objects of inquiry; the 'researched', by external 'researchers' (McKernan, 1988b).

The existing rhetoric of educational research would have one believe that research is indispensable for practice and highly valuable for practitioners. It is the writer's belief that only a small segment of the research done in curriculum and education is important for practitioners. Educational research is an industry complete with its own laboratory staff, funding agencies and publications outlets. The net result of this is that teachers' scope for decision-making and autonomy is being continuously eroded (Apple, 1982) in the face of this flight towards the technologization of teaching. One way of throwing off the bonds of the research industry is for teachers to emancipate themselves by gaining control over curriculum and educational research policy. In effect what this amounts to is that practitioners take the added and onerous burden of curriculum research into their own work and have more say about the issues deemed important for inquiry by professional educational researchers. It is time that research about curriculum be given back to practitioners.

THE SCHOOL AS A CENTRE FOR INQUIRY: TOWARDS A NEW PROFESSIONALISM

The argument thus far is that the school community — which includes not only teachers and pupils but also parents, external support agents, inspectors, research workers, etc — comes together to build a new work ethic and tradition of school-based curriculum making. Such a conception acknowledges several a priori principles:

1. A new professionalism and attitude is required which will imbue teachers with a research mentality — an action research perspective which suggests that teachers can find out what they need to know to sort out their particular difficulties. This curriculum inquiry attitude needs to be carefully established at the pre-service teacher training level. Through initial and inservice work and collaborative projects in real classroom settings, teachers would learn the joy and intellectual pleasure of working on real problems.
2. How little we really know about curriculum and theory, as well as learning and teaching must be admitted up front. By admitting to our lack of knowledge and understanding we would be able to start from a position of strength rather than

one of weakness. To understand that the curriculum continues to pose problems is to recognize the fact that teachers experience these problems and should take on the role of solving them. To begin a career in teaching is to know that one is at once not only a teacher but a researcher into the problems of teaching, solving puzzles that currently and historically have bedevilled some of the finest minds in education — an incentive offered by very few professional posts.

3. We need to learn to ask questions that are researchable, there being little point in asking ones that are not vital or testable. There is no substitute for the ultimate 'test of action'.

4. The teacher-researcher must be well equipped with the skills for doing inquiry — this is a major objective of this book. Lecture-based teacher training courses and a few hours a week in schools is not a sufficient preparation for work in a school which makes curriculum development and inquiry top priorities. Teachers will need a sound grounding in reactive and non-reactive research methodology and other action research techniques.

5. The school timetable must make available sufficient *time to conduct action research.* Time is perhaps the most identifiable constraint on action. Not only should teachers be timetabled out for curriculum planning but also for whole school review and for inquiry work. Just as scholars working in university environments are entitled to periodic sabbatical leave for study, research and writing, so too should teachers enjoy this professional benefit, and be made accountable for the time they spend away from teaching.

6. The school as a centre for research will not support the present artificial division of labour between external experts as researchers and teachers. Curriculum inquiry should be defined by practitioners and practitioners should be able to bring external researchers into the inquiry on an equal basis. Research should be controlled by practitioners since it is based upon their work.

7. The problem of language in curriculum research must be acknowledged and efforts made to rid curriculum research of special linguistic codes that only serve to promote the frames of reference of social scientists. Research language should be the language of the participants. Researchers need to agree on a language with which to communicate. This is a good starting point for serious action research discussion as there are those who use the critical social science jargon, those who use a scientific argot, and those who use the practical everyday discourse of the staffroom.

8. It must be acknowledged by central education authorities that

the practitioner has a major role in the task of formulating curriculum policy. For too long curriculum policy-makers have been influenced by the so-called experts in the discipline of education, and by distant central office staff in the company of remote politicians. Curriculum policy is the business of each school and should be worked out by students, staff and parents in conjunction with other authorities.

One is compelled to ask then, what sort of conditions are required to turn the school into a centre for research? In addition to problems such as time, support and division of labour, teachers will require improved training courses, research skills, money and other resources, collaborative opportunities, and, of course, experience of curriculum inquiry. One must try to solve problems. There is no better teacher than the teacher known as 'experience'.

THE TEACHER AS RESEARCHER: THE AUTONOMY OF INQUIRY

The idea of the teacher as a researcher is of crucial importance for the future development of the profession and the curriculum in general. It is a firm conviction of the author that if this idea were taken more seriously then the curriculum would be improved dramatically. Curriculum inquiry belongs to the practitioner and there are signs that suggest this is an idea whose time has come.

We must also acknowledge that we have a right to respect the intellectual health and interests of teachers wishing to gain knowledge about the effects of their practice, and thus making the school possible and attractive as a centre for research. A school that is only a distributor of knowledge serves not to liberate teachers and pupils but to place them in bondage as it disinherits them of their intellectual rights.

It is a major theme of this book that various areas of knowledge, e.g. the disciplines of the curriculum, are not the exclusive colony or preserve of specialists with qualifications in that field or form of knowledge, but that such colonies are, by right, open, free and independent. All comers to inquiry are welcome — the truth does not respect personal qualifications as the criterion for entry. This unilateral declaration of curriculum inquiry freedom is referred to as the 'autonomy of research'. It stands upon the bedrock principle that the pursuit of truth is accountable to nothing and no person not a part of that pursuit itself. There are no boundaries on the road to knowledge.

Hitherto there has been an attitude that only scientifically trained and qualified staff could engage in educational and curriculum research. This attitude suggests a belief which is often articulated as 'practitioners simply do not understand such problems.' This view has served to cut practitioners off from increasing not only their knowledge of practice and problems, but also their own understanding and control over the knowledge which has been created by external 'expert' researchers.

Note that by asserting that inquiry is an autonomous matter it is not being said that the researcher is not accountable. Every profession has standards of conduct: a code of practice, if you like. One of the pressing areas of concern at present is the development and dissemination of just such a code for curriculum practitioners. The work of Hugh Sockett (Sockett, 1983; 1984; 1988; 1989) is exemplary in this area. For example, there are accepted canons of inquiry and principles of procedure for doing quantitative and qualitative inquiry. This is also not to say that the *methodology* of doing research is a finite and closed field. Innovations are coming in the method of scientific research just as they are in the curriculum of schools. One of the major goals of this book is to commit to the view that there are new strategies for doing action research and to say something about this methodology. We must not be allowed to become prisoners of the 'myth of objectivity and methodology' which suggests a particular stance and mode of collecting and analysing data. If a field of knowledge is not open to new ways of inquiring then it is in mortal danger of losing its creative and imaginative potential and will serve as a barrier to scientific progress. The modes of doing research and the standards acceptable must originate in the community of discourse itself.

For the teacher to be a researcher it seems that one must first be a competent *observer*. Without accurate observations scientific progress would be a nonsense as science depends on them. Suppose for a moment that all scientists since Newton were blind, one wonders what, if any, progress in science would have been made. Thus, the first point is that one cannot call oneself a teacher without being a *participant* and more accurately a *participant observer*. The same is true for the physical scientist who can no more discuss nuclear physics without entertaining questions about peace and destruction, than he or she can talk about peace or violent conflict without thinking about nuclear physics. It is not good enough to be an inquirer, we must ask the right questions for we are all seekers rather than knowers and we shall only make progress if we ask the most important questions.

The point about asking questions is that since the curriculum is not a finished entity, for teachers to stay abreast of the demands of a changing culture and curriculum they will have to take on responsibility for asking and attempting to answer extremely difficult and embarrassing questions. This is the spirit of curriculum inquiry and it cannot forge ahead unless there is also a commitment to the philosophy of teaching as an inquiry-discovery occupation.

The task of teaching does not require that pupils' heads are filled with information and outdated knowledge; rather its purpose *is to help pupils to learn to inquire and to think rationally for themselves — critically and reflectively.*

New knowledge is discovered not by rigidly holding on to past belief but by questioning the status quo. When faced with pressing problems the teacher should not hand over research to others, but press ahead with a commitment to seeking out a solution. This is the meaning of curriculum action research. The teacher takes the intitiative by saying 'Look, this is not right. I think it might be better if I tried X or Y.' The essence of science is that it has this self-correcting mechanism for solving problems, and we should not be so gullible as to believe that there is one right and correct curriculum which, if we go on searching, we will discover. This is not the manner in which advances of importance are made in any field.

The second major point is that *advances in knowledge do not come about through the efforts of any one individual's charisma or skills but are the aggregate result of the community of discourse and researchers in that field.* Developments are made through sharing research work through publication, conferences and other forms of dialogue. The community of discourse is very wide indeed. The reflective practitioner does not fear failure and he or she does not take critique as a personal attack, but rather is able to 'distance' his or herself from any sense of personal failure.

This is one of the most important lessons to be learned in becoming a competent researcher. The attitude is akin to saying 'well I tested this idea or hypothesis and it did not work out; yet it was an idea I feel was worth testing. I am not saying I am correct, only that I have a hunch worth testing.' The reflective practitioner does not advance a hypothesis as being *correct*, rather as being worth testing empirically. He or she claims to be intelligent; not correct. Moreover, I think that teachers feel extremely threatened by professional critique when they should rather adopt the stance outlined above — i.e. they are simply educational scientists investigating how worth while various courses of curricular action are.

Practitioners need to be keen observers of their practices — that is, they must develop research skills and expertise which will allow them to 'see' their innovative actions. They must become inquirers into their own practice. Secondly, for curriculum to develop, and consequently teaching performance, it would be best if curriculum inquiry were conducted by and based on the work and discourse of practitioners. What is being sought is a community of teacher-researchers. In saying this note that a community of university teachers as researchers is being talked about as much as elementary or secondary teachers. The situation as it stands at present suggests a strong division of labour between researchers and teachers. On the whole, teachers are not brought into the community of discourse, and when they are brought in it is more likely that teachers and schools will act in a 'cooperative' way rather than a 'collaborative' one, schools being made available for research and seen as 'clients', not 'partners'.

What has been posited is not novel. Over the years a number of distinguished writers have argued the case for the school to become the centre for inquiry and for teachers to be full research partners in the creation of curriculum knowledge (Dewey, 1929; Corey, 1953; Schaefer, 1967; Stenhouse, 1975). During the past 15 years there has been a concerted effort to revitalize and reconstruct a new action research role for the teacher. This movement has largely been the catalyst for the present work.

Following the seminal lead of Lawrence Stenhouse, Jean Rudduck and John Elliott, several teacher networks, or associations, have pursued the development of the teacher-as-researcher role. In the UK, there is the National Association for Race Relations Teaching and Action Research (NARTAR), and in the case of the Ford Teaching Project, the Classroom Action Research Network (CARN) based at the Centre for Applied Research in Education, University of East Anglia. The Association for the Study of Curriculum (ASC) was established in 1978, and the British Educational Research Association (BERA) in 1975, both of which promote teacher-researcher groups. In Ireland, the Educational Studies Association promotes educational research, and more than half of its 400-plus membership are school practitioners. In Ulster, there is the Educational Action Research Network for Northern Ireland (EARNI). In Australia, action learning and research are promoted by the networking of Zygonet — a group originating at the 1990 First World Congress on Action Research at Griffith University, Brisbane.

The goal of understanding was paramount for Stenhouse. At the Centre for Applied Research in Education, University of East Anglia, where Stenhouse held the Chair of Education, there is a plaque which reads: 'It is teachers who, in the end, will change the world of the school by understanding it.' Elliott, a colleague, summed up: 'What Stenhouse offered teachers was a curriculum conceived as a set of hypotheses they could experiment with as the basis for a reflective translation of educational ideas.' (Elliott, 1983:108–109).

A second important concept for Stenhouse was emancipation, and his *Authority, Education and Emancipation* (Stenhouse, 1983) makes compelling reading. For Stenhouse emancipation is the autonomy we recognize when we eschew paternalism and the role of authority and hold ourselves obliged to appeal to judgement. Stenhouse argued that the teacher-researcher role is the route to emancipation since it eschews the authority/expert role in favour of the belief that knowledge is provisional and tentative — at best the base camp for the next attack. Stenhouse believed that research strengthened the teacher's judgement and self-directed improvement of practice; second, that the most important focus for research is curriculum in so far as it is the medium through which knowledge is communicated.

Stenhouse's effect has been quite phenomenal, in Britain at least. Since 1976, a Classroom Action Research Network has been developed by John Elliott, his colleague and Director of the Ford Teaching Project, which produced some interesting accounts of collaborative action research, particularly the method of 'triangulation' worked out with Clem Adelman (Elliott and Adelman, 1976). Working initially from the Humanities Curriculum Project, it is Elliott who has given the teacher-as-researcher movement its driving force within the British context and offered action research as an alternative inquiry paradigm.

The now defunct Schools Council in Britain sponsored Programme Two — Helping Teachers to Become More Effective — which really gave the action research movement a solid grassroots base. A number of working papers from Programme Two — Teacher Pupil Interaction and the Quality of Learning (TIQL) — are extremely enlightening (Elliott, 1981).

In the past few years a number of books have appeared on the teacher as action researcher theme, several of these written by teachers. Some of the recent British work has focused on research skills and methods for doing action research in naturalistic settings (Nixon, 1981; Walker, 1985; Hopkins, 1985; Hustler et al., 1986; Winter, 1989; Lomax, 1989) using practical methods for conducting inquiry: interviewing, questionnaires, observation, logs, diaries, checklists, case studies etc. In Australia, 'teacher-researcher' ideas and skills have been promoted by Hook (1985) Kemmis and McTaggart (1988) and others linked with the 'Deakin School'. Recently, Connelly and Clandinin (1988) have produced a teacher-researcher handbook indicating that practical teacher research has reached North American shores. Case studies of teacher experiments in action research are contained in a collection edited by John Elliott and Dave Ebbutt (1986). Richard Winter (1987; 1989) has published two important books on action research: the first is a thoughtfully philosophical book, *Action Research and the Nature of Social Inquiry,* the author being concerned with questions of the validity and nature of action research along with issues relating to professionalism. Winter argues that the purpose of action research is to 'provide an analytic theory of action research, a set of conditions for its theoretic possibility' (Winter, 1987:4). Winter followed up with a more practical book, *Learning From Experience* (1989), in which he illustrates how techniques involving narrative, writing and 'dilemma analysis' can be applied to experience. Winter's work is significant because of its concern for the development of self-reflection and the dynamic of reflexivity in inquiry; and secondly, because it lends further weight to the development of an alternative paradigm to positivism, based as it is upon the work of Habermas, Foucalt, Heidegger and other European philosophers. Yet one secretly suspects that Winter's book is unconscious of the rich and voluminous tradition of American action research — his bibliography does not adequately acknowledge this record.

What is of interest in Europe, North America and Australia is the growing band of teacher-researchers who have become teacher-writers, almost advocating a rigid separation between insiders and outsiders. This trend of reporting small, practical, case studies of action research by teachers will seemingly continue. One detects the healthy development of the increasing number of teacher-researchers towards forming a community of discourse that is willing to risk failure through inquiry.

Other useful books relating to the teacher-researcher notion describe action research projects, or are edited volumes of articles and case studies (Bissex and Bullock, 1987; Goswami and Stillman, 1987; Mohr and Maclean, 1987; Hustler et al., 1986; Lomax, 1989). An interesting collection of Lawrence Stenhouse's writings are edited by Rudduck and Hopkins in *Research as a Basis for Teaching* (1985).

Action research was not only happening in curriculum enterprises; in the 1960s and 1970s a healthy action research tradition had rooted itself in problems of industry, work organization and worker democracy in Nordic countries, particularly in Sweden and Norway, and this has continued to the present day (Selander, 1987).

The theme of my remarks is that *teaching is a profession*, and that we can no longer continue to view schools and teachers as mere distributors of knowledge. Schools and teachers are producers of knowledge. One must ask 'Where does knowledge originate?' That which passes as the curriculum is knowledge which comes from research units outside of schools (universities, laboratories and other centres for inquiry). Knowledge is created where scholars and researchers are pressing back the frontiers of the subject. The interesting thing about academic disciplines, which are well represented on the timetable, is that they possess this 'community of discourse' that has been referred to. They share a set of procedures for gathering new information and data; they have a set of key concepts which give structure and unity to their individual discipline; they have a tradition of work in the form of knowledge; and they have a method of communicating this work to others. They work within respected modes or paradigms for contributing to the development of the field (King and Brownell, 1966:68).

It is no wonder that practitioners in schools do not respond positively to much of the content of the curriculum given that ownership of this content does not originate in the teaching ranks, but in the vast research-industrial complexes outside of schools. Yet the complexities of curriculum have become so onerous that teachers have been required to study the effects of various innovatory practices and to adapt projects so that they fit local requirements and conditions. Thus school has thus become a centre for curriculum trials and implementation. Yet studies of dissemination and curriculum implementation are very much in their infancy. This is one area where teachers can make an immediate contribution to curriculum knowledge. To say that schools are producers of curriculum knowledge is to infer that schools are institutions that have purpose and look for meaning in the results of their labour.

The teacher-researcher movement is just over 60 years old, dating from the call of men such as Buckingham (1926) and Dewey (1929) for teachers to become investigators, yet significant themes have been opened up since the 1960s (Elliott, 1989). It is now instructive to turn to some of the constraints on the *teacher as a reflective professional*.

CONSTRAINTS ON CURRICULUM ACTION RESEARCH

An international survey of constraints on action research in educational settings (McKernan, 1989) was conducted among 40 project directors in the USA, UK and Ireland. Relative rankings are reported in Table 2.1. Results indicate that the major barriers to doing action research are: *lack of time, lack of resources, school organizational features, and lack of research skills.* These had been highly predicted by the literature. Stenhouse (1981:111) stated 'the most serious impediment to the development of teachers as researchers — and indeed as artists in teaching — is quite simply shortage of time.' These were followed by: *obtaining consent/support to research, language of research, pressure of student examinations* and *disapproval of principal.* At the other end of the ranking scale were human factors: *disapproval of colleagues, beliefs about the role of the teacher, professional factors (union policies, contract)* and *student disapproval.*

Most projects were self-supporting, and project leaders favoured a 'practical' approach as opposed to a 'scientific' or 'critical' model of action research. Choice of data-gathering methodology favoured the questionnaire, interview, use of field notes, diaries and direct observation. Finally, major reasons offered for engaging in action research were: to improve practice and to develop practical knowledge and reflective understanding.

Table 2.1 *Ranking of constraints on action research: means and composite rank order variables for American, British and Irish action research officers*

	N=All:40		USA=24		UK=8		NI=8	
	$\overline{X}$	Rnk	$\overline{X}$	Rnk	$\overline{X}$	Rnk	$\overline{X}$	Rnk
Obtain consent/ support to research problems	5.77	(5)	6.40	(5)	4.20	(4)	5.00	(4)
Disapproval of principal	7.08	(8)	7.68	(8)	4.50	(5)	6.75	(6)
Disapproval of fellow teachers/ colleagues	7.54	(9)	8.22	(10)	7.00	(10)	5.71	(5)
Disapproval of students	8.87	(12)	8.71	(12)	9.00	(11)	9.28	(12)
Students' examinations	6.96	(7)	7.05	(7)	6.66	(8)	6.85	(7)
Personal beliefs governing role of teacher (division of labour factor)	8.38	(10)	8.68	(11)	6.60	(7)	8.71	(10)
Lack of resources (equipment/ finances)	3.61	(2)	3.50	(2)	3.16	(2)	3.33	(2)
Personal lack of research skills/ research knowledge	5.68	(4)	5.00	(4)	6.25	(6)	7.83	(9)
School organization (timetabling etc.)	4.06	(3)	3.54	(3)	4.00	(3)	3.62	(3)
Lack of time for research	1.86	(1)	1.95	(1)	1.42	(1)	2.00	(1)
Language of research	6.74	(6)	6.47	(6)	6.68	(9)	7.57	(8)
Professional constraints (contract/union policy, etc.)	8.55	(11)	8.15	(9)	10.0	(12)	8.83	(11)

Note: Figures shown are the mean (X); in parenthesis is the composite rank order.

THE TEACHER AS A REFLECTIVE PRACTITIONER

There has been a return to the call for 'reflective teaching' (Zeichner and Liston, 1987; Bonser and Grundy, 1988; Brennan and Noffke, 1988; Noffke and Brennan, 1988). That is, teaching that is not a knowledge-bounded set of competencies which are learned during student teaching, but on the contrary teaching that reflectively supports teacher growth and professionalism through the questioning of policies, problems and the consequences of actions. These commentators (Brennan and Noffke, 1988) argue that action research is a highly suitable approach to reflectivity since it is personalized and politicized; their concern is with exploring how action research can contribute to the empowerment, and therefore liberation, of teachers in schools. The present writer would argue that action research will result in the empowerment of students equally. Much of this new, accumulating literature on reflection in teaching is directed at teacher educators and at the student teacher in particular (Noffke and Zeichner, 1987; Rudduck, 1989).

In a salutory warning, Giroux and McLaren (1987:286) argue that 'one of the great failures of North American education has been its inability seriously to threaten or eventually replace the prevailing paradigm of teacher as a formal classroom manager with the more emancipatory (*sic* reflective) model of the teacher as critical theorist.' This statement simply acknowledges the prevailing balance of power in teacher education as a 'technical', as distinct from a 'moral-critical-reflective' conception. The technical-behavioural model dominates curriculum (Schubert, 1986); a natural consequence of 73 years of curriculum planning driven by 'objectives' and managerial effectiveness, which I would date from the work of Franklin Bobbitt, *The Curriculum* (1918).

It is paradoxical at a time when many countries are talking of greater centralized control over national curriculums and standard modes of assessment of pupils, that the cry for greater critical reflection in teacher education is also being sounded. Rudduck (1989) describes one interesting UK experiment in critical thinking in initial teacher education at Sheffield University. In the Sheffield programme student teachers are afforded several critical-reflective opportunities:

1. Peer review by another student teacher of the same discipline.
2. A three-day 'analysis' student teacher workshop to explore issues of concern to the student teacher — e.g. working with special educational curricula or cooperative work.
3. Collaborative group projects involving students and school staff working on problems identified by school staff.

There have been various usages of reflection discussed in the 'reflective teaching' literature. From Dewey (1910) to the Holmes Group (1986) reflection is a central concept. The latter group argued that 'reflective, practical experience' was to be part of the prescription for ensuring a more 'intellectually sound' approach (Holmes Group, 1986: 62).

THE TEACHER AS A REFLECTIVE PROFESSIONAL

Perhaps the most outstanding feature of the professional is the capacity for self-evaluation and self-improvement through rigorous and systematic research and study of his or her practice. The image of the reflective teacher is an attractive one in which the problems of practice are open to reflection and inquiry. Several academics, but as yet few teacher-practitioners (Calderhead, 1988; Hoyle, 1972; Schon, 1983, 1987; Munby, 1986; Zeichner and Liston, 1987), have attempted to capture the implications of the reflective, learning professional. Hoyle (Stenhouse, 1975:143–144) offers a conception of the 'restricted' and 'extended' professional.

The restricted professional

The restricted professional has the following characteristics:

1. A high level of classroom competence.
2. Child-centredness (sometimes subject-centredness).
3. A high level of skill in handling children and in understanding them.
4. Derives a lot of satisfaction from personal relationships with pupils.
5. Evaluates performance in terms of own perceptions of changes in pupil behaviour and achievement.
6. Attends short courses of a practical nature.

The extended professional

On the other hand, the *extended professional* has all the qualities of the *restricted professional*, plus:

1. Views work in the wider context of school, community and society.
2. Participates in a wide range of professional activities (subject panels, teachers' centres, conferences).
3. Has a concern to link theory and practice.
4. Has a commitment to some form of curriculum theory and mode of evaluation.

The extended professional has an inquiring attitude to the profession and to personal performance, and a broad understanding of curriculum. The late Lawrence Stenhouse (1975:144) argued that the outstanding characteristic of the professional teacher (or administrator) is 'the capacity for autonomous professional self-development through systematic self-study, through the study of the work of other teachers and through the testing of ideas by classroom research procedures'.

PROMOTING TEACHER PROFESSIONALISM

One cannot be a teacher-professional without engaging in research in order to improve one's performance. In an ironic twist, research then becomes the basis for teaching. As inquiry, teaching becomes a sort of scientific activity founded on curiosity and the desire to understand the effects of one's behaviour. Research is essentially utilitarian-inquiry applied to action to determine if it is worth while. Research activity is the *sine qua non* of the professional. It is crucial to make the distinction which Sockett (Sockett, 1989) draws between *professionalism and professionalization*. By professionalism is meant the manner of conduct within an occupation — for example, the instrumental values which guide behaviour such as honesty and punctuality. By *professionalization* is meant the process by which one becomes a 'professional', or by which the occupation becomes a profession, thus signalling a socialization into the profession through some educational route, rites of passage etc. Professionalism is essential for those claiming the status of teacher or educator.

The school curriculum, as presently structured, emphasizes the mastery of large bodies of skills and knowledge, leading the teacher to focus on *an instructional role* to the exclusion of inquiry and other professional endeavours, and thus signalling the status of 'manager' described above by Giroux and McLaren (1987). This concentration on 'covering the ground' is deprofessionalizing for the teacher as it strips him or her of engagement in the 'community of discourse' and from making a more constructive contribution to the advancement of teaching and learning. Teachers need to know better about the effects of their work and to help others to know better and do better as teachers and as teacher-researchers.

What counts as *professionalism*? Some concept of professionalism should be defined if this idea is to be promoted. It seems that a professional must have a *large store of knowledge and the competence to practise his or her art and craft of teaching.* He, or she, would also posess *considerable research skill and expertise — a theoretical knowledge.* In addition to possessing a theoretical knowledge, the professional would have to be able and competent to *teach well.* Such a person would possess a disposition that allows them to behave 'professionally' — one might call this having a 'professional attitude' (Gaden, 1988).

Let us examine a case of a teaching skill — knowing how to plan units of work in curriculum development. Many teachers know how to plan lessons so that they hang together as a unit. This is no mean achievement, calling into play skills, knowledge and pedagogical understanding. Knowing how to plan units is evidence of *being able.* Knowing in this sense is a function of existence. Knowing how to act as a professional then is a function of existence rather than thinking. A professional thinks by reason of what he or she is, rather than existing by virtue of what he or she thinks. Learning how to develop curriculum units does not depend upon instruction gained during teacher training, but upon modes of terminal and instrumental human values which govern modes of behaviour and are supported by an ethos complementary and sustaining to such professionalism.

Inquiry is a form of professional knowledge-getting, and is developed through experience of inquiry. The skills of the grafitti artist, dancer and composer are gained through the practice of their art or craft. The concept of apprenticeship is an excellent notion which conveys this idea. One learns through experience and through a community; not necessarily through schools and schooling. Ivan Illich's idea of 'learning webs' and Toffler's 'networks' are apposite here (Illich, 1971; Toffler, 1971). To behave professionally one must reveal some essence of one's self or character — what Polyani (1973) calls 'personal knowledge'. It is not of the 'knowing that' but the 'knowing how' variety.

The professional teacher must have an answer for those who ask the question 'What is the purpose of teaching?' To my mind the purpose of teaching is to understand the nature of knowledge. There will be many other key goals, such as the promotion of critical thought, but with regard to the knowledge dimension understanding is the aim.

Some have argued that teachers, through their posts of authority in schools, serve to restrict pupil freedom rather than to liberate it. That is, teachers dominate rather than emancipate pupils. The central problems of schooling are those of power and control and the difficulties inherent in the authority role of the teacher. The professional teacher will seek to understand the effects of his or her role through self-evaluation and action research.

Sockett has argued (Sockett,1983) that three aspects of the art of teaching require attention:

1. The continual improvement of practice and a solid commitment to that improvement.
2. The development of skill, insight and critical reflection which

must be couched within a framework of theoretical understanding.
3. The development of a community sharing practical and theoretical understanding within a commitment to common ideals.

It would be best if the further development of a *code of professional practice* were to emerge from the rank and file members of the school community itself, for in the final analysis any code of practice contains a statement of what those in the profession regard as legitimate rules of engagement; it sets out the desires and mores of members for their own behaviour.

Teachers and administrators must accept the idea that their practice can be improved. Teachers *qua* instructors can leave content alone. Teachers *qua* professional educators must be imbued with a spirit of inquiry. Such educators thirst after the knowledge and wisdom that they do not yet possess, but which it is in their power to grasp. The contemporary concern for 'mastery learning' and its counterpart in 'mastery teaching' suggests that some ultimate level can be reached; educators must work to develop the craft, art and science of teaching *not simply to master it.* For teaching to improve, educators must submit their work to the critical scrutiny and appraisal of those within the community of discourse.

EDUCATION AND TEACHING AS A PROFESSION

Thus far it has been put forward that teaching is a profession but this is only an empty platitude without sound criteria being offered to defend the claim. The following criteria go some way towards establishing the parameters of the claim to being a profession.

Criterion 1: Qualifications

It is usual in any profession for a member to have attained certain academic qualifications, knowledge and skills, such as a degree or certificate of competence validated by an authoritative body like a university. It would be unusual to allow someone to lecture in anatomy or curriculum development without some training in medicine or education. For teaching, it would seem that a minimal requirement would be a university degree in curriculum subjects together with an approved course of teacher education and training.

Criterion 2: Theoretical knowledge

Here a body of knowledge, concepts, frameworks and theories are referred to that make sense of the art of teaching for the teacher. Through study and experience models are built up which explain good practice. That is, a teacher lays claim to the profession by virtue of possessing a deep knowledge of the theoretical foundation of work within that tradition.

Criterion 3: An association with restrictive entry

The argument here is not one of 'elitism' but rather of the need for a defined community of fellow professionals who through their group membership are enabled to continue the 'discourse' and debate methods, practices, research, knowledge, innovations etc. in the field. By restrictive entry one argues that membership could not be open to all, for clearly all would not have succeeded in gaining qualifications, theoretical knowledge etc. A secondary purpose of the association would be to protect members from outside interference. This would dictate that some form of register of members be kept, which is the usual function of the many teacher registration councils operating internationally. The fact that membership is defined would allow for meetings of members to take place at which practice could be debated and criticized.

Criterion 4: Commitment to continuing education and training

If an association is to behave professionally, then it seems that members must keep abreast of recent developments in practice and that a vital function of the association is to educate its members. A commitment to recurrent and permanent teacher training, as opposed to initial teacher training, is at the heart of the quest for professionalism.

Criterion 5: Code of ethics/practice

Conduct and behaviour of members would be subjected to a code of professional behaviour. That is, members must comply with special rules in the conduct of their duties. We have such codes operating in medicine and law, yet little has been written about those for educators (see Sockett, 1983; 1984), despite the many claims of teaching to be a profession. For example, regarding confidential personal information teachers would have to ensure that pupils' privacy and rights be respected. Ethics are further discussed in Chapter 8.

Criterion 6: Commitment to service function

The 'service' function is linked to the idea that a professional is willing to help others when his or her services are required. In university teaching, for example, it is not uncommon for lecturers in education to 'service' courses managed and administrated in departments other than education. The author teaches curriculum planning to external students — nurse tutors pursuing a Bachelor of

Nursing degree course — as well as to pre-service education students. The basic notion here has been touched upon by Hoyle (1984) in his discussion of professionalism in education by reference to a 'primary concern for the client'. Thus, something of the intricate teacher-pupil relationship enters into our thinking about delineating professional criteria. If there is to be a truly educative and caring relationship in teaching then surely the pastoral role of the teacher must be a starting point. How does the school best organize its curriculum to serve the varied needs and interests of its clients — the pupils and the community from which they emanate?

Allied to this caring or serving role, it is usual for teachers to induct new members into the profession, as in the service performed by the 'cooperating' or 'master' teacher who takes on the student teacher in the school setting as an apprentice and acolyte educator. It may seem obvious, but should be said, that the purpose of the teacher is to educate — that is to educate students, student teachers and other teachers as well.

Criterion 7: Commitment to the caring-helping function

Education and curriculum in particular is a highly moral as well as practical endeavour. It is argued here that for education and the 'educative' relationship to grow and flourish then an 'I-Thou' relationship must be nurtured between teacher and taught. A teacher must care about the development of his or her pupil in intellectual as well as social, personal, emotional and vocational terms. In taking charge of young persons one is acting legally *in loco parentis*, i.e. taking the place of parents. Given this condition it would seem reasonable to conclude that teachers must then be concerned to help with the development of these characteristics and put resources before the pupil to assist in their development. Caring is a much neglected aspect of teaching which at base shows one's true moral metal. Teachers need to work at *showing* they care, *evoking care* from pupils and *teaching with care*.

Criterion 8: Self-autonomy

This is the democratic argument for professionalism. That is, that teachers have the right to make crucial decisions about curriculum content, method and assessment of pupils. Members need to be free of the constraints of bureaucratic agents external to the school setting so that the school becomes a centre for development and research. Teachers need to participate in democratic decision-making which affects the historical process in which they work and celebrate their identity.

The fact that so many teachers are exempted from crucial curriculum decision-making is testimony of the low level of professionalism accorded practitioners. What is needed is wholesale commitment to the concept of school-based curriculum research and development. Autonomy is also required in making decisions regarding entry to the profession, curriculum development and the ongoing critical discourse which is associated with any professional body.

Criterion 9: Commitment to ground theory in teaching practice

Teachers do not easily take on board educational literature, ideas and theories. To the majority, research is an exotic activity carried out by university academics and has little practical benefit for those in schools. Action research seeks to redress this perception. Teachers are in the best position to contribute to curriculum theory because they can ground their theorizing in practical experiments — what Glaser and Strauss (1967) refer to as the discovery of 'grounded theory'.

Rather than beginning with 'grand' or 'middle-range' theories, practitioners would engage in inquiry and experimental work to derive more adequate concepts from which their frameworks of understanding can emerge. One of the most urgent tasks in the years ahead is to expose the unwholesome idea that theory and practice are divorced and separate entities. This is one of the great educational myths of our time and is a good example of the distortion of knowledge by a particular intellectual tradition which has sought vigorously to keep questions of theory separate from questions of practice. The key thing here is that practitioners are skilful in crafting conceptual models and theories from their day-to-day work.

Criterion 10: A commitment to research one's practice

The notion of the research teacher is crucial for the improvement of the art of teaching and for the advancement of our curriculum knowledge about pedagogy and learning. This is not simply a matter of having a research project up and running; the research project must be an inquiry into one's own practical performance. One needs to have a set of questions to which answers are sought through some sort of research agenda into one's professional practice.

ACTION RESEARCH AND THE REFLECTIVE-TEACHER PROFESSIONAL

Research must not be monolithically viewed as the work done by the rocket scientist in the laboratory, or the social scientist who spends long hours in libraries running down reference material for the writing of a piece of basic or 'desk' research. Action inquiry is unlike this 'traditional' approach to research. The political context is crucial. One of the first starting points should be an analysis of the constraints on one's action. Thus, action research is a form of *applied* or *operational* field research. Its purpose is not the generation of reports, articles or books on the problem; nor is it about the advancement of one's professional career through publication — although this may be important for the researcher. The real reason is the lifting of the oppressive situation; the freeing of blockages and barriers to effective action; in short, the improvement of life quality in the research setting. Action inquiry is the lever for increasing teacher autonomy and control over curriculum.

The teacher as researcher is tough-minded and thoroughly professional. This is the 'empowerment' of teachers so that they can take charge of their own professional lives. In the same vein, the main problems of teaching and curriculum are the twin problems of authority and emancipation. We must work towards being 'in authority' rather than posture as 'an authority' on matters curricular. The goal is not only to emancipate practitioners but to allow such a strategy to empower students so that they are emancipated as learners. What this will mean is that students take the responsibility for thinking and learning, making rational choices, and so forth. If students do not become involved in critical thinking and inquiry learning while they are at school then it is highly likely that they will go on 'leaning' on authorities in their future lives — thus minimizing the chance of developing as self-autonomous individuals.

Research yields knowledge. Yet knowledge as 'instruction' is merely a rhetoric of conclusions — a rehearsed set of authoritative statements. Knowledge has an in-built capacity for self-destruction and needs updating; this is why a strategy of teaching based upon inquiry is sound. Inquiry will help to yield that knowledge which we do not yet possess. Research by teachers can provide a curriculum knowledge in the same way that research by mathematicians and sociologists provides a basis for teaching those disciplines. Research into teaching will yield up new curriculum knowledge and contribute to the construction of new understandings and more sophisticated theories of curricularizing. *Applied research* is such a conception of teacher inquiry; it suggests that not only will practitioners learn from such a course of action, but students will likewise be enlightened.

Practitioners must make an attempt to discover the effects of implementing a defined line of teaching practice. This might mean that teachers need to monitor their work carefully. The unique contribution of this book is to provide a range of research techniques for studying one's work and for getting feedback on teaching. For example, a teacher might use a *video recorder* to trap teaching performance as evidence or 'data' to be analysed. More importantly, such a film becomes a critical documentary for reflecting on practice and for helping other teachers to reflect collaboratively. Research can be undertaken by reactive methods such as *observers, questionnaires, interviews, dialogue journals*, or through such non-reactive techniques as *case studies, field notes, logs, diaries, anecdotal records, document analysis, shadow studies.* The community of discourse created by cadres of teacher researchers will find enthusiastic support and credibility from rank and file practitioners, where traditional curriculum research has often been regarded as dubious and uncreditable.

CONCLUSIONS

In this chapter it has been argued that the major rationale for teachers as researchers is in terms of *a professional response* and democratic notions of *teacher autonomy* in professional curriculum judgement. Other arguments could be advanced — for example, the lack of credibility of much traditional educational and classroom research, which conceives a strict division of labour between professional 'experts' trained in evaluation and social science type research methodologies, and practising teachers, whose role is to teach, not to enage in research. Moreover, much traditional educational research is extremely difficult if not downright impossible to apply to classroom practice.

Schools will serve as centres for curriculum inquiry to the extent that they achieve a true understanding of the nature of their curriculum problems and foster the ideals of emancipation, participation and reflection on practice. The key values here are: freedom, autonomy, equality, democracy and professionalism. We know what the virtues are. Now we have to act.

Part of the solution is financial; it would cost to allow teachers time to do inquiry work. Part of the answer is ideological. That is, teaching is about instruction and not inquiry. But the argument in this book challenges this authority model of teaching as mere instruction; we should remember that all knowledge is won through inquiry. Of course teaching needs instruction but it must also adopt the courtesy that knowledge is subject to change and that its very essence makes it provisional and tentative. The teacher who sees his or her role as an authority sets herself or himself up as Promethean; while the inquiry-oriented teacher evokes a Promethean response from the students. Society cannot afford to accept two quite separate views of the relationship between teaching and knowledge; one for the universities and one for school teachers.

The tasks of teacher research are onerous. The present situation would seem to suggest that a strengthened school-college partnership should be undertaken in which collaboration may be started. The book to this point has tended to focus on the mind of the action researcher, or the individual in the research process; note that the institutional and political issues governing the success or failure of the action research perspective have not been taken into account. However, the political dimension is crucial (Sockett, 1989) and it is fundamentally true to note that all researchers require support, but also that it is because institutions of higher education should not become too detached from the real rough-and-tumble world of curriculum reality that such a school-college partnership is essential.

Three prescriptive suggestions: first, school practitioners need *time* and *resources* to engage in practitioner research. Can ways and means be found to redirect current expenditure on educational research, particularly at school district level, to allow for support in addressing these major constraints so that curriculum may be improved at local levels? Second, action research writers, particularly second-order university facilitators, need to have ongoing involvement in action research projects if they are to be credible speakers; the gap between meta-theory and practical theory is too large. They must get their feet wet with the water of practice. Third, action research writers should make a sustained effort to publish and disseminate their work abroad in order to overcome the *transcontinental curriculum ideological divide.* This refers to the tendency to work within the national paradigm — e.g. the 'self-monitoring teacher researcher' characterizes much of the UK 'practical' experience, while in North America the RD&D external support team of researchers utilizing the 'technical' model is paramount. Moreover, publishers do not disseminate books internationally and often good exemplars of action research practice are unavailable from continent to continent. It is time to recognize that action research is an international phenomenon.

PART 2

Action Research Methodology

Action research permits a wide variety of reactive and non-reactive research methods and techniques. Part 2 is divided into four chapters. Chapter 3 looks at those research methods dealing with *observational and narrative* techniques for the conduct of action research. Observation is the fundamental basis of educational research and action research requires rigorous and systematic methods for data collection. Various types of observation are discussed: *participant* and *non-participant*; obtrusive and unobtrusive. Schools and classrooms are complex settings; it is crucial that researchers use research methods suited to the purposes of their inquiries. This chapter also offers a variety of *narrative* techniques, for classrooms are naturalistic settings where the spoken and written word abounds. Narrative accounts include *anecdotal records, action research reports, analytic memos, case studies, diaries, field notes, stream of behaviour chronicles* (the 'shadow study'), *photography, video,* and *audio-tape slides.* Chapter 3 concludes with a discussion of 'structured observation' techniques, including the use of *checklists, personal action logs,* interaction analysis protocols and *rating scales.*

Chapter 4 introduces a variety of *non-observational survey and self-report research* techniques for the conduct of curriculum action research. Standard and conventional data collection methods are discussed: *questionnaires, attitude scales,* interviews and *key informant interviews,* along with self-report techniques of *projective methods,* and the *life or career history.* Unobtrusive data are supported through the use of the *physical traces techniques:* the use of artefacts and physical objects present in the research setting.

Chapter 5 presents both *discourse analysis* methods and *instructional and pedagogical* problem-solving techniques that might be employed in teaching and learning scenarios. Since the basic data of action research evolves around discourse and unconstrained dialogue between and among participants, experimental methods for the analysis of discourse hold promise for the advancement of research methodology. Techniques discussed include: *dilemma analysis, constraints analysis, content analysis, document analysis, personal time analysis, sociometric analysis* and *episode analysis.* The second part of Chapter 5 focuses upon the use of instructional problem-solving strategies for use in action research projects: *action inquiry seminars, brainstorming, discussion groups, problem surveys, small deliberative working parties* and *neutral chairperson.* Thus action research can be undertaken within the context of teaching and learning in the classroom and in settings where teachers and other educators meet in small reflective groups.

Chapter 6 completes Part 2 with a discussion of *critical-reflective and evaluative* research techniques. The focus of concern in this section is primarily upon techniques that can provide detailed description, interpretive asides and evaluative accounts of action, planning, observation, and reflection on one's action. Further, they seek to expose constraints on human action and provide the basis for further action to emancipate and liberate. *Triangulation,* developed in the Ford Teaching Project, examines triangular perspectives offered by researchers, teachers and pupils in order to monitor human action. The use of *quadrangulation* allows the researcher to go one step further by 'triangulating' research methods, theories, actors' perspectives and the accumulated case data gathered in the setting. Professional critique is afforded through the use of *collegial review, lecture feedback, lesson profiling* and *student course evaluation instruments.* Finally, three experimental modes of 'critical-emancipatory' evaluation are given through the use of *curriculum criticism, discourse evaluation* and *critical trialling.* These methods will be of use not only to field action researchers but to professional evaluators of curriculum. In all some 48 methods, resources and techniques are included.

Space limitations have prevented the inclusion of other, often obvious techniques for gathering data: for example, formative tests, pupil profiles, item sampling and record cards.

Action research has re-emerged at a time of great upheaval and concern for professional development in classrooms and schools. As the teacher-researcher movement gains pace and as teachers continue to monitor their actions, new and more potent research techniques will appear. Curriculum, teachers and pupils will be the principal beneficiaries of this extended reflective professionalism.

3 Observational and Narrative Research Methods

> If you want to understand what a science is, you should look in the first instance not at its theories or its findings, and certainly not what its apologists say about it; you should look at what the practitioners of it do.
>
> Clifford Geertz (1973:5)

Observation is not only a fundamental activity associated with action research but is a requisite tool for scientific enquiry. Observation may be *obtrusive and interactive*, as in the case of 'participant observation', or *unobtrusive and non-reactive*, as in the case of 'non-participant observation'. The style will depend upon the nature of the research problem and the skills or preference of the researcher. It is even fair to comment that the observer is observed as he or she makes observations — a dimension little discussed in the literature.

Observational data are principally of three types: *narrative, structured protocols (checklists, interaction analysis categories etc.)*, and *ratings*. Observations are also either *structured* or *unstructured*.

Observation may be further understood by reference to *structure*. We can classify observational studies as either *unstructured*, as in the case of anthropological or ethnographic type inquiries (Smith and Geoffrey, 1968) or *structured*, as in the case of using interaction analysis protocols, checklists and so forth (Flanders, 1970).

NARRATIVE DATA

Unstructured observational studies

1. *Field studies: narrative.* Field studies use naturalistic observation in the natural setting of the behaviour researched, e.g. a university researcher sitting in classrooms to discover the effects of a pilot programme. Often, anthropological methods of ethnographic data collection are used, such as case study, field notes, diaries, journals, audio and video film footage. The aim is description and interpretation from the inside rather than strict measurement and prediction of variables using a quantitative approach.

2. *Participant observation: narrative.* Participant observation is employed when the researcher wishes to understand by engaging in the roles of those studied. It is unstructured in the sense that strict controls are not placed on the context, action or the type of data collected, as well as there not being any a priori research hypotheses to test in the field setting. The crucial problem is to be able to render interpretable the process of events and behaviour as it occurs naturally. Becker (1958) discussed the process as follows:

> The participant observer gathers data by participating in the daily life of the group or organization he studies. He watches the people he is studying to see what situations they ordinarily meet and how they behave in them. He enters into conversation with some or all of the participants in these situations and discovers their interpretations of the events he has described. (Becker, 1958:652)

3. *Specimen records (stream-of-behaviour chronicles/shadow studies).* Behaviour is observed in a natural setting, but over a brief period of time (e.g. a full day) in the original context. A good example would be Barker and Wright (1951), *One Boy's Day,* in which a researcher 'shadowed' a seven-year-old child, chronicling all the episodes of behaviour and interaction throughout the day and ending up with rich, detailed descriptions of episodes. See also Barker and Wright (1955).

4. *Anecdotal records: narrative data.* Widely used by historians and educators for unstructured observation. These are simply brief accounts of action or events that are written-up verbatim — it is a 'word imagic picture of action'. Best used to record *unanticipated behaviours*, preplanning becomes virtually impossible outside of several general headings (see section on anecdotal records on p. 67 for examples).

5. *Diaries/dialogue, journals/logbooks: narrative data.* These techniques are unstructured in the sense that they permit maximum freedom of response and invite the researcher to collect a continuous stream of events and behaviours.

Simple naturalistic observation using narrative techniques such as field notes, anecdotal records, diaries and logs as discussed above are used in naturalistic settings by an observer who is ordinarily unobserved. Such distancing from subjects buttresses the research project from 'reactive' effects. There is the principal gain of gathering the data first-hand in the natural setting where it ocurred.

Structured observational techniques

1. *Checklists.* A device permitting the observer to 'check' to see if a

pre-specified behaviour is present or absent during observation.

2. *Rating scales.* Using coded scale procedures, the observer 'rates' a particular behaviour using graphic, numerical or categorical rating scales.

3. *Interaction analysis protocols.* Use of pre-specified categories of verbal and non-verbal behaviour, which are 'ticked' during the cycle of observation (cf. Simon and Boyer, 1975; Galton, 1978)

Styles of observation: participant and non-participant

In participant observation the researcher is a normal member of the group — this would seem axiomatic for action research work — and he or she joins in wholeheartedly with the activities, events, behaviours and culture of the group. Although the true identity and role of the researcher may not be fully known to the group, this does not rule out cases where it is.

In non-participant observation, the researcher is unobtrusive and does not engage in the roles and work of the group as a group member, but remains aloof and distanced from the action (perhaps hiding behind a two-way mirror as in some psychological studies); further, the researcher deliberately does not feign membership of the group. The researcher is more concerned with *participants' behaviours* than with gaining meaning through *personal participation.* The focus is on valid recording of behaviours using an unobtrusive strategy of data collection so as not to interfere with the natural sequence of events; care is taken not to disturb the ethos and culture of the setting by intrusive activity. Non-participant observation is increasingly being used in educational anthropological studies (Smith and Geoffrey, 1968; Erickson and Mohatt, 1982), mainly through use of video-tape technology.

Advantages of observation
Observation has certain decided advantages as a research technique:

1. *Naturalistic enquiry.* The study takes places in the 'natural' environment of the participants rather than an artificial or contrived laboratory reconstruction.
2. *Time sampling.* Unlike the survey researcher, the observer can take as much time as is required to gain a representative sample of behaviour — ensuring that trends and behaviours are representative. The advantage is that unlikely as well as likely occurences will probably be sampled.
3. *Non-verbal behaviour.* The observer can make notes on non-verbal behaviour, like facial and body movement and gestures, which are not available to the sample survey researcher.

Disadvantages of observational studies

The following are the disadvantages of observation as a research technique:

1. *Data difficult to quantify.* Unstructured modes of observation rely heavily on description rather than measurement and counting procedures. It is often difficult to impose a coding frame on massive amounts of qualitative data.
2. *Small size of population observed.* The fact that a group or individual is the focus of the observation may permit discussion of results only in relation to the case studied.
3. *Generalizability.* This is related to point 2 above; since cases studied are small, it is impossible to generalize the results to larger populations.
4. *Reactivity.* With an observer present *in situ*, a reactive effect may be introduced into the setting which distorts behaviour and produces unnatural results. That is, with a researcher present, respondents may behave uncharacteristically.

In conclusion, it can be said that observational data can be attempted by trying to get whole pictures of events through video-audio taping, through the collation of narrative data, using structured checklists and category systems and by using ratings.

Observational roles

An interesting analysis of the variant conceptions of observation has been provided by Gold (1958) who discusses four roles: *complete participant, participant as observer, observer as participant*, and *complete observer.*

Complete participant

In this role, the researcher is a complete participant; he or she never makes his or her real identity known to the group being observed. The researcher is, in the fullest sense, a 'participant observer' joining intimately in the life of the group. The observer learns the role, language, mores and world-view of the group. The researcher may employ 'triangulation' by utilizing various methods to check on perspectives and results (triangulation being a nautical concept which allows the correct position of a ship to be checked by comparing its position with the position of two known navigational points (Bailey, 1978: 239).

Participant as observer

This position is similar to the complete observer role, but differs in the sense that the observer and the subjects 'know' that this is simply a 'field relationship' and that the researcher is there only as long as the study continues. This is typical of community studies and is well demonstrated in the field relationship enjoyed by Carlos Castaneda (1970) in his bewitching studies of Don Juan, the Sonoran sorceror.

Observer as participant
This role is typical of studies where the researcher conducts one-off visits, e.g. interview settings and formal observation using checklists. The role does not call for unstructured, but highly structured techniques, and the researcher has only a brief relationship with subjects in many settings.

Complete observer
Here the researcher is a true 'non-participant' and he or she is throughly removed from any human interaction or reactivity with the subjects. It is akin to professional eavesdropping as in the case of the child psychologist observing behaviour from behind a hidden mirror or camera. The researcher does not take any risks.

PARTICIPANT OBSERVATION

Participant observation may be defined as the practice of doing research by joining in the life of the social group or institution that is being researched. Thus the researcher has a twofold goal: to take on the role of a participant in a setting and to inquire into the ethnographic character of the setting. By participating, the researcher gets the feel of what it is like to be an actor in the social situation and is able to comprehend and understand behaviour. Participant observation is axiomatic in both teaching and action research since the practitioner must be committed to the study of his or her practice. In the opinion of the author, participant observation bears the highest fidelity with the methodological purpose of action research and is the foremost technique for use in the study of classrooms and curriculum. For a good discussion of participant observation see Spradley (1980) and Goetz and LeCompte (1984) for applications to qualitative educational inquiry. It is not a single strategy but a methodology for field work studies.

Perhaps the greatest benefits of participant observation are in terms of collecting authentic accounts and verification of ideas through empirical observations — do the actors do what they, or the researcher, believes they are doing? Yet it is more than mere looking; data must be systematically recorded through such means as interviewing, or keeping a diary or set of field notes. The written record ought to include both objective information — i.e. facts or events which occurred — as well as subjective ruminations in the form of beliefs, feelings etc. One must become experienced at differentiating between what does and does not need recording — long-term residency will help sort this out.

Guidelines for the conduct of participant observation

The following suggested steps are offered not as a blueprint to be followed religiously in a lock-step fashion but as criteria considered worth treatment in an action research study:

1. *Defining the ethnographic problem.* One must not assume that the reader knows the purpose of the project. Define the puzzle that has prompted research into the issue, e.g. bullying behaviour in the school. Illustrate with examples from actual experience.
2. *Negotiating access/entry.* Discuss how the researcher obtained permission to proceed from authorities, pupils, others. It is understood that the teacher is already strategically placed to do participant observation, yet this role is not assumed in other social settings such as factories, community clubs, etc. Provide examples of letters written to secure access to research settings.
3. *Define the research group/population.* Who is in the research setting? How was membership acquired? What are the names of these characters — make them human for your reader.
4. *Making a record of events and activities.* What is going on in the setting when you are there? Who talks with whom? What is the content of messages passed? What rituals, duties, activities transpire? Write descriptive accounts of when events happen and with what regularity. Making a record will entail a variety of ways of looking — eavesdropping, focused interviews and casual conversations with actors in the setting. The record can consist of notes, videotapes, photos, diaries and any other method for documenting the study.
5. *Describing the research setting.* Map out the setting by drawing diagrams, maps, etc. which illustrate space and how it is used. What special resources, equipment is needed? Key concepts here are *space* and its use, *artefacts*, *symbols* and other *objects* found in the setting. Try to answer the question: What do these objects or artefacts mean to the actors?
6. *Analysing the data.* Search through the data for themes, recurring ideas etc. Make a components analysis by describing the frequency with which themes occur. For example, by emptying the contents of an infant's schoolbag one could find: reading books, workbooks, a lunchbox, pencils, some football cards and some earmuffs. One could divide these into two domains or components: schoolwork objects (books, workcards, pencils, etc.); and personal artefacts (earmuffs, lunchbox, football cards).
7. *Closure and exiting.* When a thorough cycle has been observed and action monitored the time will come when it is necessary to

retire from the study, though in the case of the teacher not from the setting. Certain civilities and courtesies should be observed here — thanking people for assistance, promising a report, etc.

8. *Writing up the study.* Write up the study in the units or cycles in which it unfolded. A case study is an ideal method for reporting an ethnographic piece of action research. Be sure to dwell on what was learned from the research experience.

9. *Disseminating the study.* The results should be fed back to the setting and the community of action research discourse as soon as possible for others to learn from and to criticize the report. Research is not research without some holding out of the work to public scrutiny for criticism.

One must try to keep a happy medium between juggling the observation and the participation element, yet this is a problem which each researcher must face and solve.

Finally, mention should be made of the problem of 'going native' — that is, the tendency to become so emotionally involved with the subjects one is researching that any sense of rational reportage is totally lost. To wit, the story cited in Lang and Lang (1960) concerning participant observers who became *participants.* It would appear that two researchers present at a Billy Graham crusade made their 'Decision for Christ' and left their fold of observers to walk down the aisle!

SCHOOL AND CLASSROOM OBSERVATION: *AIDE-MÉMOIRE*

These are some points to keep in mind when observing in schools and classrooms. They may act as an *aide-mémoire* in this respect. These items are not intended to beg the question, i.e. item 1 does not imply that all schools should be orderly and quiet when classes are changing — the purpose is to make an empirical and *factual* rather than a *value* judgement of the setting.

Corridor traffic/behaviour

1. How *orderly* are halls and corridors when classes are changing?
2. Do students talk with one another? Do students and teachers interact?
3. Is the traffic fluid — does it move efficiently?
4. Are teachers in the crowds?
5. Is there evidence of student work on the bulletin boards and walls of the corridors?
6. What artefacts are celebrated, e.g. trophy case for sporting activities.

Classroom Ethos

7. Does the class begin precisely on time?
8. Does the room have bright lighting? Windows?
9. Is student work posted on walls, boards, etc?
10. What strategy of pupil organization is used in the class: whole group teaching, small groups or independent-individualized instruction?
11. Is the class streamed by ability, mixed ability etc?
12. Do the students get straight down to work?
13. Is the class coeducational?
14. Is the register taken?
15. Is anyone late?

Teaching and learning

16. Describe the lesson activity and teacher's strategy in opening the lesson.
17. What seems to be the objective?
18. Does the teacher have a lesson plan with objectives and activities planned in advance and written up?
19. How does the teacher provide for individual needs?
20. Are students attentive?
21. Would you deal with this lesson in an alternative fashion? How?
22. How would you describe the climate in this class: authoritarian/democratic/chaotic?
23. Does the teacher act in a supporting way which facilitates learning?
24. Is the lesson relevant?
25. Was homework or out-of-school project work given?
26. Does the lesson connect with previous learnings?
27. To what extent do students participate?
28. Was the lesson plan carefully and systematically implemented?
29. Did the teacher make any effort to evaluate learning through questioning, pupil work, etc?
30. Describe how the lesson terminated.

Afterthoughts

31. Did students dash quickly out of the room?
32. Did students react to your presence as an observer? How?
33. What problems does this school have which you have observed?
34. What are some of the strengths of the school and its curriculum? What are its disadvantages?
35. What values are celebrated in the 'hidden curriculum'?
36. What things concern students in this school/class?

37. What role do parents play in school curriculum and decision-making?
38. Are there regular staff meetings?
39. Did the teacher *evaluate* his or her own performance? How?

Conclusions

The above questions can be used to structure observations when one is looking from a *non-participant* role. The richness of the notes taken are vital to capture the ethos or climate of the school. Look out for rituals (assembly, prayers, etc.) and symbols (flags, statues, etc.). What does the surrounding community look like — affluent or poor? How does the community support the school and curriculum? Are parents frequent visitors to the school? Is the school used by the wider community? Write up what you have witnessed, being sure to record dates, times, events, persons interviewed etc. accurately.

ANECDOTAL RECORDS

Anecdotal records are narrative-verbatim descriptions of meaningful incidents and events which have been observed in the behavioural setting where the action takes place. Each anecdotal account is written up immediately after it happens. They focus on narrative, conversation and dialogue and provide short, sharp incisive summaries of points that stick in our mind long after the event. Anecdotal records are useful in action research because they are directly observed behavioural data which enable the researcher to 'see' the incident and gain an 'insider' perspective. Brandt (1972) suggests that the anecdote has been the most widely used method of recording naturalistic behaviour — having served the policeman, journalist, doctor and novelist as well as the teacher.

Collected over a period of time, the anecdotal record provides a running commentary of an ethnographic type on particular individuals and cases. With the heightened interest in the qualitative-ethnographic methodology of educational research, anecdotal data can prove to be an easily mastered technique for capturing the social reality of the research setting. Every day the practitioner is exposed to a wealth of data: for example, that Ross is always on time while Sarah is continually late; that Paul only talks to Ross; and that Mark has problems with reading. Such observations are only likely to provide an incomplete picture of behaviour unless they are supplemented by more systematic data collection. To systematize such random events and incidents, the anecdotal record can be employed. One must, however, limit the amount of inference permitted.

Nature of anecdotal records

Anecdotal records are factual descriptions of the meaningful incidents and events which the teacher has observed in the lives of his or her pupils (Gronlund, 1981). Anecdotes serve as word descriptions of behavioural episodes. One of the key tasks for the researcher is to watch for the beginning and ending of 'episodes' of behaviour. To this, the author would add that interpretive asides can be added to the factual descriptions rendered, and further, that these can be used in any social setting or activity space — not only by teachers in classrooms. They are extremely useful when focusing on particular individuals over a period of time and can be effectively used to monitor social-psychological development such as attitude change.

The method is somewhat selective in that the researcher decides what incidents to pick out from the action. Yet, they are objective accounts and can be an accurate sampling of behaviour when kept over a continuous period. Anecodotal records are particularly fruitful in exploratory work where one wishes to generate new hypotheses. Piaget (1926) used the anecdote method widely in reporting children's cognitive development.

Keeping anecdotal records

It is highly advisable to keep anecdotal records on index cards. A file of cards can be set up for each pupil or case unit. This can be cross-indexed to a more detailed set of field notes kept for pupils in notebooks. Sometimes a notebook for each student will be preferred as a strategy. Selltiz et al. (1959:227) have described the anecdotal record as 'the most widely used unstructured method for describing behaviour in natural settings'. By cross-referencing to other methods, i.e. interviews, field notes, a more complete composite can be erected. In the example used opposite, Jim Jones' development of understanding controversial social issues can be monitored by reference not only to the anecdotal record card itself, but by cognitive and affective achievement tests in social studies.

Suggestions and procedures for writing anecdotal records
1. Accounts should focus on a clear description of the facts of the event, behaviour or incident.
2. State what actually happened and the context which promoted its occurence.
3. Write the facts first, then offer an 'interpretation' as a separate entity on the anecdotal record card.

Sample anecdotal record card

Class: 11A   *Pupil:* Jim Jones   *Observer:* JMcK
Date: 15 May 1985   *Place:* Classroom, Roosevelt High

The incident observed:

Before beginning the social studies lesson I overheard Jim Jones talking about the police incident at Osage Avenue in Philadelphia where 11 members of the MOVE group were burned to death after the police dropped a fire bomb on their home. The issue is clearly a controversial one as half of the group took the side of the MOVE folk and the others, the authorities. During the lesson I raised the issue and encouraged a discussion. Jim Jones was very upset by the resultant deaths and seemed depressed after.

Interpretation:

This is clearly an issue of concern for the students. The issue offered itself as a 'teachable moment' so I permitted the discussion. As a follow up I called for a vote from the class on approval for the police action — the vote was 21 against, 10 in favour. I have set up a small working party of pupils to collect data of a factual nature and to keep a file which they can present in a seminar at a later date. Jim Jones seemed eager to be involved so I appointed him Chair of the working party. The group have confirmed my belief about the importance of this as an issue and I notice a new interest in the discussion work in social studies.

JMCK, 15 May 1985 10.30 a.m.

---

4. Each record should be concerned with a separate incident and have clear boundaries.
5. The incident should be chosen because it represents an important learning experience or issue in the life of the individual, class or group.
6. Employ verbatim accounts or direct quotations to illustrate action.
7. Endeavour to preserve the sequence and continuity of behaviours and events as they unfold in the research setting.
8. Write the anecdotal record at the time the incident occurs, or shortly thereafter. If a time lag is necessary between observation and writing, jot down a few 'organizers' or 'key descriptors' of the incident that will assist in jogging the memory of events.
9. Include responses of others to the chief character's behaviour.

10. Detail the setting, where the action happened, who was involved, what the key point was, etc. by keeping good/neat records and files.
11. Concentrate on a single or a few behaviours.
12. Restrict use to behaviours that cannot be evaluated by other means.
13. Cross-reference to other files.

Advantages of anecdotal records

1. They provide factual description of a single case through direct observation, which might not be captured by other methods of inquiry.
2. They may be the only technique available for use with extremely young pupils who cannot yet write themselves.
3. Over a period of time they present a composite or running ethnographic picture.
4. By focusing on a single unit or pupil they sharpen observation.
5. They promote observer growth in understanding pupils.
6. They provide a more vivid snapshot than ratings, checklists or sociograms as a lot of information is conveyed through short sharp detailed description.
7. They provide both objective and subjective accounts.
8. They can be used by all participants: teachers, counsellors and tutors.

Disadvantages of anecdotal records

1. They require extensive time to observe, write and interpret.
2. Maintainenace of 'objectivity' is difficult.
3. Observers require training in the use of anecdotes.
4. They are often reported *without taking account of setting.*
5. Read out of context, they can be misunderstood and misinterpreted.
6. Some observers focus on 'negative' or 'undesirable' events only.

SHORT ACTION RESEARCH CASE REPORTS

The short action research case report is a technique for telling a story in a concise manner. The problem with much curriculum research is that it is long-winded and therefore eats into the precious *time* available to practitioners. A brief report will suffice to enable busy practitioners to report on what they are experimenting with, the outcomes of action research hypotheses, etc.

Short case reports can often be used simply to open up discussion of an important issue in teaching and learning among colleagues. They can be used as the basis for staff discussions, collaborative curriculum development and even publication.

The action research report that follows is drawn from the author's Cultural Studies Project files made while working as a 'second order action researcher' in getting teachers to develop group discussion as a teaching strategy for handling controversial issues. Similar action research reports are described in recent British work (Hustler, Cassidy and Cuff, 1986: 18). Such reports could only be written and discussed in a school where teachers and pupils were highly supportive of the action research perspective with a view to learning from one another's experience — otherwise research would be quite pointless.

The following example serves to illustrate an issue identified by the teacher (and pupils) as a pressing practical problem in need of further investigation. Indeed, only issues seen as important to the practitioner should be researched. Keep these cases short, preferably to one side of a page.

Example of short action research case report

NI Schools Cultural Studies Project
Greenhill High School

REPORT No. 47   17 November 1978

Pupil involvement in group discussion
I am concerned about the number of pupils not joining in the work of the discussion groups. I have discussed it with the class teacher (Mr Mike Murphy) and also with the class (4S, fourth years/age 15–16). The pupils say the sessions are not satisfactory. But what can I do to make pupils more interested? This is my problem.

Doing reconnaissance
The pupils say the groups are too large and that it is impossible to allow all to speak. Second, they say they don't know enough about some of the topics to talk about them — this is a really basic difficulty.

Action step 1
I am going to try something new. I will form up two discussion groups of 14 boys each and leave one of the groups with either Mike Murphy or the star pupil, Sean Kelly, while I chair the discussion work with the second group. Mike says he can tape record the lesson so that we can verify pupil involvement later.

Observation of action

After three lessons it is clear that still about half the group do not participate. So, I will prepare detailed handouts on the topics for discussion and pass these around beforehand.

Action step 2: prepare handouts

Further reflection on action

By the sixth class I find that 12 of the 14 boys are participating — except for Sammy and Aidan. I also sense a growing 'espirit de corps' in the group. They know I have wanted this to work and they also know how important the topics are — 'assassinations and violence in Ireland'. Yet, I think that we all need a short set of discussion rules as guiding principles — but that is another day's work.

Jim McKernan, Project Team

ANALYTIC MEMOS

Analytic memos are documents written by the researcher in order to systematize his or her thoughts on a stage or cycle of action research. Elliott (1981) suggests that analytic memos 'contain one's systematic thinking about the evidence one has collected, and should be produced periodically . . .'

Memos would ordinarily record such information as:

1. Hunches that emerge during the research act.
2. New concepts ('grooving the kids'; 'rapping' etc.) which explain data and can be used to link ideas into more coherent explanations.
3. Construction of models to dictate the type of data required in future, i.e.
    *   Arriving (at school)
    *   Working
    *   Playing
    *   Being bored
    *   Getting praise
    *   Having status
4. Discussion of ongoing difficulties with fieldwork, respondents etc.

Analytic memos are personal-conceptual field notes written by the researcher to him or herself. They are akin to 'methodological' and 'theoretical' notes developed in the section on field notes on p. 93. Analyses can be kept quite short and could be usefully cross-referenced to other observational data, e.g. diaries or logs. Analytic memos force one to reflect on the volume of field notes which are piling up in the study. They serve to take stock of important issues and are written up as reminders to oneself to investigate some particular issue or other. If for every five to ten field notes recorded a researcher decides to write one analytic memo, that memo would count as an observer's comment to him or herself on the story unfolding through the field note journal. As the field notes continue to develop they do become more analytical — perhaps centring around one question, issue or idea. Then the memos can serve as reminders that certain other themes and problems need to be explored.

These analytic field notes are simply 'notes about the notes', yet one must bear in mind that other types of notetaking are done in field research (Glaser and Strauss, 1967; Schatzman and Strauss, 1973). Memos are important in that they force the researcher to read and reflect at frequent and periodic intervals in the research project.

An example of a field note memo is provided below.

Example of analytic memo

A/M. October 7th 1976

(Cross-reference to Field Notes for September 10, 1976 through September 14th.)

Emergent issues in need of further exploration and discussion which have appeared since visiting Greenhill High.

A. *Student dress code*

This is interesting as I see a pattern, very distinctive, along religious/cultural lines. The Catholic boys wear boots, jumpers and heavy coats (some military). Protestant-Loyalists wear school sweaters, blazers, ties. Both groups like high black bootboy shoes. Neither group likes to wear hats. Is this universal with adolescents?

Task: Draw up a chart to show cross-cultural wearing of 'gear'.
For example: Ties, coats, scarves, shoes, jeans, etc. Does the dress code reveal something of the hidden values curriculum of school authorities? Is it social class forced? By this I mean is it legislated because funds do not exist for Catholic families to use school uniforms? Can this be arranged in table form?

B. Northern Ireland conflict as a 'game'

Field notes suggest that some of the pupils see the ongoing 'troubles' as a game (the Northern Ireland Conflict). For example, one pupil, commenting on the shooting of a soldier said, 'It was like a match (football game) Sir, they score one and then we score one.' He meant that on this occasion the IRA got one back by shooting this soldier. Another pupil chipped in, 'You are shooting at the uniform (Brits) not the man in it.' This reminds me of my time in Vietnam. Watching the attack bombers and knowing that the pilots cannot feel any identification with the humans they maim and kill from 50,000 feet up. Do the Derry kids share this same sense of psychological distancing which makes the war more tolerable? Ask Sean, Fintan and Michael to elaborate when we go for basketball.

Follow up on dress code, school rules governing this and explore pupil understanding of the 'war as a game'.

Note: Taken from the author's doctoral thesis (McKernan, 1978) 'Teaching Controversial Issues: Beliefs, Attitudes and Values as Social-Psychological Indicators in Some Northern Ireland Secondary Schools', University of Ulster, NI

THE CASE STUDY

A case study is a formal collection of evidence presented as an interpretive position of a *unique case,* and includes discussion of the data collected during fieldwork and written up at the culmination of a cycle of action, or involvement in the research. Hopkins (1985) suggests that educational case study is a 'relatively formal analysis of an aspect of classroom life'.

The case study reports on a project or innovation or event over a prolonged period of time by telling a tale or story as it has evolved. Narrative, description and explanation are highly valued and utilized in this methodology. Stake (1985) argues that case study methodology is becoming more widespread and defines case study as:

> the study of a single case or bounded system, it observes naturalistically and interprets higher order interrelations within the observed data. Results are generalizable in that the information given allows readers to decide whether the case is similar to theirs. Case study can and should be rigorous. (Stake, 1985:277)

Case studies are a mode of reporting on the status of particular projects or cycles of inquiry; they bring things 'up-to-date', so to speak. Lawrence Stenhouse (1978) has distinguished between case study, case data and case records. *Case studies* are reports on a full cycle of action; they aspire to completeness. That is, they contain a rich slice of the action and behaviours of participants including *case data* and *case records* (Stenhouse, 1978; Rudduck, 1984).

Case data include everything in terms of evidence collected — the sum total of transcripts, diary entries, field notes, video or audio recordings, letters, documents, etc. The case data consist of the *total data base* upon which the case study is erected. The case data are the entire collection of information organized during the inquiry.

The *case record* is a theoretically parsimonious record, consisting of a condensing of the total action and data. The case record, according to Rudduck (1984: 202), is a 'cautiously edited selection of the full data available, the selection depending on the fieldworker's judgement as to what was likely to be of interest and value as evidence'. The case record consists of an ordered selection of evidence from the case data, which is organized in terms of its relevance to the issues addressed in the case study (Elliott, 1981).

Case study methodology

The case study has become a research technique that is much celebrated in scientific research, as witnessed by its increase in such diverse fields as anthropology, education, law, social work, medicine, psychology and psychiatry, to name but a few. The method of case study has become something of a workhorse in qualitative research generally, and a careful examination of the literature suggests that there is growing evidence for its use in educational research work, such as in curriculum inquiry (Simons, 1980), in curriculum evaluation (Center for New Schools, 1972, 1976; Simons, 1987) and in educational action research (Elliott and Ebbutt, 1986). Indeed, one of the most useful collections of case studies is that of Elliott and Ebbutt (1986), *Case Studies in Teaching for Understanding,* in which teachers identfy, diagnose and attempt to resolve major problems they faced in teaching for 'understanding'. These teacher reports of their experiments represent teachers' contributions to the development of a practical domain of knowledge about the art of teaching, as well as serving as examples of case study work in curriculum. Perhaps the following definition might be proposed as a starting point:

A case study is a study of a bounded system, in which the unity of that system is retained as the focus, and in which the researcher uses a variety of data-gathering methods to identify and record the particular features and characteristics of that system and employs a conceptual

> framework to assist in the identification and explication of significant
> patterns and recurrences.   (Glatthorn, 1985a).

Glatthorn's definition is useful because it is a composite one. First, Glatthorn argues convincingly that a case study is of a 'bounded system', i.e. a clearly defined population with specific roles, duties and goals. In this method, the study could be of one person, say the school vice-principal, or it could be of a classroom, or the entire school. The vital component is that it constitutes a single case or system. The task of the researcher is to stay within the boundaries of this system, noting relationships with external connections.

The second feature of Glatthorn's definition is that the researcher employs a number of research methods to secure data — possibly observation, questionnaires, interviews and documents. Thus, 'triangulation' (Denzin, 1970) is used to see the case from various vantage points and to correlate methods with perspectives. It should be noted that case study employs many research methods and that it is not a single method that can be packaged and used as a prescription.

Thirdly, the researcher uses a 'conceptual framework' to make sense of the rich detail and evidence. This framework may be borrowed from existing social science or developed as constructs which are grounded in the particular case. So, the researcher employs various concepts to make sense of his or her world. By examining recurrent patterns of thought, activity and behaviour concepts may be suggested; these may be aided by the researcher's own personal knowledge of theory. Howard Becker (1958) suggests that these concepts may be gleaned from examining the massive amounts of data collected and noting their frequency of occurrence.

One should not equate case study synonymously with ethnographic research. Some teacher-researchers discuss case study and ethnography as if they are the same. To write a simple descriptive account of a case does not constitute an ethnography. The function of ethnography is to produce 'analytic descriptions or reconstructions of intact cultural scenes and groups' (Spradley and McCurdy, 1972). The notion of culture is centrally tied to ethnographic perspectives. For a detailed description of ethnography in education see Goetz and LeCompte (1984).

Advantages and disadvantages of case study research

Advantages	*Disadvantages*
1. Reproduces phenomenological world of participants through detailed description of events.	1. Extremely time-consuming

2. Presents a credible and accurate account of the setting and action.
3. Uses multi-methods to corroborate and validate results.
4. Tells a story in language layman and practitioner can understand.
5. Data are 'representative'.

2. Results are suspended until action is concluded.
3. Researcher may have a priori assumptions which bias interpretations.
4. Researcher can be 'taken in' by respondents and informants in the field.
5. No generalization.
6. Idiosyncratic and interpretive nature.
7. Data base usually supplied by researcher.
8. Costs
9. Training

Case study attempts to bring into focus the in-depth features and characteristics of the case being studied; it goes for 'depth' rather than 'breadth' of coverage. It is phenomenological in that it represents the world as the participants and researcher experience it. It is therefore more than a description of characters and setting — it seeks to disclose the 'milieu', which itself influences an innovation, system etc.

Case study can be used to generate new concepts, conceptual frameworks, models and even theories. Indeed, Glaser and Strauss (1967) suggest that the best theory is 'grounded theory' — the kind generated from concrete cases of a naturalistic and empirical type. It is difficult to refute concrete case data. Case study methodoloy can also be used in exploratory descriptive research where theory development is not the primary concern.

Case study is eclectic, using a variety of research styles and methods; it is idiosyncratic and specific; it is process- rather than product-oriented; and it is rich in description, interpretation, explanation and narrative, working more for understanding than for rigorous scientific measurement, prediction and control of settings, respondents, actions and so on. It is qualitative as opposed to quantitative, yet a good case study worker knows how to quantify masses of qualitative data.

The essential character of the case study suits it to rendering an account of all pertinent aspects of an event, thing or situation, employing as the unit of study an individual, institution, community or any group considered as a unit. The case consists of some phase of the *life history* of the unit, or the entire life process, whether the unit be a person, family or social group. Case study is not the same as *case work* or *case method*. Case study refers to intensive inquiry into a system or unit. *Case method* is a term for describing a plan of organizing and presenting materials, therapeutic interventions, actions, and so on in a given field such as law or medicine. The case materials used are often the product of a case study.

Case work and case study

Careful distinction needs to be drawn between *case study* and *case work*. Case work is the process of rendering help, advice or service to the individual, unit or system. It thus refers to the mental, adjustmental, remedial or corrective measures required following diagnosis during case study. For example, following careful case study of a needy family, a case worker might provide the family with advice and financial assistance to put right some lack of resources, such as inadequate housing. Case study and case work, even though they may not be conducted by the same individual are complementary affairs. In the conduct of *case work* there are five distinct stages:

1. Description of the status of the situation, unit or person.
2. Collection of case data and records (life history).
3. Diagnosis and examination of causal factors.
4. Prescription and administration of treatments, therapy or remedial correctives.
5. Follow-up of the remedial action.

Returning to *case study* proper, one should be aware that it is not simply a chronological record of events and actions. It is not a listing of the bald facts; although, of course, these are necessary they are not sufficient to count as a full-blown case study. One must go beyond the facts and render interpretation and explanations. Case study is appealing to the practitioner because it does not require advanced expertise in statistical usage. It provides what Stake (1967) usefully calls 'naturalistic generalizations', though these results must not be generalized to other populations. Indeed, the temptation to over-interpret and to generalize beyond the bounded system is very great indeed, but it must be resisted.

Case study method

The same sort of procedures apply to doing case study as with the conduct of ethnography or community studies generally. The major concerns should be with rigorous procedures, systematic collection of data; hypothesis testing; sensitivity to the natural setting and the reactive effects of a researcher *in situ*; confidentiality; and negotiation of any publications emanating from the work.

Stages of doing case study research

1. *Define the unit or case.* Who or what population is to be studied (Class 3C at Roosevelt High; the Principal at Roosevelt, and so on). Here the concern is 'get to know the people'.

2. *Define the nature of the behaviour.* What is the focus of the study? What problem, ritual or other aspect will count as the subject of study? (For example, teaching controversial religious and political issues/examination of texts' treatment of controversial issues; introducing computers to schools.)

3. *Characterization: portraits, glimpses.* Describe (fictional names, of course) the principal actors in the setting. I think it is important for the reader to 'see' the plot and get a feel for the characters who people the case so that illumination can occur.

4. *Read some exemplary case studies beforehand.* Orientate your thinking into the canons of inquiry in case study paradigm. Read some case study work before conducting such inquiry. See, for example, exemplary studies such as Burgess (1984), Hustler et al. (1986) Reid and Walker (1975), Wolcott (1973), and Elliott and Ebbutt (1986). Such exemplars will critically focus on strategies for data collection, data analysis, reporting and scores of other practical considerations for doing case study work.

5. *Negotiate entry to the research setting.* Here the researcher must formally gain access to the setting for the purposes of research. It may be that the researcher is already teaching in the setting, but it is vital nevertheless to gain official sanction for the inquiry so that rights are protected. Researchers from external agencies must take special care in gaining access. Many school authorities require written approval before studies can proceed.

Negotiating entry is crucial for the success of the project. Perhaps the best way forwards is to submit a formal proposal outlining the purposes of the study; the researcher's role; how the study will impinge upon other actors in the setting; the expected outcomes of the study; the time required to conduct the research; the form of support or help the researcher requires from the actors/authorities; a note stipulating the confidentiality of responses and how this will be observed; how much the study will cost; what resources are requested; what gains will accrue for the setting, system or unit being studied; and finally, how the researcher will benefit from the study (increased awareness, improved teaching skills, a thesis for a higher degree, and so on.).

6. *Development of a research plan.* This step will incorporate a breakdown of who will be studied, when and why. It will also offer a critical time analysis of the various stages of work — a time line schedule for the project. This time schedule will show what research activities will take place and when they will be brought to closure.

7. *Statement of hypotheses.* A statement of the major ideas, hunches, hypotheses or questions to which answers are sought. There is no need to stipulate these as statistical hypotheses but simply to list the important themes and questions up front. There is no doubt that new questions and hypotheses will be suggested once the study gets under way, but it is useful to identify initial issues and queries.

8. *Review literature related to the case.* Assemble a working draft of relevant literature related to the project. This review will alert the reader and the researcher to the major issues and concerns of the research project. It will also allow for suggested questions to be tested in the study.

9. *Detail the methods of inquiry.* Here one needs to link questionnaire items, interviews and observations to the research questions listed above. Attach any protocols to the proposal. How do you propose to collect information about the case under study?

10. *Collect data and record systematically.* Record data regularly and develop a filing system. Data must be collected often and as soon after observation as is possible to ensure that alteration and distortion does not occur. (See the section on field notes on p. 93.) It can be useful to write up data on different coloured paper to indicate whether they are *descriptive-factual* or *interpretive-value laden.*

Case study data are sometimes called 'thick data' not because of their density but because of the interrelationships between and among the data of the case — they are 'thick like spaghetti' says Geertz (1973), referring to this interconnectedness. The researcher appreciates the contextuality of the milieu and seeks to disclose something of the quality of the case.

11. *Begin formal analysis of data.* Assemble the data and read them over several times. Sound out the results with colleagues. Ask questions of others relating to the study. Try to keep factual observations separate from methodological notes and interpretive

asides. Search for patterns, recurring ideas and key concepts. Begin to identify gaps in the information collected and decide what else is needed for the study.

12. *Write an interim case report.* Prepare a formative research report (along the lines of *critical trialling,* see Chapter 6) on the case study and circulate this to key participants for comment. Collect their responses and try to build these into the writing of any 'final' report of the case study. Don't be afraid to make the case sound like a good thriller novel — it is about real people in real heart-rending scenes. Use characterization, metaphor and other descriptive tools with effect.

The principal purpose of *case study* is to appreciate and understand an innovation from the inside, and to convey this understanding to others. A separate point concerning case study refers to the *style of writing,* which should be less scholarly or formal and more like the approach of an investigative journalist or literary critic. This is not to say that quantitative data may not be used — indeed, they may strengthen a case study where that particular form of data is required to address specific research issues.

The value of case study methodology

Case study methodology may make the greatest contribution where project purposes or aims are unclear or ambiguous. The research may tend to clarify and tidy up misunderstandings.

Special problems of validity, time, cost and difficulty of training (Stake, 1985:282–283) often make case study research prohibitive. Yet ironically, practitioners are often drawn to case study methods because of their honesty and clarity; they do not hide behind second and third order statistical abstractions. Special attention needs to be devoted to the provision of case study methodology for pre-service and inservice teachers as part of teacher training. If this type of inquiry can satisfy users' questions and the coveted 'need to know' factor, then it may be a powerful tool for naturalistic classroom and curriculum inquiry.

Case studies may be useful in a number of ways:

1. They may be used with pre-service and inservice teachers to demonstrate aspects of real curriculum problems.
2. They can serve as examples of how one can get started with inquiry and how a case study is actually reported.
3. Teachers who are already in service can study case studies to compare and contrast problems, solutions and persistent difficulties.
4. Administrators can use case studies to form the basis of school-wide discussion on common problems.

5. Practitioners in general may query whether they can 'generalize' from case studies to their own experience.

CASE RECORDS/CASE DATA

The *case record* contains an edited or condensed version of the entire *case data* and action. Rudduck (1984:202) has stated that it is 'a cautiously edited selection of the full data available, the selection depending on the fieldworker's judgement as to what was likely to be of interest and value as evidence'. Building a case record then amounts to an ordering of data and evidence picked for their relevance to issues being addressed.

Contents of case records

Clues as to what might count as the content of a case record might include some or all of the following:

1. An account of negotiations in a project, including the initial proposal documents, memos, letters, conference minutes and proceedings, minutes of meetings and so on.
2. Log notes of vital telephone conversations, visitors to the project, etc.
3. Extracts of video and audio transcripts.
4. Background dossiers and information on project personnel, such as application forms, curricula vitae and contextual discussions.
5. Sequence of events charting project developments in the order in which they transpire.
6. Description of settings (behavioural and activity spaces).
7. Field notes and sessions with actors.
8. Transcripts of meetings.
9. Official reports, newsletters.
10. Fieldworker's reflections: factual and evaluative.

The case record requires careful sequencing and collation. Some attention should be given to the protection of individuals' rights to privacy and anonymity; therefore a 'need to know' policy might have to be put into operation regarding who can see such records. Data need to be cleared and negotiated for release with participants. Copyright exists and must be respected. This could mean that a final report might have to be negotiated for accuracy before being published for consumption. Case records can serve to inform participants in the event that the final report may be some time in coming to them. The case record is shorter and sharper in its contents than either the case data or even the case study report.

The case record might be preferred over the more final case study for a number of reasons. First, if a researcher must write up a report on a multi-site project then this report will be subject to some editing and data 'mutilation' which comes about as a direct result of second order abstracting. By mutilation is meant that a certain degree of erosion occurs. The conclusions are often eroded by the second order generalizations that occur as a result of this 'knock-on' approach. Imagine a central team project evaluator writing a case study from a number of records supplied by several fieldworkers. Some of the close-up richness and quality of action will be sacrificed in moving from case data to case records to case study.

A further problem concerns the fact that much case study data is selected and constructed by the researcher. The evidence is supplied by the researcher alone. The case record can help in that fieldworkers should be concerned to put their own case data alongside public records so that the creation of *public documentation* occurs, thus providing the opportunity for the action researcher's record to be compared against public evidence. This is not dissimilar to the approach adopted by some historians; for example, when a particular historian is provoked by one account of evidence then he or she may attempt a reinterpretation of events, drawing on the same source of evidence. This is what Lawrence Stenhouse had in mind when he discussed the notion of *public records*. That is, we can create careful records that become public as part of our research remit:

> At present most reporting ... of case study seems to me both idiosyncratic and superficial. This is attributable less to the fault of the author of the reports than to the absence of a disciplined convention which could support scholarly work in this genre.
>
> I see the best promise for such a convention as lying in the recommendation that case study workers produce *case records* (sic) from their field data which can serve as edited primary sources accessible to other scholars.
>
> (Stenhouse, 1977:2)

One feels that Stenhouse has grasped an important nettle here by arguing for a discipline of keeping records as evidence open to interpretation much as records are kept in official public records offices. The idea is that case study data and case records form a valuable archive and become primary source documents in their own right which future researchers can consult with some degree of confidence. We must rightly question the interpretation of action researchers and case study writers. Researchers often report their biases and often do so unconsciously. Furthermore, we must surely admit to the possibility of alternative interpretations of our records and reports. It is also a curious fact that *case records* of projects are fundamentally important as historical documents, records and resources in their own right.

While the history of doing 'case studies' is a long one, training in communicating the methodology is immature (Stake, 1985:283). Added to this, the case study researcher often violates the 'privacy' of the 'researched' (Jenkins, 1980), and Jenkins goes on to warn that protection of personal feelings may not justify perpetuation of social inquiry due to data/information denied. However, when all is said and done, if one really wants to know something of the complexity and contexuality of single cases, then case study and its allied records and data are necessary.

DIARY/JOURNAL

A curriculum can be understood in a more personal and humane way by keeping a personal diary or journal. Allport (1942:95) has made the point that 'the spontaneous, intimate diary is *the* personal document *par excellence*'. Allport was writing in connection with the use of personal documents as research strategies and placed the diary at the top of his rankings. Hook (Hook, 1985) states:

> Diaries contain observations, feelings, attitudes, perceptions, reflections, hypotheses, lengthy analyses, and cryptic comments. The entries are highly personal conversations with one's self, recording events significant to the writer, they are not meant to be regarded as literary works, as normally the accounts or remarks are read only by the writer and no one else. (Hook, 1985:128)

The journal is a general tool which can have more than simply a research purpose: a diary can be used to promote educational objectives, such as enabling pupils to communicate through the written, as well as the oral mode. The use of the personal diary, or journal as some action researchers prefer to call it, can be employed to encourage description, interpretation, reflection and evaluation on the part of the teacher as well as the pupil.

For the purposes of action research, the diary is a personal document, a *narrative technique* and record of events, thoughts and feelings that have importance for the keeper. As a record, it is a compendium of data which can alert the teacher to developing thought, changes in values, progression and regression for learners. It summons up feelings and beliefs captured at, or just after, the time they have occurred, thus providing a 'mood dimension' to human action.

In the diary, one can express feelings not normally made public and it is unsurpassed as a method of recording continuous events in one's life. Furthermore, it allows one to store information without the distortion effects of memory and past recollections.

Types of diaries

1. *Intimate journal.* This is the most personal of documents. It is a set of personal notes, a log of events rich in personal sentiments and even confessions. Entries are usually made on a daily basis, or at a regular interval.
2. *Memoir.* The memoir is impersonal as a document and often written in fewer sittings than the intimate journal. It tries to aspire to being more objective and does not concentrate on personal feelings. The records of war correspondents are good examples, such as Michael Herr's *Dispatches*, based on daily dispatches sent to his magazine, *Esquire*, from the jungle war in Vietnam. The diary kept by Ann Frank is a memorable example of a child's experience during war.
3. *Log.* The log is more of an 'accounts' record. It is a running record of transactions and events, such as a list of contacts or telephone calls made during the day, of meetings or of signatures of persons entering a building; or it may be the sort of written log-record kept by a ship's captain.

The diary may be kept by the teacher to document his or her own classroom as a case history. The notion here is one of evaluation of teaching actions, intentions, outcomes and unanticipated side effects or objectives achieved. For teacher-kept journals, I would propose a three by two classification which sets out to illuminate *affect vs objectives, content and teaching methods.* This can be illustrated as follows:

The diary matrix: affect and process

Type of affect	Intentions	Transactions	Outcomes
Positive/successful			
Negative/frustrating			

In the matrix it is envisaged that a teacher proceeds with some goals, or *intentions,* which result in *transactions* between teacher and pupils, leading to *outcomes* or the results of teaching and learning. Further, it is envisaged that two kinds of affect can result from any of these three elements: *frustrating elements* and *positive elements*. The idea of the diary is to organize entries by reference to these desirable or undesirable elements.

Positive features
These would count as rewarding moments, and positive and exciting developments in which curiosity, discovery and inquiry are realized. It could be that intentions are achieved and that some goals not set have been reached. It could also be the case that interaction in terms of the transactions was successful and that in terms of outcomes significant progress has been made.

Negative features
The entries in the diary here would focus exclusively on constraints, barriers, problems, areas of conflict and tensions experienced in the classroom. Unrealistic intentions may have to be revised — lessons that were not successfully implemented, strategies that failed and poor outcome results in terms of achieving stated objectives would be entered.

Keeping the diary

If a decision is made to keep a diary, then it should be realized that this will require time each day. The benefit of keeping a diary is that it forces one to reflect, describe and evaluate daily encounters. The following points should be remembered:

1. *Keep the diary regularly.* Since it is a running account of facts, anecdotes and thoughts, these may quickly be forgotten if left for completion later on.
2. *Entries should be dated and cross-referenced to other entries where relevant.* Recording the date and time of entries will place events in a clearer context of sequence. The human memory often lets one down. Try to link similar themes, concepts and recurrences through a system of cross-referencing.
3. *Diaries should record both facts and interpretive accounts.* The first task is to describe what actually happens; after this has been done, offer some analysis and interpretation — an analytical note. I have suggested a three by two matrix for considering entries: good and bad features relating to intents, happenings and results.

Pupil diaries

Getting pupils to keep a diary will serve a number of educational objectives: it will help to increase writing, thinking and communication skills. A variation on the private diary is the *dialogue journal* (Kreft, 1984), developed as a separate action research strategy in this work. The diary is normally a private enterprise, whereas the dialogue journal is a running conversation held between the tutor and the pupil. The teacher could instruct the pupils that beginning on a certain date, say 2 January, all pupils will keep a diary, completing a separate five- to seven-minute entry each day.

It is important to instruct pupils that they should feel free to write whatever they wish concerning their work in school. The classification used in the teacher diary could also be used in pupil-kept diaries by asking pupils to write about frustrating and successful experiences in school; identifying good experiences and transactions and objectives they have achieved or not achieved.

Alternatively, diary entries could be organized around topics or subjects of pupils' choosing. The topic or entry could evolve out of a *discussion, confrontational comment* posted on the wall or simply be a commentary about themselves — 'What I experienced today' or 'What I learned in school today.'

It is crucial to note that pupils ought to reread their entries for personal growth and reflection. They are putting a little piece of themselves on paper and not asking for this to be turned into a point of contention, as so often happens with pupil written work. Indeed, this is writing for personal awareness and growth not writing out of fear (the end of term essay).

Some of the side effects of keeping diaries have enormous educational potential. Most teachers are unhappy with pupil writing abilities — diary writing can help to improve these. In addition, pupils will learn to develop ideas and communicate these through writing.

Of course, pupils may share their diaries with one another, or with the teacher, but this should be a matter for negotiation with the author. Remember, pupils are protected by copyright laws as well! There is some research that indicates that peer evaluation is associated with improvement in writing skills among pupils (Kreeft, 1984).

Ira Progoff (1975), a humanistic psychologist, suggests keeping an 'intensive journal' or diary with sections given over to special topics such as 'dreams' or 'dialogues'; in the entries, which are recorded on a frequent basis in an exercise or notebook, the writer confronts others and is asked to 'free-associate', imagine and meditate. An interesting feature of Progoff's clinical diary is that the writer of the diary is asked to have regular confrontations and face-to-face dialogues with others about the diary. This sharing of one's feelings, ideas, fears and so on is viewed as having importance for personal growth. Thus, pupils could keep a series of diaries concerned with specific content topics, e.g. 'My Friends', 'Leisure Time' and so forth.

Concluding comments on diary writing

Keeping a diary or journal forces the teacher or pupil to assume a reflective stance. One not only reflects on events, but is faced with the physical confrontation of the diary. The diary can be used as an historical account, a tool for personal redirection and growth, or both. A teacher diary is also a very valuable tool for self- and course-evaluation and will provide a running ethnography of life in the classroom and thus be a rich source of data. Mary Holly has produced guidelines on keeping a professional diary (Holly, 1984; 1989). Janesick (1983) offers guidelines on using a diary to develop reflection and evaluation skills.

Working as a prison teacher in Northern Ireland, the author kept a diary of his teaching encounters to help him to reflect on his work with prisoners, mainly incarcerated in connection with offences arising out of the violence in Northern Ireland. A sample entry follows:

Extracts from the diary of a prison teacher

Date: September 13th, 1976, 2200 hrs

Tonight I attended my first 'orientation' session at H.M. Prison Magilligan, in Northern Ireland. I met Mr X, the Education Director, and he thoroughly explained the procedures. This meeting takes two hours but one of the negative features of this position is security — it takes more than one hour of my two hour assignment to pass through the various security barriers, where my briefcase is searched, clothing etc. The British Army and the prison guards even flash large mirrors under the trucks carrying the visitors and teachers to see that weapons or bombs are not hidden there.

The prison is a grim exclamation mark on the otherwise beautiful and soft green Irish countryside. The thirty foot high walls are decorated with machine gun posts and the British Army patrols outside the prison with the regular prison officers and guards taking care of the internal area.

The German 'Z' wire is quite nasty and clings to one's clothing if one gets too near. And the wire makes a monsterly moaning sound when the wind runs through it — almost eerily human, speaking for this terrible place. This all sets a sombre mood.

I meet my class — political category status Irish Republican Army men (I.R.A.). The class is large — about 20 of us huddled in a small Nissen hut. No chalk, a blackboard about two feet square and my single textbook! What a challenge — eh? We have tea and talk about our work. Next time we start in earnest. I am on at the same time as *Top of the Pops*. How will I be able to compete with that?

Source: McKernan, J., Cultural Studies Project Diary, 1976

DIALOGUE JOURNALS

Dialogue journals are interactive personal journals — written in notebooks, in which pupils write to their teacher as much as they please and on any topic of their choice. Some writers prefer to use the term 'personal journal' to describe this, usually daily, self-initiated journal writing. A more formal definition would be 'the practice of communicating in writing about topics of mutual interest through continuous, functional conversations between teachers and pupils' (Staton et al., 1985). While there is not a tradition of dialogue journals between teacher-researchers conducting action research, the technique holds out real promise of return for the energy invested in this unexplored area of curriculum inquiry. That is, teachers participating in a project could communicate through written journals with one another, particularly if a multi-site project is underway. One way of conducting this is through the technique of *electronic mail,* whereby computer messages can be transmitted from one researcher to another on the network; or through *fax messages* and/or *video conferencing.*

In using dialogue journals the teacher is obliged to respond to each writer with a written entry, continuing the discussion, clarifying issues, inquiring, and so on. Journal writing is seen as a valuable method of achieving social and personal development, as well as the more obvious goals of improving writing skills. Some of the outcomes or objectives of dialogue journal writing are:

1. It provides opportunities for pupils to communicate by writing and reading.
2. It creates an educational 'I-Thou' humanistic relationship between learner and teacher.
3. It provides the teacher with a mode of assessing each pupil's potential for development in that dialogues are occurring in the pupil's 'zone of proximal development'.
4. It provides a rich base for lesson planning and curriculum development.
5. It allows pupils to have access to the tutor on a one-to-one basis.
6. It provides the teacher with a technique for researching his or her own teaching and curriculum.
7. It allows pupils the opportunity to criticise and evaluate curriculum experiences; thus serving as an evaluative data base.

Dialogue journals provide a running commentary, or conversation, between teacher and pupils, carried on in a private capacity through written symbols (Staton, et al., 1988).

Procedures

At the start of the term, or school year, the teacher explains carefully the idea and benefits of journal writing. It is often the case that pupils will experience difficulties in getting started on writing — they will not know how to proceed. To overcome this constraint the teacher should have a few simple ground rules for journal writing, which should be communicated clearly to all participants orally or posted as ground rules:

1. Pupils must write a minimum of three to four sentences each day — most pupils will want to write more.
2. Pupils may choose any topic to write about — school work, personal interests, etc.
3. Journal writing may be done when all other school assignments have been completed, or it may be used as part of language arts curriculum.
4. Journals are written in private and no one has access to them but the teacher.

The teacher has responsibilties as well. He or she must answer each journal writer by writing back to the pupil for each entry logged in the journal. Staton (1980) suggests that pupils view the major advantage of journal writing to be in terms of teacher-pupil interpersonal relations — as one pupil put it, 'Your teacher gets to know you better, and understand your problems.' Problems for pupils might include how to get along with fellow pupils or the pressures of succeeding in school. Journal writing is helping researchers understand what good writing is and what school conditions are necessary to lead to good pupil composition. Journal writing would appear to have consequences for inquiry learning by teaching pupils to ask questions; for writing ability and motivation; for fostering personal reflection and awareness; and, of course, for personal development.

The use of journals comes close to fulfilling a 'counselling' role, but one in which the *pupil* is able to initiate the questions or problems of concern without being labelled a 'problem pupil'.

Examples

Kreeft (1984) provides an example of a dialogue journal entry for pupil and teacher. Jay is an 11-year-old sixth grade pupil in a Los Angeles elementary school.

> *Jay:* 'Potting was really a lot of fun. I liked getting dirty. I can't wait for the hoot (a school Halloween party). I rilly hope there is dressing up but I still think this one will be fun all of them.'

Teacher: 'How would you like to dress up? Thank you for your help in potting the plants. They should be a super addition to the hoot.'

Journals have been used with elementary, secondary and college student levels, as well as with adults and pupils in special education. Farley (1985) reports on his work with mentally retarded students (chronological age 18.1 years, mental age 10) and found that the topics discussed in their dialogue journals do not necessarily reflect their mental age, but rather their chronological age. They discussed driving, employment, marriage planning and parenthood:

> *Male student:* 'Some persons are nice and other persons like to do things like to sing play the radio, go to the movie. Some person don't like to work in their house and some are very good for working on a job or some . . . peoples like to have things like money, new car, house, and some people like to read and some don't like to read a books. I sometime like to read a book but I like to put think to gathir and I like working with my hand and I like to play on a football team.'

The above students consistently produced functionally interactive communication. It may prove helpful, though not a necessary pre-condition in contributing to the success of dialogue journal work to:

1. Allow class time to write journals.
2. Have a small class of pupils.
3. Understand pupils' strong and weak points.
4. Use small composition-size notebooks rather than large notebooks.
5. Number and date entries (see example below). Numbering lines allows for ease of analysis later.

March 3rd
    Jay
    70 The art was wiley fun. it makes my eyes go wird because of the three demeshnal I will make a few at home.

    Teacher
    70 The geometry project if done correctly is supposed to create movement — an illusion. We'll do more and more difficult ones whenever Math is cancelled.

    Jay
    71 We did make more harder piicturs. did you see mine? I think I will do that piicture. When I was a kid I wanted to be a artist but now I dont know . . . When I grow up I want to be a rock star that is my dreams now.

Teacher

71 It is good to have dreams! Would you play an instrument? Do you play any musical instrument now?

In this exchange Jay initiates the discussion of art (70) and also the discussion of music (71). The teacher questions but the purpose is not to initiate discussion, rather to continue one already begun. The teacher builds on Jay's comments, helps him concretize his thoughts, and encourages him. Thus a form of 'interactional scaffolding' has been erected by the teacher for the pupil to gain a foothold and to take a step upwards, then the teacher provides a new foothold.

With the teacher's help the writing can proceed from a simple conversation to shared experiences and true interactive writing in which the pupil is anticipating questions and providing responsive answers. Writing skills then begin with the teacher as a faciliator or guide.

Characteristics of dialogue journal writing

To conclude, one should be aware of central concepts characterizing dialogue journal work:

1. Journals are *pupil-initiated*. Pupils choose the topic and start the discussion.
2. Writing is *interactive*. The journal allows for a conversation or dialogue to be sustained.
3. Journal writing is *functional*. By advocating literacy skills and writing skills language and communication work can proceed through a plan (Staton et al., 1988).
4. Journal writing may be *evaluative*. Pupils will render normative statements regarding classroom life. Teachers ought to be trusting and supportive rather than providing answers; suggesting alternatives may be the best strategy for them to follow, rather than being judgemental.

Some research evidence

In a résumé of teacher research on writing by Cazden et al. (1988) dealing with teacher authors, two emergent findings were cited: first, the teachers report a clearer understanding of their learning, use of classroom time, and the needs of their pupils; and second, other teacher-researchers point to. the effects of particular classroom practices or argue that a certain teaching approach works. A key idea developed by Cazden et al. concerns the ways in which the results of teacher research on writing can help teachers to 'recalibrate' their pedagogy and the deep structure of their own understanding of their work.

Action research studies of writing have been reported by Awbrey (1989) in her study of kindergarten pupils; by Bissex and Bullock (1987); and by Perl and Wilson (1986). See also Miller (1990); Mohr and Maclean (1987); and Goswami and Stillman (1987) for portraits of North American teachers as researchers.

FIELD NOTES

Action research is by definition *naturalistic* inquiry, in that it refers to 'investigation of phenomena within and in relation to their naturally occurring contexts' (Willems and Raush, 1969:3). It is thus field study based, and can make optimum use of the principle method of field study inquiry — namely *field notes.*

The first systematic work to address the taking of notes was published by the Royal Institute of Anthropology of Great Britain and Ireland in 1874 as *Notes and Queries.* This is perhaps the first ethnographic manual for those interested in tracing the history of ethnography. It is interesting to recognize that it was designed as an aid for non-anthropologists so that they might make more informed observations and thus supply anthropologists with second order data, for example missionaries, travellers and civil administrators.

A diverse set of scientists, such as anthropologists, sociologists, psychiatrists and zoologists, take detailed and extensive field notes during the course of their inquiries because observation of behaviour in its natural context is the principal mode of the scientific method. Field notes have entered educational and curriculum research through the work of educational ethnographers (Smith and Geoffrey, 1968; Bogdan and Biklen, 1982; Goetz and LeCompte, 1984); socio-ethnographers (Henry, 1963; Hargreaves, 1967; Hammersley and Atkinson, 1983); psycho-ethnographers (Barker and Wright, 1951); and qualitative evaluators (Parlett and Hamilton, 1972), to name but a few examples.

Field notes have come with the territory of contextual-qualitative curriculum study which is concerned to see educational actions in their socio-cultural settings and milieu. Moreover, many fieldwork-minded social scientists are not only interested in recording behaviour in the field setting, but in participating in that behaviour. The field study method is attendant to the interdependence of data, roles, etc., and the researcher is keen to see how holistic configurations relate to discrete facts.

Field notes often provide clues to fundamental issues of importance and group dynamics for the actors involved. More structured instruments such as questionnaires and checklists may not be sensitive enough to these underlying and often subtle themes and occurrences. Despite their inherent subjectivity field notes remain a major scientific tool; how would Darwin's theory of evolution ever have come about were it not for the meticulous attention he paid to recording details in the field?

A major strength of the field note approach is that it is not rigidly structured and thus leaves the researcher open to the unanticipated and unexpected; the researcher sees it as it is, not as it is programmed.

Field notes: types and procedures

Regardless of how a researcher collects and records data, whether through audio or video tapes, or longhand-written field notes he or she must eventually classify and order these observations (Schatzman and Strauss, 1973:99) Three types of field notes are suggested here: *observational-descriptive* notes, *conceptual* notes and *procedural* notes.

1. Observational field notes (ON)

These are field notes that have a bearing upon events experienced through direct listening and watching in the setting. They are a form of non-interactive interpretation which describes the action. One should learn to write these first. Observational notes focus on description rather than interpretation and should be made as accurately as possible. The present writer found difficulty in remembering all the details of the school day when researching the teaching of controversial issues in Northern Irish schools (McKernan, 1978) and learned to take field notes using a short pencil that could be hidden in a pocket. So as to write down interesting details as they happen and during vital conferences with actors, use a small notebook concealed within one's clothing; this does require some skill and a certain determined attitude but can be mastered with practice. It should be noted that the greater the lapse in time between the observed event and the writing up of the field notes, the greater the likelihood of distortion and of being unable to reconstruct the sequence of the action and behaviour with total accuracy.

Each observational note represents a happening or event — it approximates the who, what, when, and how of the action observed. It describes settings, who talks with whom, and so on. Observational notes can stand as discrete units by themselves. If actual conversation is recorded one can quote verbatim accounts; these often add to the lucidity and relevance of final reports as well. Verbatim narratives should always be quoted, cited, dated and cross-referenced where possible. Remember, inferences and interpretations do not enter into the writing of observational notes — when they do, then it becomes a *conceptual note*.

2. Conceptual field notes (CN)

These count as self-conscious attempts to glean meaning from observations. It is vital to look at the facts and then to construct a personal statement of their importance and significance. Conceptual notes also count as crude attempts to construct concepts and conceptual frameworks from raw data. The key notion behind CN is inferring, interpreting, hypothesizing, conjecturing, and developing concepts, models and explanations of theory.

3. Procedural field notes (PN)

Such notes are classified as *procedural notes* when they describe procedures, methods and operations. For example, *aide- mémoires,* notes to instruct oneself; they note sequencing, timing and other procedural matters. They are a form of observational note on the research process itself or on the researcher's work.

After field notes have been written up it is wise to place various types on different coloured paper for filing purposes, e.g. white notebook paper for observational notes, green for theoretical notes and pink for methodological notes. Following this 'colour code sorting' process the next step is to 'process' or 'boxwrap' the data. To 'boxwrap' the data try to write 30 lines (a full side of 8×10 paper) containing, say, 10 lines of the observational notes, followed by 8 to 10 lines of conceptual notes and concluding with 10 lines of decision-tactical remarks: the procedural notes.

It is useful to do this packaging shortly after the initial writing as later it will stand out as a cameo or coherent unit for analysis. The key concept operating with large amounts of data is *structure* when one is working with units of information. Even if inferences are made in the form of strategic suggestions later these can form a new package. The thing to keep in mind in the heat of battle is to record all that is thought significant.

It is important always to leave page margins for notes and descriptors that might help when scanning during later analysis. Secondly, be sure to date and record every page, place and character carefully. Cross-reference to other data collection techniques used so that filing is not a problem. Try to keep an extra copy if at all possible.

Analytic notes can be used to summarize stacks of field notes. These analytic notes are kept separately, and rather than expanding on the 'packages' a separate analytic note can be written (see section on analytic memos on pp. 72–4). At the end of the day the heart of the research report will contain a good deal taken from the analytic notes as they bring a sort of termination to field note writing.

Interview notes (IN)

It is vital to keep interview notes separate from field notes and analytic notes. These are the running accounts of conversations with key actors and participants, usually based on the career histories of these people. One way around the problem of bulk in record keeping is to place a 'top sheet' on each case record containing a list of interviews, analytic notes and field notes relating to particular cases, units or individuals.

Advantages of field notes

1. They are simple records to keep requiring direct observation.
2. No outside observer is necessary.
3. They are excellent as a 'running ethnographic record' of the action.
4. Problems can be studied in the teacher's own time.
5. They provide a useful data base for the writing of a solid case study.
6. They can function as an *aide-mémoire.*
7. They provide clues and data not dredged up by quantified means.

Disadvantages of field notes

1. It is difficult to record lengthy conversations by longhand field notes.
2. They can be fraught with problems of researcher response, bias, and subjectivity.
3. It is time-consuming to write up field notes on numerous characters.
4. They should triangulate with other methods, e.g. diaries, analytic notes.
5. They are difficult to structure and file.

Sample specimen field note

Date: 18 September 1974
Time: 9.55 a.m.
Nature: Observational-descriptive note/theoretical-conceptual

Concepts: Identity; Reciprocity; Territoriality

'No Man's Land'

I am struck by the 'territoriality' of the Northern Ireland conflict. It is raining. I have just alighted from the train in the city of Londonderry. A taxi driver approaches me and asks my destination. After replying 'to the Bogside' (Republican Nationalist territory), the driver walks away. A second driver takes me. I ask the second driver why the first would not give me a lift to the Bogside. He confides that only Catholic drivers will enter Catholic-Republican-Nationalist neighbourhoods. Not being a Catholic, the first driver gave his fare to a Catholic colleague (this also indicates 'reciprocity'). 'I would do the same for him,' the driver remarked. The area around the taxi halt is vandalized and there are massive amounts of 'New York subway-style' but highly politicized graffitti. 'Brits Out', 'I.R.A. Rule O.K.', 'Throw Well — Throw Shell' (a reference to tossing Molotov Cocktails), and my favourite . . . '8 Years is Enough' (reference to the eight-year terror campaign waged by the I.R.A.) and directly underneath a response from an I.R.A. sympathizer . . . 'And Eight Hundred Years Is Too F—ing Much!' (pointing out that the British have been in Ireland for eight centuries). I am beginning to think that private property is not the target of these wall artists: they use public walls, derelict buildings on which to write — the purpose seems to be to advertise their political beliefs. The places where they write are more often public property — it is a sort of 'no-man's land'.

Source: McKernan, 1978, p. 155

STREAM-OF-BEHAVIOUR CHRONICLES: THE SPECIMEN RECORD OR SHADOW STUDY

Stream-of-behaviour chronicles were first used by the ecological psychologists (Barker and Wright, 1951; Barker, 1963). The research act consitutes the recording carefully of continuous streams of human behaviour, dividing these into 'episodes' and analysing and interpreting them. They are invaluable for gaining process data, e.g. manipulation of materials, or the study of teaching strategies (Goetz and LeCompte, 1984).

Behaviour is observed scientifically by trained observers and the units or episodes are recorded in narrative form on a minute-by-minute basis. Naturally occurring behaviour can be identified. They are in essence naturalistic field studies using narrative form.

> A specimen record is a sequential account of a long segment of a person's behavior and situation as seen and described by a skilled observer. It reports in concrete detail a stream of behavior and psychological habitat. Specimen records do not interpret behavior within the framework of psychological theories; they describe in the concepts and language of laymen; they provide analysed theoretically neutral data that can be used for different purposes.
>
> (Barker et al., 1961:vi)

The classic study of the specimen record is the extreme case of Barker and Wright's study of a seven-year-old Midwest boy from 7a.m. until 8.33 p.m., and faithfully recorded one might add in 435 pages as *One Boy's Day*. It should also be noted that the Barker and

Wright (1951) study used a form of triangulation in that photographic data was accumulated alongside drawings and, of course, the extensive narrative chronicles. This particular stream of behaviour is also referred to as a 'shadow study' or specimen record, since a subject is targeted for study and followed, or 'shadowed', by an unobtrusive researcher. Chronicles may be audio or video taped, or simply recorded as written narrative notes.

Example of stream of behaviour chronicle

Scene 5: Classwork   *Time:* 10.21 a.m. to 11.31 a.m.

The classroom is in turmoil. A few children are in their seats but most of them are in the process of getting settled.

10.21 a.m. As Frank skipped down the aisle towards his desk, he glanced around the room.

Whenever his glances met those of other children, his face lit up in friendly greeting.

At his desk he paused, as if undecided whether to sit down immediately or to find something else to do.

Suddenly, he turned and went to the back of the room.

He climbed on to a window sill.

10.22 a.m. He (Frank) walked briskly to his desk and sat down, leaving his feet in the aisle. His gaze wandered around the room.

While the teacher walked to the front of the room she said 'There isn't much time to tell stories this morning. Sit up straight now! Sit up straight and put your feet under your desk where they belong!'

10.23 a.m. Susanna Hall was the first speaker . . .

10.24 a.m. Frank slid further down in his seat.
He arched his back tensely for a moment, as cats do, and then relaxed.

Studies of this ilk help us to focus on time, physical activity, spatial relations, and mapping the physical environment. Yet, such data may need triangulating with other data such as key informant interviewing, observations, and so on. But when all is said and done, such faithful recording can only help us to see and feel the living classroom more vividly.

Innumerable parts of the stream of behaviour exist in classroom discourse — a teacher's question, a pupil gazing out of the window, a game of jacks, etc. The total narrative data base can be broken into episodes or what Barker (1963) calls 'behaviour units', consisting of the segments of the total stream of behaviour. The parameters of behaviour units occur at those points of the stream where changes occur independently of the researcher. These units are naturalistic, rather than induced or summoned by the researcher — for example, children playing with toys. The second type are 'behaviour tesserae' — those created by the researcher as part of his or her mosaic. For example, when a researcher intrudes to ask a question this form of behaviour is interactive and behaviour tesserae. Whenever there is feedback between subject and researcher, behaviour tesserae is present — there is feedback between the researcher and the stream of behaviour.

Stream of behaviour chronicles face the 'time-sampling' problem — that is, unusual or atypical behaviour may be present and ordinary behaviour missed in short chronicles like, say, a class period. The risk is that the sampling may catch an unusual population. This can be overcome by *saturation* chronicling, i.e. taking numerous episodes in the continuous stream as evidence — say a full day or the same class subject on a daily basis for a week or month. Yet this would be a herculean data collection exercise. the transcripts of even a class period would be weighty indeed. Despite such constraints, Webb et al. (1966:137) conclude that these limitations are 'no more punishing than the limitations of other approaches, and the subtlety of links between behaviours can hardly be better described'.

Sample stream-of-behaviour chronicle

Behavioural setting: Junior class at Archbishop Ryan High School, Philadelphia, Pennsylvania

Subject: Mr Ray Scalio — English teacher   *Date:* 7 June 1985

Observer: Dr J. A. McKernan

Activity space: Students have just returned from lunch. Windows wide open. Hot humid summer day.

Note: Episodes refer to utterances by multiple speakers; *monologues*, to utterances by one subject; *social interaction unit* is numbered and bracketed.

Episode 1* 'Directing'	1:15 p.m. Mr Scalio makes announcement about school examination for the next day. 'Be sure you understand Walt Whitman's *Leaves of Grass*.'

	Pupil: 'Sir, are we also responsible for the Modern period?'
	Teacher: 'You are responsible for all the work covered since Christmas.'
	Class accept generally this directive.
Episode 2 'Querying'	1.16 p.m. *T:* 'All right then, let's get on with the review.'
	T: 'Peter, name two works by Hemingway.'
	P: '*The Old Man and the Sea* and *For Whom the Bell Tolls.*'
	T: 'Good.'
Episode 3 'Boardwork'	1.17 p.m. *T:* Moving to blackboard. Bends and picks up chalk. Draws columns on the blackboard.

---

* Episode 1 'Directing' contains social interaction unit 1 which is bounded by the narrative beginning at 1.15 and ending before the narrative at 1.16 p.m. Social interaction unit 2 begins and includes two teacher statements followed by a pupil response and teacher close.

PHOTOGRAPHY

An underdeveloped resource in the conduct of curriculum action inquiry is the use of the still photograph. Photographs count as documents, artefacts and evidence of human behaviour in naturalistic settings; in short, they function as windows into the world of the school. Photography and social research have a long history in social anthropological work, and early accounts demonstrated poignantly London street life (Thomson and Smith, 1877). What person does not remember the two vivid photographs of the Vietnam War: that of a young girl, running naked down a road and screaming in terror after being burned by napalm; or that of the execution of a suspected communist by a Saigon police officer firing a hand pistol at point-blank range? Yet it is only within the recent past that photography has been used by classroom researchers (Adelman and Walker, 1975). Commenting on the fact that educational ethnographers have not paid sufficient attention to the use of film, photographs and other visual material, Walker (1985) argues that educational researchers tend not to treat schools and classrooms as culturally exotic or indeed as problematic settings. One recent study using photographs in curriculum inquiry is that of using photographs in curriculum inquiry is that of Walker and Weidel (1985), whose study of school children in a London secondary school focused upon collecting evidence of children's experience in a range of timetabled subjects over the period of the academic year. Pointing to some of the practical applications of this project, 'Pictures: A Collaborative Project' (1977–1979), the initial photos were placed in an exhibition with teacher and pupil interpretive comments juxtaposed, e.g. one photo shows a teacher looking quite stressed as she examines the work of two students at her desk — it is titled 'Maths: Ten Minutes at the Teacher's Desk in an Individualized Maths Class'. A commentary including teacher and pupil comments was later included which reads:

> *Teacher:* This was a bad day for me! I don't really like sitting at the front but prefer to move around the room . . . when they all start collecting around my desk I feel like shouting 'Go away!'

Secondly, the display was used as a basis for discussion with teachers and pupils in the maths department, and finally it was used by the department for an evening meeting with parents. Bogdan and Biklen (1982) suggest categories of photography which may be useful:

1. *Found photographs.* For example, yearbooks, class pictures newspaper photos. These can provide a sense of the setting and its characters. Found photos have been taken by others and therefore one is not always certain of the reasons or purposes for the pictures. Undoubtedly many are self-explanatory, as in the frontier schoolhouse photographs of the last century. Yet Sontag's criticism (Sontag, 1977) must be answered — that photography as an objective accounting is useless because it distorts that which it claims to illuminate.
2. *Researcher-produced photographs.* The second category of photographs are those made by investigators themselves. Often observers in research settings use photographs to supplement other data collection techniques, such as artefacts, documents, etc. Bogdan and Biklen (1982) argue that the complete photographing of a classroom can count as a *cultural inventory.* Yet cameras can be hazardous to the health of fieldwork rapport. The author was denounced on a gypsy camp in Ireland for photographing individuals: the 'Travellers' felt this was an invasion of privacy, a capturing of one's soul on film. Permission must always be sought and granted before photographing individuals. Indeed, release forms must be signed by authorities and parents in most US states before taking photographs in schools.

In the Ford Teaching Project in Britain, an action research project designed to promote teachers' use of inquiry discovery methods, photographs were used to capture essential moments when pupils were working; these were then linked to audio tape recordings of the action.

Often photos can only be secured with the services of a surrogate researcher; to find out, for example, what is going on behind the teachers' backs. Yet there is quite a lot the teacher as researcher can do alone and with the aid of pupils as photographers. In fact, the use of pupil photographers may present itself as a motivational teaching strategy.

At a minimal level, photographs can provide the basis for thorough discussion among members of an action research project, or with the participant pupils. Always try to link photographs with other case data such as memos and so on.

What is most controversial about the use of photos in curriculum research lies in their analytic or interpretive function. Do they convey objective meanings? Can they reveal the quality of life and action in school settings? All that this researcher can say is that they are artefacts, resources which represent the culture of the school, and must be viewed as resources or tools for inquiry.

While skill in taking photographs is an advantage, even the amateur can capture something of curriculum life with his or her camera. A good 35mm camera will suffice for most research tasks; high-speed black-and-white film that can be shot without a flash is recommended as the flash will disturb even the most non-reactive pupils.

Finally, an important distinction has been made by Berger (Berger, 1980) between two uses and intentions of photography. First, there is the public photograph which presents an event which has nothing to do with the reader, or with the original event itself. It merely offers information, yet information cut off from experience. It makes the statement 'Look!' On the other hand, we have the private photograph, which belongs to lived and personal experience — the high school graduation snapshot or family portrait. The private photograph, says Berger, 'remains surrounded by the meaning from which it was severed. A camera has been used as an instrument to contribute to a living memory. The photograph is a memento from a life being lived (Berger, 1980:51–52).' Personal experience would suggest that private photographs are the best type for the purposes of curriculum inquiry.

VIDEOTAPE RECORDING

The VTR, or videotape recorder has become the most indispensable tool for all those conducting observational studies in naturalistic settings. The VTR allows either the teacher, or the teacher accompanied by a cameraperson/observer, to record and feed back aural and visual images. Because audio-visual technology is increasing so rapidly, no attempt will be made here to recommend various apparatus. Both colour and black-and-white VCR (video cassette recorders) can be found in most schools.

Essentials

At least three pieces of equipment are needed: first a video camera and blank casette, second a video recorder and third a monitor (often a television can accomodate). Since video technology became popular in the 1970s both Beta and VHS (video home systems) have become popular, but the two systems are not compatible and require separate machinery. VHS dominates today.

The research and instructional uses of video equipment are unlimited. Every curricular moment can be filmed; what is more, one has a valid and reliable record of the human interaction, which can be retrieved for interpretation and reinterpretation. In addition to revealing teacher behaviour (quite useful for any self-evaluation by the teacher), the video can be trained on pupils and pupil behaviour can be filmed which would ordinarily be missed by teacher observations.

Procedure

First decide what aspect of classroom life is to be observed. Record the lesson and then ask: What is happening here? What is the issue or problem being examined? How can I as a teacher improve this? Can I share this experience with colleagues?

Operational guidelines

- Connect camera-to-camera input on the deck (10 to 10 pin cables on the portapak); switch the deck to camera.
- Connect power source to wall socket.
- Turn on power button.
- Push VCR 'eject' control and insert cassette; push button down.
- Uncap lens on camera.
- Put deck in 'standby' slot (press 'record' and 'forward').
- Allow several seconds to warm up.
- View picture on in-camera monitor (a small TV screen in the camera).
- Set the shot; adjust aperture; zoom lens in for close-up; focus.
- Check audio level.
- Set counter index at 000.
- Press camera trigger to 'record' (red lights appear in viewfinder).
- Allow film to roll for count of five.

- Record.
- To playback on a portapak, unplug the camera cable and connect the monitor with an 8 (monitor) to VTR pin cable.
- Rewind and press 'Play'.
- Switch monitor to VTR; adjust for brightness/contrast.

Note: Do not wave or move the camera about rapidly when recording — move it slowly to get a sweep of the area. Remember, all connections go into, or out of, the deck. The camera is connected to the deck by a coaxial cable. If the camera has a built-in microphone no further connections are necessary (this is an omnidirectional microphone, picking up sound in a 360 degree pattern).

Dos
1. Label all tapes for future reference and viewing.
2. Rewind the tape when finished.
3. Avoid extreme temperatures.
4. Cross-reference tape data with other research methods (diaries, interviews, anecdotal records, field notes, and so on).

Don'ts
1. Touch tapes with fingers.
2. Store tapes near a magnetic field (be careful at airport security checks that film is not erased through X-ray).
3. Move camera too quickly when recording.
4. Film subjects with their backs to sunlight — get the camera with the sun behind.

Checklist for teachers using video

1. What do you wish to observe (aspects of behaviour, problems, for example)?
2. What are the positive features of the performance?
3. Are the goals of the lesson clear?
4. What is the role of the teacher (e.g. expository, inquiry)?
5. Are students involved/interested?
6. Who is doing the talking?
7. What type of utterances are made?
8. What type of questions are asked (convergent/divergent)?
9. What type of pupil involvement is there?
10. Is the pace right?
11. What style of classroom/pupil organization is used?
12. What negative features of this performance present themselves?
13. What non-verbal behaviour is present?
14. What symbols, icons, rituals or artefacts are observed?
15. Are the voices clear?
16. Is language formal/informal?

17. What mannerisms are evident?
18. Do any distractions occur?
19. What things have you learned from this analysis?

In classroom action research the VTR can be used to tape lessons (or other settings) in whole or in part. It is suggested that an observer use the equipment while the teacher and class go about their work. Portable cameras are perhaps best since they permit shots to be taken from all angles, whereas fixed cameras may have black spots.

Elliott (1981) comments that researchers will benefit most by reviewing the tape first, stopping at insightful events, and then transcribing the relevant episodes. Transcribing videotapes by hand can be extremely time-consuming, but may well be worth the effort. Walker (1985) reminds us that videotape has made it possible to solve some of the problems of previous eras, such as inter-observer reliability, selectivity and validity, yet new problems have been introduced by the video — such as the intrusiveness or reactivity effect of observers and high technology in the setting.

The use of video has the benefit of assisting others. Take the case of the teacher educator who has exemplary examples of teacher questioning, small group work, etc. and who wishes to use these with pre-service student teachers. The present writer has used videotapes of teachers engaged in discussion work and the implementation of new curriculum materials with interested schools wishing to adopt this new discussion approach in life skills coursework.

All visual recordings are basically case studies. As such they are selections from the action and not a full account — thus an interpretive point of view is present. All video researchers must keep this in mind since it will have effects on what is edited and how the final version is arrived at. If one is interested in teacher behaviour it may be best to place the camera at the rear of the room and use a wide-angle lens. Using a height of approximately two metres will permit uninterrupted views. Take care in setting up sound equipment. Ensure that equipment is set up before a class begins.

Advantages and disadvantages of video

Advantages	*Disadvantages*
1. Provides a comprehensive record.	1. Transcription is a chore.
2. Reliable/accurate.	2. Requires expensive equipment.
3. Provides visual recreation (valid record).	3. Reactivity effects (to camera/observer) occur.

4. Can be used as exemplars.

4. Distortion may occur through editorial effects

5. Teacher and pupil can be recorded.

5. Demands an observer/cameraperson.

AUDIO/TAPE-SLIDE RECORDING

While tremendous advances have been made in the observational hardware now available — mainly the use of videotape equipment — the use of the audio-tape recording should not be overlooked. Small portable and inexpensive tape recorders can capture verbal interaction and record utterances accurately. Furthermore, FM stereophonic-receiver recorders can be used to capture the verbal behaviour of a subject up to 50 feet away, and a second microphone can be connected for the observer. The advantage is that an observer is able to record conversations that are often inaudible.

Audio-tape recording is still a popular technique for the classroom researcher since it allows for the recreation of verbal interaction and its transcription. Transcripts, though time-consuming to prepare, are an ideal way of exploring the narrative aspects of segments of a lesson or problem being investigated. The playing back of tapes can also reveal qualities that may illuminate one's knowledge and understanding concerning teaching performance and professional practice. When linked with some method of creating visual insights into the action in the form of a *tape-slide presentation*, the medium is enhanced even further.

One promising technique is that of photographs of action research 'moments' linked with sound recordings of participants (Walker and Adelman, 1972). The audio-tape recording is useful for identifying broad patterns of verbal behaviour and the selection of episodes for more extensive micro-analysis.

One technique that has been investigated by the writer has been use of photographs, taken at minute intervals during the analysis of a lesson, linked with audio recordings. Other variations which combine the visual and audio perspectives include:

- The use of time-lapse photography and recording (Kerkman, 1964).
- 'Stop-frame-cinematography' (Walker and Adelman, 1972).
- Audio-tape and 35 mm colour slides.
- Freeze-frame video technique (a feature of modern video recorders).

The use of tape recordings provides a multiplicity of participants' perspectives within a naturalistic setting. It is thus a complete and accurate account of verbal behaviour which can be extended through the use of visual aids, such as video, photographs and colour slides. The researcher should experiment first with a machine so that the sound level is set properly — this should be done before the class meets so that he or she is ready to shoot the scene with the start of the action. Remember that the recorder only monitors sound within the range of its microphone.

The students will need to be inducted into the reasons for employing the tape recorder. While the students may at first demonstrate atypical behaviour, prolonged contact with the equipment will lessen its reactive effects.

In summing up, it can be said that tape recordings provide a great wealth of data and can be strengthened considerably when used in connection with slides or photographs of students and teacher working. Such activities may be diagnostic, acting as a survey tool to pick up problematic situations or provide stimulus for the development of further discussion and inquiry. The use of the tape recording also enables the teacher to be free to conduct normal classroom routines. The use of tape/slide recording has advantages and disadvantages.

Advantages and disadvantages of audio records

Advantages	*Disadvantages*
1. Easy to record.	1. Problem of data overload.
2. Provides a total account of verbal behaviour.	2. Biased towards the articulate.
3. Narrative style is in natural setting.	3. Time-consuming to process.
4. Allows for verbosity/ anecdotes, metaphor, etc.	4. Does not capture visual/ non-verbal behaviour.
5. There is freedom of response.	5. Reactivity factor.
6. Data are verifiable.	6. Contextual bias.
7. Provides an objective type record.	7. Needs corroborative data.
8. Gives multiple perspectives.	8. Requires some technical know-how.
9. Appeals to practice.	9. Expense incurred in purchase.
10. Does not require observer.	10. More baggage to carry.
11. Allows other teachers to respond who are not present.	11. Concentrates on individuals and small groups.
12. Permits normal class teaching/duties/routines.	12. Slides may not be of 'typical' situations.

CHECKLISTS

Checklists are structured aids to direct observation. A most basic example is the housekeeper's shopping list or the criteria ticked off by the pilot before taking his aircraft up. Where specific conditions must be present, then the checklist approach is very useful. At base it amounts to a series of questions one administers to oneself. The checklist is somewhat similar to the rating scale in that it tells us if a given behaviour is present but it does not tell us anything about the degree of the behaviour in terms of its range or quality. The checklist calls for a decision or judgement as to whether some criteria is present or absent.

Definition

The checklist is one of several instruments (including interaction analysis protocols, and rating scales) for use in *structured observation.* Hopkins and Antes (1985: 467) define the checklist as 'a list of points to notice in *direct observation.* It is used to focus the observer's attention to the presence, absence, or frequency of occurrence of each point of the prepared list as indicated by checkmarks.'

The checklist is a tool for aiding observation by focusing the action researcher's attention on pre-defined points or criteria-attributes. The arrangement of the points is crucial, in that sequence in task completion should be logical and sequential. In developing a school-based instrument ensure that:

1. Points to be observed are listed in their actual sequence of happening.
2. All similar traits/attributes are included in categories.
3. All the relevant and specific points are listed.
4. Space is provided for tallying marks on the form itself so that analysis is eased.

An illustration of two items on a checklist are described below:

Pupil cooperation in play

_____ 1. tends to be dominant

_____ 2. shares toys and cooperates

_____ 3. accepts rule of majority

_____ 4. some difficulty in cooperating/sharing play

_____ 5. is solitary/outside the group

Pupil participation

_____ 1. takes part eagerly in all educational activities

_____ 2. makes major contributions to group work

_____ 3. interested and alert but rather quiet

_____ 4. a passive spectator

_____ 5. opts out of all work

The checklist allows the researcher to record data without making value judgements at the time of observation, thus making this an ideal approach for some classroom research projects.

Checklist data

1. *Static data.* These are highly stable data which can be ticked off by mere observation, such as race, sex, weather conditions and time. These independent variables may be highly correlated with aspects of the study itself. An example of classroom static data is provided below.

2. *Action data.* These are data which are ticked when observing human behaviour itself. For example, in the checklist item cited above it can be determined by observation alone if a pupil is cooperative or non-cooperative in play activities.

A checklist with action data variables can be used to examine the practical problems of children queuing at the teacher's desk, children talking, or pupils using the correct procedures in setting up a laboratory experiment. 'Action checklists' may prove remarkably helpful in action research owing to their focus on active behaviour and implementation.

The recent increase in interest in accountability has made the checklist a high priority method for conducting teacher evaluation, particularly in the field of supervision where checklists and rating scales have been widely endorsed. In the United Kingdom a number of local education authorities have asked school teachers to use checklists to keep schools under review. If conscientiously constructed they can highlight glaring omissions in behaviour and problem situations which can then be tackled by grass roots school-based curriculum development.

Checklists are singularly appropriate when evaluating performance skills that can be broken up into smaller units or operations and where appropriate behaviours are known or predicted, for example in correct procedures for operating a wordprocessor or lab equipment. Further, checklists can be drawn up for observation regarding a single pupil, a small group or a whole class.

A supervisor may draw up a checklist along the following lines:

Action checklist of basic teaching skills

Behaviour	Skill observed	
	YES	NO
1. Indicates lesson objectives.	X	
2. Implements lesson systematically.		X
3. Uses audio-visual aids correctly.		X
4. Gains and holds pupils' attention.		X
5. Displays enthusiasm in teaching.	X	
6. Speech is audible.	X	
7. Pupils actively participate.		X
8. Deals with any pupil difficulties.		X
9. Writes an evaluation of the lesson.	X	

Here the student has a prepared plan with appropriate objectives but fails to show skill in implementation, use of aids, gaining pupil attention, getting pupils to participate in the lesson and attending to pupils experiencing learning difficulties at the time. On the observed side positive traits such as lesson planning, speech audibility, enthusiasm and evaluation skills are evident. The negative or not-observed skills should become the subject for a conference between the supervisor and the teacher.

'Action lists' examine behaviours, while 'static lists' are where objects etc. are observed. For example, a static list may be used to gain an inventory of classroom furniture and objects such as audio-visual aids, chalk and texts, whereas an action list will have as its focus behaviour such as pupil talk, teacher talk, and so on.

Static checklist of classroom objects/equipment

Object	YES	NO	Object	YES	NO
Wall charts	——	——	Cabinets	——	——
Blackboard	——	——	Maps	——	——
Teacher's desk	——	——	Television	——	——
Pupils' desks	——	——	Video	——	——
Pupils' tables	——	——	Globe	——	——
Overhead projector	——	——	Flag	——	——
Film projector	——	——	Religious objects	——	——

Object	YES	NO	Object	YES	NO
Screen	——	——	Posters	——	——
Chalk	——	——	Pens/pencils	——	——
Album	——	——	Newspapers	——	——
Bulletin board	——	——	Paintings	——	——
Collage	——	——	Feltboard	——	——
Textbooks	——	——	Calculator	——	——
Filmstrips	——	——	Sports equipment	——	——
Laboratory equipment	——	——	Curriculum kits	——	——
Library	——	——	Mobile	——	——

This is an example of a 'static checklist' of materials found in a classroom; it is only used here for illustrative purposes as a technique for tallying or accounting for the material aspects of classroom culture. For example, it might prove of interest to tally the number of religious objects, such as pictures, crosses and books, found in denominational schools; these exert some impact on the 'hidden curriculum'.

PERSONAL ACTION LOGS

Personal action logs are record sheets which document a researcher's activities over a specified time period, e.g. a day or a week, and which record the bare essentials of human behaviour. Logs (Herron, 1983; Kemmis and McTaggart, 1988; Walker, 1985) are useful when kept over a lengthy period of time and in connection with more extensive accounts, such as field notes, diaries and audio transcripts, as they lend a triangulation aspect to validate findings. For example, a log can be used to study the dominant events and activities engaged in by an individual over a period of time: imagine a study which focused attention on 'the role of the vice-principal'. The vice-principal might decide to log his or her activities every 15 minutes over the course of one month to get a full-blown representation of the working day.

Logs may be kept in chart summary form (see example on p. 112) or in a more descriptive form; yet the latter verge on the boundaries of becoming a diary. For example:

---

15 September 1988

Began the day at 9.00 a.m. Taught the new Health Education Worksheet No 1.
Attendance is down from full (39) to 32.
Went to assembly at 10.00 a.m. Principal addressed pupils.

Personal action log

Date _____ Log No. _____ Researcher _____ Project _____

Time	TG	TE	ADM	CNF	RCH	CD	OBS	SUPV	INS	LEI
8:30 a.m.										
8:45										
9:00										
9:15										
9:30										
9:45										
10:00										
10:15										
10:45										
11:00										
11:15										
11:30										
11:45										
12:00										
12:15 p.m.										
12:30										
12:45										
1:00										
1:15										
1:30										
1:45										
2:00										
2:15										
2:30										
2:45										
3:00										
3:15										
3:30										
3:45										
4:00										
4:15										
4:30										
4:45										
5:00										
5:15										
5:30										
5:45										
6:00										

Codes: TG=Teaching; TE=Telephone; ADM=Administration (paperwork/office); CNF=Conferring with others; RCH=Research; CD=Curriculum Development; OBS=Observation; SUPV=Supervision; INS=Inservice Education and Training; and LEI=Leisure/relaxing.

Pupils worked on art project until lunchtime at 12.45 p.m.
Met the new music teacher at lunch.
Afternoon trip (nature trail) and visit to the zoo.
Arrived back at school at 3.30 p.m.

Logs thus serve a useful *monitoring function* in a project.

Herron (1983) provides an interesting example of the log method in his study of the role of the primary school principal. (I am grateful to Don Herron for use of this instrument.)

Principal's log

PART I
What time did you arrive at the school?_____
What time did you depart from the school?_____

Was there any *unusual feature* to this school day? (describe below)

Instruction: Enter a tick (√) for activity engaged in.

LUNCH TIME	EVENING	
Which best describes lunch period?	Please record school activities engaged in by you with their number or duration	
Alone ____	Meeting ____	Duration ____
With staff ____	Callers at home ____	Duration ____
With visitor ____	Telephone calls ____	Number ____
Missed ____	Desk work ____	Duration ____
Supervising ____	Games ____	Duration ____
Tended injury ____	Purchasing ____	Distance ____
On telephone ____	Other ____	(Describe) Round Trip____
Other ____		

NOTE: Parts II and III OF FORM TO BE COMPLETED FOR EACH HALF-HOUR OF THE SCHOOL DAY.

PART II

Instruction: Please list the activities you engaged in for this half-hour.

CORRESPONDENCE   No.
Letters (in)   _____
Letters (out)   _____
Memos (in)   _____
Memos (to staff)   _____
Memos (to parents)   _____
Other   _____

PART III
Instruction: For the main activity of this half-hour, please fill in the details by ticking the boxes.

1. ACTIVITY   *DURATION (minutes)*

Unscheduled meeting ____   ____
Scheduled meeting ____   ____
Desk work ____   ____
Phone ____   ____
Tour ____   ____
Teaching ____   ____
Announcing ____   ____
Maintainance ____   ____
Other ____   ____

2. WHO INITIATED   *LOCATION*

Self _____   Office ____
Other _____   Staffroom ____
_____   Classroom ____
_____   Corridor ____
_____   Off Premises ____
_____   Home ____
_____   Other ____

3. WITH WHOM   *WHAT ISSUE?*

Alone ____   Finance ____
Teacher ____   Discipline ____
Pupil ____   Pupil (other) ____
Parent ____   Staff relations ____
Management board ____   Public relations ____
Inspector ____   Curriculum ____
Ancillary staff ____   Instruction ____
Sales rep ____   Clerical ____
Staff — other school ____   Admin ____

Medico-socio-psych ____   Personal ____
Community assn ____   Other ____
College of ed staff ____
School attendance officer ____
Student teacher ____
Past pupil ____
Chaplin ____
Foreign visitor ____
Other ____

INTERACTION ANALYSIS PROTOCOLS

One of the most widely used strategies for the analysis of classroom behaviour is *interaction analysis.* Interaction analysis takes place through a wide variety of structured checklist-type observation instruments, which appear to be direct descendents of Bales' work in the observation of small groups (Bales, 1950), with the work of Ned Flanders being perhaps the best known today — Flanders interaction analysis categories (FIAC) (see figure 3.1).

Flanders has described interaction analysis as helpful 'to decide how teachers and college students can explore various patterns of interaction and discover for themselves which patterns they can use in order to improve instruction' (Flanders, 1970:17). Thus, Flanders would see interaction analysis as a tool to be used by non-participant observers to improve curriculum. Given this premiss it is put forward as a possible, though limited tool for action research.

Interaction analysis refers then to a checklist of criteria for the classification of communications of a verbal nature and a method for arranging these in matrix display for the purpose of analysing teaching behaviour. Simon and Boyer have classified more than 200 interaction analysis instruments for use in classroom observation (Simon and Boyer, 1975). Most of these systems for the analysis of interaction are North American in origin, although Galton (1978) reports in *British Mirrors* some 41 developed in the UK. The focus of these instruments is to record modes of human interaction. The protocols are founded on operationally defined sets of criteria or categories, e.g. TEACHER TALK: LECTURE (Code 5).

Procedure

1. Most systems require the presence of a non-participant observer who sits in the classroom and ticks one of the categories every three seconds which best represents the behaviour present at that moment.

2. The coder, or observer, uses a 'tally sheet' with minutes and columns for making these tallies. For example, an observer using FIAC should ideally make 20 tallies every minute.
3. A pocket timer can be used to ensure reliability for making tallies and a second observer for inter-observer agreement and reliability correlation of tallies.

Some problems with interaction analysis categories, especially those of Flanders', are that they do not take sufficient account of the substantive content of the behaviour or message. That is, they may tell us that the teacher is talking during 75 per cent of the class time but they do not tell us what he or she is saying.

As Lawrence Stenhouse has so aptly remarked, 'Interaction analysis systems provide *Mirrors of Behavior* (Simon and Boyer, 1975) but they are distorting mirrors' (Stenhouse, 1975: 148).

Flanders limited his number of categories to ten — seven for teacher talk, two for pupil talk and one for silence or confusion. By writing down the numbers best representing each of the ten categories every three seconds in succession, one is enabled to comprehend the sort of behaviour which preceded particular behaviours and thereby the original sequence is maintained. A sample tally sheet might look like this:

Sample tally sheet for FIAC

Class: 3C   *Teacher:* John Simpson

Lesson: History — Voyages of famous explorers

Minute tallies

| 01 | 5 5 5 4 8 5 5 5 9 10 10 7 7 5 5 5 6 6 2 2 |
| 02 | 6 6 6 6 5 5 5 5 5 10 4 8 8 8 5 5 5 9 9 2 |

Interpretation and analysis of observational data above
During the first minute some 20 tallies are made — one at every three-second interval, in accordance with the ten categories of the Flanders system. For the first nine seconds the teacher was providing the class with factual information (dates, names etc.) thus category No. 5 is ticked three times. The teacher then asks a question (4) and is given a pupil response (8); the teacher immediately begins to provide more information (5×3) followed by a pupil-initiated response (9). There then follow six seconds of silence (10×2), after which the teacher seizes an opportunity to criticize the class for not paying attention (7×2). The teacher then lectures for three units (5×3); gives directions as a command (6×2); and follows on with encouragment to the class (2×2).

Teacher talk	Indirect influence	1. Accepts feeling: accepts and clarifies the feeling tone of the student in a non-threatening manner. Feelings may be positive or negative. Predicting and recalling feelings are included.
		2. Praises or encourages: praises or encourages student action or behaviour. Jokes that release tension, not at the expense of another individual, nodding head or saying 'uh huh?' or 'go on' are included
		3. Accepts or uses ideas of student: clarifying, building, or developing ideas or suggestions by a student. As teacher brings more of his own ideas into play, shift to category five.
		4. Asks questions: asking a question about content or procedure with the intent that a student answer.
	Direct influence	5. Lectures: giving facts or opinions about content or procedures, expressing his own idea; asking rhetorical questions.
		6. Gives directions: directions, commands, or orders with which a student is expected to comply.
		7. Criticizes or justifies authority: statements, intended to change student behaviour from non-acceptable to acceptable pattern; bawling someone out; stating why the teacher is doing what he is doing, extreme self-reference.
Student talk		8. Student talk-response: talk by students in response to teacher. Teacher initiates the contact or solicits student statement.
		9. Student talk-initiation: talk by students, which they initiate. If 'calling on' student is only to indicate who may talk next, observer must decide whether student wanted to talk. If he did, use this category.
		10. Silence or confusion: pauses, short periods of silence, and periods of confusion in which communication cannot be understood by the observer.

Source: Flanders, 1970.

Figure 3.1 *Flanders' interaction analysis categories*

Critique of Flanders interaction analysis system

First, it should be stated up front that the Flanders approach has both strengths and weaknesses. On the plus side FIAC is clear and easy to learn to use and decipher. Secondly, it provides reliable results and the data can be used in quantitative analysis — for example the calculation of teacher response ratios (TRR), or teacher question ratios (TQR) (see Flanders, 1970).

Yet FIAC has its limitations. First, interaction analysis does not take account of the cultural setting or ethos in which the research is carried out. We do not have descriptions of the surroundings and the artefacts and other objects therein. Second, the parameters of behaviour are fixed a priori, in advance of instruction, so this means that the observer must confine his or her observations to the pre-specified categories — as a consequence rich slices of behaviour do not fully fall in to the research category net and are lost. Third, interaction analysis fails to take notice of the 'hidden curriculum', or what Smith and Geoffrey (Smith and Geoffrey, 1968) have called 'the silent language of the classroom' — thus not taking into consideration the intentions and purposes which give rise to the behaviour researched. Fourth, the system does not take account of the message or the content of what is actually said. Fifth, and severely limiting, is the view of teaching presumed; FIAC systems seem based upon a formal class system of organization in which the teacher is a didactic leader. They do not seem appropriate for more open structured classrooms where informal methodology is the keynote.

Interaction analysis can help one to examine both verbal and non-verbal behaviour rigorously and can act as a catalyst for action. Combined with qualitative analysis using ethnographic approaches to the study of one's teaching, a holistic profile may be made.

Use of observational category systems

The concern with using category observation instruments is with standardization of behavioural components in the setting. The central features of any observational system (including Flanders' system) are: first, a *pre-specified set of behaviour categories,* for example, 'teacher questions'; second, *a set of rules for employing the system*, for example, tallying behaviours every three seconds; third, *rules for analysis of data recorded;* and finally, a *standard observation form.*

Category observations assume typicality of teaching and learning behaviours — that is, that classrooms everywhere embody these rules and criteria and that the chief objectives appear to be stating law-like generalizations about the patterns found.

It should be borne in mind that researchers can and should create their own category systems to fit the design of the research study. One need not be restricted to the work of Flanders, Bales or other classroom analysts. In devising a category system several points should be kept uppermost in one's thinking: define the purpose of the inquiry — what is it in aid of? Decide upon the number of categories to be used. Decide on the frequency of recording tallies. Provide training in the use of the category system before entering a classroom for the purposes of data collection. Employ a team to design the system.

The following questions can be answered using FIAC: the amount of time used by teachers and pupils to talk; how much silence or confusion exists; type of questions asked by teachers and pupils; the amount of praise, reward or encouragement given by teachers.

RATING SCALES

Rating scales are used to make evaluations of human behaviour and activity by asking the rater to assess, along a continuum, some characteristic from high to low, good to bad, etc. They are mainly used in structured observation. While there are various styles — category, numerical, graphic and pictorial rating scales — they all share the same common feature of having a rater place an object, person or idea along a sequential scale in terms of estimated value to the rater. Rating scales are described by Gronlund (1981) and Kerlinger (1986), and are recommended for use in action research projects by Hook (1985).

Rating scales can be used both by the pupil, as an activity and learning experience in its own right (see group skills: self-rating sheet on p. 122), and more specifically by a teacher, as a method of gaining evaluation data and feedback on curriculum.

Category rating scales

Here the rater picks out the category or classification which best depicts or describes the object of the rating:

Item: To what extent does the pupil participate in discussion?

Never ____ Seldom ____ Occasionally ____ Frequently ____

Always ____

These category ratings can thus provide the teacher with observational data in order to assess pupil achievement of curriculum objectives. They can also be completed by the pupils. Such data can be a very powerful in making crucial curriculum selection decisions. The following example is designed to allow pupils to provide evaluation of a trial curriculum unit on American Indians:

Item: How would you rate the unit on American Indians?

Extremely imaginative ____

Very imaginative ____

Imaginative ____

Very unimaginative ____

Extremely unimaginative ____

Numerical rating scales

These are perhaps the simplest to construct and interpret. The trait being rated is presented on a scale, usually from one to five, but it could be constructed from one to ten or any other continuum desired.

Item: To what extent does the pupil participate in discussions?

____ 0. Never
____ 1. Seldom
____ 2. Occasionally
____ 3. Frequently
____ 4. Always

Item: The aims of this project are?

1	2	3	4	5
Very clear		Middling		Very unclear

One of the positive features of the numerical-type rating scale is that the teacher or pupil analysing the scale items can arrive at a mean score for a person by adding up the number value for each item and dividing by the number of items asked. Similarly, when a group of persons are completing the items a mean score for each one can be obtained by calculating the number value for each item and dividing by the number of persons completing it. Mean scores will act as an important *index of affect/belief.*

Graphic rating scales

The graphic rating scale is probably the most widely used type. In this format, the rater, or observer, indicates a rating of an item by placing a check mark or tick along some point on a line or continuum. The tick can be placed at any point along the line, thus not restricting the rater to ticking discrete categories or numbers. Their visual stimuli make them easiest to perceive and complete. They may, or may not include numbers.

Item: To what extent does the pupil participate in discussions? (Please tick at the appropriate point on the continuum X)

(Always)	(Frequently)	(Occasionally)	(Seldom)	(Never)
4	3	2	1	0

X

Item: Interviews make me:

_____I_____I_____I_____I_____
Extremely   Very   Anxious   Somewhat   Not at all
anxious   anxious   anxious   anxious

Pictorial-type rating scales

Pictorial rating scales are especially useful with non-readers and/or very young children, though they are novel and have been used with highly educated respondents. Pictures are used instead place of numbers and the respondent selects the 'face' or picture that best represents how he or she feels.

Item: When I have to make a public speech I feel:

Sample item A:
(tick one face)

_____   _____   _____

Item: How do you feel when you are asked to read aloud to your teacher?
Sample item B:
(tick one)

_____   _____   _____   _____   _____

Notes for raters

Rating scales can be used to evaluate/rate any number of goals or outcomes. They are most helpful in some non-cognitive areas, for example social and personal development (Gronlund, 1981, McKernan et al., 1985), where a teacher is interested in cooperativeness, industriousness, tolerance, enthusiasm, group skills, etc. Some rules would be:

1. Attempt to rate *observable behaviour* occuring in a natural setting.
2. Attempt to rate significant outcomes as opposed to minor or trivial behaviours.
3. Employ clear, unambiguous scales — never use less than three, nor more than ten points on a scale.

4. When possible, arrange for several raters to observe the same phenomena as this will increase the reliability of ratings.
5. Keep items short and to the point — avoid double negatives and items based upon value judgements or opinions.
6. Watch for the *response bias*, that is observer bias, in rating all observations near one end of the scale.

Rating scales are similar to checklists since the behaviours are known in advance and encourage focusing on these behaviours. The two crucial aspects of developing rating scales are: (1) the behaviour to be rated, and (2) the degree or scale which is used to rate the behaviour observed.

Group skills: self-rating

After working in small groups, read and respond to each item. Please tick, or circle the number on the scale that best describes *you as you behave in the small group.*

1. Participates in discussion in a positive manner
(Never)   (Always)

| 1 | 2 | 3 | 4 | 5 | 6 | 7 | 8 | 9 | 10 |

2. Able to influence other group members
(No influence)   (Highly influential)

| 1 | 2 | 3 | 4 | 5 | 6 | 7 | 8 | 9 | 10 |

3. Supports/defends other group members' views
(Never)   (Always)

| 1 | 2 | 3 | 4 | 5 | 6 | 7 | 8 | 9 | 10 |

4. Tendency to trust group members
(Distrusts)   (Trusts)

| 1 | 2 | 3 | 4 | 5 | 6 | 7 | 8 | 9 | 10 |

5. Willingness to discuss personal feelings/values/beliefs
(Not at all/reticent)   (Open/Free)

| 1 | 2 | 3 | 4 | 5 | 6 | 7 | 8 | 9 | 10 |

6. Personal reaction to critical comments about self
(Defensive/hostile)   (Receptive/open)

1	2	3	4	5	6	7	8	9	10

7. Ability to listen to others in understanding manner
(Inattentive/insensitive)   (Attentive/sensitive)

1	2	3	4	5	6	7	8	9	10

8. Builds friendships/relationships with others in group.
(Not interested)   (Actively interested)

1	2	3	4	5	6	7	8	9	10

9. Contributes 'evidence', ideas, to the group work
(Not at all/never)   (Always)

1	2	3	4	5	6	7	8	9	10

10. Inspires enthusiasm, solidarity in pursuit of group aims.
(Not at all/never)   (Always)

1	2	3	4	5	6	7	8	9	10

4 Non-Observational, Survey and Self-Report Techniques

Each classroom should not be an island. Teachers working in such a tradition need to communicate with one another. They should report their work.

Lawrence Stenhouse (1975:157)

ATTITUDE SCALES

Action research as a reflective human activity needs to uncover human beliefs and attitudes in arriving at understanding. The tools of educational and psychological research, particularly techniques of attitude scaling and measurement, can make an important contribution to inquiry into human belief systems. Action researchers can construct their own scales to reflect issues and concerns at local level.

Using attitude scales helps the inquirer to determine the strength of attitude or opinion held by the respondent on a variety of attitude statements. By assigning a numerical code to each item on the scale, a composite, or scale, can be determined representing the range of attitudes within the group studied. The aim is to force respondents to study their attitudes and feelings about a number of issues.

Procedures for implementing the strategy

The researcher provides respondents with a worksheet, in the form of an attitude questionnaire containing a number of statements. Pupils are asked to circle a response indicating whether they agree, disagree or are of uncertain attitude to the question.

Participants in the action research project can develop their own questionnaire attitude items using the five-point Likert-Scale technique (strongly agree, agree, uncertain, disagree, and strongly disagree). If the research involves a study of younger pupils a three- or two-point scale can be used, e.g. agree/disagree/uncertain. Alternative scales can be used — for example, very important, important, unsure, unimportant, very unimportant, etc.

Coding
Strength of attitude can be measured by assigning a number code to each attitude, e.g. strongly agree=5, agree=4, uncertain=3, disagree=2, and strongly disagree=1. By adding up the score on say 20 attitude questions a range from 20 to 100 may be obtained. For example, Professor Milton Rokeach developed an attitude scale

which purportedly measured dogmatism (Rokeach, 1960). Rokeach's scale had 40 attitude items which could be coded from 1 (low dogmatism) to 7 (high dogmatism) for each item — thus an individual could score from 40 to 280 on this scale. The higher the score, the higher the notional degree of dogmatism in the respondent's personality. Those with high scores will be interpreted as holding strong, positive attitudes on the subject, while those with low scores will hold negative attitudes to the phenomenon under investigation. Word items either all positively or all negatively so that a consistent attitude scale can be discerned. Rokeach (1973) also developed a 'value survey' instrument.

Affect/interest in subject

Attitude scales can be used to measure accurately and gauge pupil affect and interest in certain school subjects and curriculum experiences. The following questionnaire could be distributed to pupils for completion; the data would provide feedback to teachers on levels of pupil interest in subject fields.

The data yielded up by the *pupil interest* instrument can be used by teachers to evaluate their teaching — including units, teaching style and pupil affect. Thus while the instruments can have an intrinsic utility for pupils, they can provide diagnostic feedback for teachers.

Pupil interest in subject

Please choose from among the following responses that which best represents your feeling about each question.
Use the following scale: SA=Strongly agree   A= Agree
U=Uncertain   D=Disagree   SD=Strongly disagree
(Circle one response for each item)

1. I would (not) like to inquire/learn more about this unit.

    SA   A   U   D   SD

2. I wish I could take more (fewer) classes in this subject.

    SA   A   U   D   SD

3. I would like to spend more (less) school time in this subject.

    SA   A   U   D   SD

4. I enjoy (dislike) the assignments in this class.

    SA   A   U   D   SD

5. The work is interesting (boring) to me.

   SA   A   U   D   SD

6. The work is relevant (irrelevant) to my life.

   SA   A   U   D   SD

7. I hope to continue (discontinue) work in the subject.

   SA   A   U   D   SD

8. The materials/books are highly interesting (uninteresting).

   SA   A   U   D   SD

9. The teacher is very effective (ineffective).

   SA   A   U   D   SD

10. The course makes (does not make) me think critically.

    SA   A   U   D   SD

QUESTIONNAIRES

The questionnaire approach to gathering data is probably the most commonly used method of inquiry. It is a form of interview by proxy, with the interviewer removed from the face-to-face contact of the interview method. A minimal description is 'written questions requiring responses' (Kemmis and McTaggart, 1988). The respondent is presented with a pre-set list of questions which may be closed/open-ended in nature. The questionnaire technique is advocated by many action researchers (Elliott, 1978b; Walker, 1985; Hook, 1985).

As a data collection instrument the questionnaire is easy to administer, provides direct responses of both factual and attitudinal information, and makes tabulation of responses quite effortless. The questions written down must be very carefully phrased and the purpose of each should be clear.

Some disadvantages of the questionnaire method are:

1. It is difficult to get a list of good questions together.
2. Analysis is time-consuming.
3. Response rates are often low due to fear, lack of anonymity, etc.
4. Some respondents do not answer honestly.

Types of questionnaires

There are three types of questionnaires. First, the *mail (postal) questionnaire,* in which a pre-determined set of questions are posted to the respondent for answering and return. Second, *the group administered questionnaire,* in which a group of respondents is brought together in one place to complete the questionnaire (the inquiring researcher may or may not be present). This is the strategy most preferred by teachers who wish to collect data from pupils about curriculum for purposes of unit evaluation, etc. Third, the *personal contact questionnaire,* where the researcher contacts the respondent and has him or her complete the questionnaire, or where the research situation is treated as an interview with the researcher asking the questions and recording the answers in the presence of the respondents.

Types of questions

It is usual to go for one or both of the two principal types of questions: open-ended or closed response questions. Open-ended items allow the respondent to say what he or she thinks, in his or her own words; while closed or fixed (forced-choice) responses force the respondent to select a response from a pre-set menu.

Fixed response (closed) questions

1. In general, do you enjoy social education classes most of the time?

   Yes _____ No _____ Uncertain _____

2. Did you learn anything new in this unit? I learned:

   A great deal _____ Something _____ A little _____ Nothing _____
3. Corporal punishment should be outlawed in schools.

   I agree _____ I disagree _____ I am uncertain _____

Open-ended (free) questions
The major purpose of the open-ended response is to give the respondent freedom to answer — thus it probes or raises issues, but does not structure an answer. For example:

1. What should be done to benefit pupils in this school?
2. As you see it, what are the major problems adolescents face?
3. What topics should be included next year?

It should be pointed out that open-ended responses require more time and thought in interpretation as a variety of responses are possible from even a small sample of respondents.

Stages in questionnaire construction

Questionnaires are time-consuming to construct. Some steps in their construction would be:

1. Deciding what the problem really is and what information is required to provide answers.
2. Deciding what type of questions to use: fixed or open.
3. Writing a first draft of the questionnaire.
4. Piloting the draft questionnaire with a sample of respondents.
5. Revising the questionnaire on the basis of criticism — e.g. deleting ambiguous or poorly worded questions, etc.
6. Administering the questionnaire.
7. Analysing and interpreting the returned questionnaires.
8. Writing the final report of the inquiry.

Questionnaires should not be too long. Questions ought to be clearly worded and in simple non-jargonized language. Ensure that questions are important and that the respondents possess the knowledge to give an answer. Avoid leading questions or loading the items as these will tend to produce biased responses — 'Don't you feel it is wrong to work on Sunday?' Ensure that fixed response alternative answers are balanced. Finally, ensure that the items follow a natural logic, or order.

Questionnaires can be used by pupils in completing major requirements for qualifications, such as forming the basis for collecting data in connection with a group or individual assignment or project.

It is often assumed that questionnaires can only be used with large samples or populations. In fact, they can also be used in more immediate and intimate settings. Local studies can take more risks by asking probing personal-type open-ended questions, whereas this would not be as permissable in a more formal, large-scale study.

Tapping both facts and dispositional data

Questionnaires can be used to collect *facts* and/or *values/attitudes* (dispositions). For example:

Facts level:

1. How many times have you visited the teacher centre this year?

   Never _____ Only once _____ Two trips _____
   Three times or more _____

2. Name two inservice courses you wish to attend:

   (a) _____ (b) _____

Values/affect level:

1. How would you feel about teaching in the inner-city area?

   Very happy ____ Uncertain ____ Very unhappy ____

2. It is right for government to provide extra resources for those in need.

   I strongly agree ____ I agree ____ I am uncertain ____
   I disagree ____ I strongly disagree ____

Factual items request empirically verifiable information. For example, a list of the inservice courses offered will yield up the various offerings provided to verify the answers to question 2 at the facts level. Yet answers to questions 1 and 2 at the values level are *normative*, in that they express a personal preference about what government *ought to do*. Factual items collect data about *what the case is*, while value items request data about *what should/ought to be the case*.

Advantages and disadvantages of the questionnaire

Advantages	*Disadvantages*
1. Easy and quick to complete.	1. Takes time to analyse.
2. Provides direct responses.	2. Responses may not be truthful.
3. Information is quantifiable.	3. Respondents try to produce the 'correct response'.
4. Can quickly tap responses of large numbers of people.	4. Time-consuming to prepare good items.
	5. Completion depends on literacy.

THE INTERVIEW

One of the most effective modes of gathering data in any inquiry is through the interview method. Interviewing is a social survey skill which can be taught. Some of the best examples of research employ the interview method for generating and gathering information.

The interview is like the questionnaire approach, but is conducted in a face-to-face, or personal contact situation, such as a telephone interview. The interview has the advantage over the questionnaire of allowing the interviewer to probe areas of interest as they arise during the interview. The interviewer can also observe the setting in which the interview is conducted, e.g. in a prison or an old people's home, which may have enormous bearing upon the responses.

The interview is thus a personal contact situation in which one person asks another questions which are pertinent to some research problem. As such, it allows the focus to settle upon a specific issue which can be explored in some real depth and determines what an issue looks like from another's vantage point. Interviews are chiefly of three types in terms of their content and organization: *structured, semi-structured* or *unstructured.*

Structured interview

Here the interviewer has a list of specific questions — an orally administered questionnaire if you like. The interviewer does not deviate from the wording of these questions. Questions are often 'fixed-response' types. For example:

How important do you believe the topic of drugs and alcohol are to adolescents? (tick one):

Very important _____ Important _____
Of little importance _____ Not important _____

Semi-structured interview

Here the interviewer has certain questions he or she asks of all interviewees, but also allows the respondent to raise issues and questions as the interview progresses. It is important that these are not tacked on to the end of a pre-set list of questions, but are allowed to occur naturally throughout the course of the interview. In addition to the 'fixed choice' type of question, the interviewer may wish to ask 'open-ended' questions. These are especially useful in a semi-structured or unstructured style of interview. For example, 'What do you think about sex education?' 'How do you feel about nuclear power plants being built?'

Unstructured interview

In this style, the issues and topics to be discussed are left entirely to the interviewee. Once the interviewee has touched upon an issue or topic, the interviewer can ask him or her to explain and expand. During the initial stages of an inquiry this style is preferred as it allows respondents to raise issues which may not be tapped by other styles of interviewing.

Implementing the strategy

In the classroom the teacher can ask for volunteers who wouldn't mind being interviewed on particular topics. The task of the interviewing panel or interviewer is carefully to frame the questions to be asked. The interviewee would sit at the front of the room from where he or she would answer questions and make comments.

It ought to be stressed that in such an interview situation there are no right or wrong answers and that personal information is to be discussed on a voluntary basis. The interview is not the place for a heated debate or discussion to prove one's position.

Questions should be probing and not mundane. It is important to stress the asking of questions to which answers are needed, i.e. don't ask questions for the sake of it. Teachers could point to effective television interviewers as examples or models.

Pupils ought to always hold the right to 'pass' on a question by saying 'no comment' or 'I pass'. Pupils can certainly demand the reason for a question before answering. The interview is over when the interviewer ceases asking questions or when the interviewee breaks off the interview. Interviews are best when brief and to the point of a problem inquiry. Answers ought to be tape-recorded or written down for further discussion and as a reliable record of the event.

Pupils ought to be allowed to select problems/issues they wish to explore in greater depth and design a schedule of interview questions of the fixed-choice or open-ended variety (or both) to ask of respondents outside the classroom. Such work could be co-ordinated with project or fieldwork, such as a survey of shopping needs, a survey of old-age pensioners in the community, a survey of attitudes towards a variety of issues like nuclear power or civil liberties. What is of significance here is the learning of how to use the interview as a tool for gathering data in inquiry work.

Pupils can best generate questions by working in groups as one researcher may not be able to think of all the pertinent questions working in isolation.

Types of questions

A variety of question types can be used to interview respondents:

1. *Why questions.* These are used when one wishes for greater depth or detail or to simply fill in the gaps: 'Why was the SRA reading kit adopted?
2. *Normative queries.* Used to assess values, beliefs and dispositions. For example, 'Should the principal be free of teaching duties?'
3. *Affect questions.* To assess feelings and emotions: 'Did this bother you?'
4. *Leading questions.* Sometimes used to explore or open up a new line of inquiry or topic: 'What do you think about the problem of teachers not having enough time to do research?'
5. *Recall of events.* Used to tap respondents' ability to recall information, events and so on: 'What do you remember about the opening-day conference at school?'

6. *Comparative questions.* Here one is asked to make comparisons: 'What curriculum packs did you find the least attractive?'
7. *Experience/behaviour questions.* The purpose is to elicit what the interviewee can do, or has done.
8. *Demographic queries.* To find out how the respondent describes him or herself.

For further details about interview construction and question type see Spradley (1979), Denzin (1978) and Schatzman and Strauss (1973).

KEY INFORMANT INTERVIEW TECHNIQUE

The key informant interview technique is a variant of general interviewing with the special proviso that the interview is with an individual who possesses unique or specialized knowledge, skills or expertise within an organization and who is willing to share these with the researcher (Zelditch, 1962; Goetz and LeCompte, 1984).

Key informants are chosen because they have the time and special knowledge to give purposeful and insightful accounts and comments that are often denied the researcher through randomized designs. It is wise and instructive to note that key informants are often atypical and need to be chosen with care to ensure representativeness. Key informants are informed about the issues and tasks because of their experience and cultural background. Because they are in key positions they often have high education and reflective skills which may produce hypotheses and further lines of inquiry for the researcher. An interesting study using the key informant procedure is reported by Jackson (1968), who used his students to corroborate his own observations of classrooms transactions and encounters.

The strategy is simple but has the advantage of involving a steering committee which will result in involvement of even more authority in the welfare of the project. The method thus invests the results of the project in the institutions represented on committee and as informants, thus going some way towards implementation of the action suggested. Picking a good steering committee seems vital. Pick individuals who are organizationally active and involved.

The research procedure

The process of using key informants (Freilich, 1970; Goetz and LeCompte, 1984; Hagedorn, 1984; and Spradley, 1979) is well documented. The methodology proposed by Hagedorn may be of interest for teachers and other educational action researchers:

Step 1: Select a small steering committee (three to six members)
Pick a small committee who in turn will have the task of defining a small target population of key informants. If the research problem is examining some programme then it will take on the responsibility for reviewing goals, outcomes, action etc. For example, a teacher participating in a pilot curriculum development project might ask several other project teachers to identify persons within the wider community of teachers who might be interested in implementing, or 'buying into', the trial project.

Step 2: Draw up list of potential informants
The small committee then draws up a list of potential key informants. The criteria for selection might be that the informant: has special knowledge; will be a potential user; ensures geographic representativeness; ensures inter-organizational representation; is a person who has some purchase on policy decisions. Some typical groups might be students, teachers, trade union officers, teacher educators etc. Let's say 20 are selected from a preliminary list of 50.

Step 3: Design the research instruments
Research instruments are then constructed, e.g telephone interview schedule, structured interview. Face-to-face contact is most desirable although questionnaires and telephone interviews can be employed.

Key informant interview items

Health Education in Schools

1. How important do you believe the following topics are for inclusion in the secondary high school programme? Please tick (√)

Issue	Very important	Important	Not at all important
• AIDS	___	___	___
• Alcohol	___	___	___
• Sexually transmitted diseases	___	___	___
• Communication skills	___	___	___
• Valuing skills	___	___	___

---

2. What are your views on sex education topics in the curriculum?

---

3. Below are three course units designed for high school health education. Please rate *usefulness* and *appeal* values.

	Usefulness			Appeal		
	HI	AVG	LO	HI	AVG	LO
Unit 1 . . .	—	—	—	—	—	—
Unit 2 . . .	—	—	—	—	—	—

Step 4: Analysis of data
Once data have been collected they need to be tabulated. Codes will have to be implemented for both open-ended and closed-response items. With qualitative data examine the similarities of response across interviews and look for recurring themes and critical points: What are the disadvantages/advantages, etc? What concerns interviewees?

Step 5: Feedback to key informants
Summarize the findings and call a meeting of all those who were key informants in the study. Let them review the results and call for a frank and open discussion of the findings. A summary sheet or abstract of the study would be most useful at such a meeting.

Step 6: Write a final report
In any final report include the research brief or statement of problem; objectives of the study; methods used for collecting data; results; and a discussion of the results for practice and action. Send copies of the report to the informants and key organizations concerned.

The key informant interview technique ensures that the researcher gets access to individuals who 'know their stuff' or who can provide valuable data. Often the informants can point to chief value issues underlying the study. The technique is biased towards the perspectives of the selected informants and this should be recognized from the start. The technique is used increasingly in curriculum evaluation and is cheap and efficient.

PROJECTIVE TECHNIQUES

Projective techniques allow researchers to understand how respondents see, perceive and interpret objects and events. In curriculum action research the projective technique gives respondents opportunities to 'project' themselves by completing open-ended questions, and revealing and exploring attitudes, values and emotions. In short, the subject is presented with a probe, or stimuli, which calls for a response — thus the idea of projecting oneself into the situation. The more general the situation, the more opportunity there exists to make this projection. In action research, projective techniques provide self-report data.

Projective techniques may take several forms: open-ended stories, unfinished sentences, role playing, word association tests, etc. Some require clinical training to use, such as the classic Rorschach inkblot test or thematic apperception test (TAT), and these would clearly be inappropriate for teachers untrained in their specific use.

The technique considered here is just one type of projective technique; it has been labelled 'incomplete sentences'. What things emerge are often indicators of values or special needs. Projective techniques are fun and ego-involving. In addition they throw up important personal data — information which begins to reveal the concept of 'self'. These techniques should not be associated with negative or malajusted cases, but used to explore creativity and beliefs, and thus put pupils in closer touch with themselves. Besides, classic test situations give pupils little opportunity for personal expression of feelings; this could be a major reason why creativity is not nurtured in curriculum.

Projective techniques can be used quite effectively with embarrassing topics or questions. For example, some respondents do not like to discuss private matters with an interviewer but might risk this in a third-person, or fantasy-type, format: 'Some teachers who use this reading programme find a lot of fault with it. I wonder if you can guess what it is they object to . . . ' The ultimate aim is to assess the respondent's views but the respondent might answer truly as he or she thinks another would answer.

In the technique described below the respondent is presented with unfinished sentences and asked to complete them. If spontaneity is desired then the researcher might think of placing a time limit on the completion of the task.

Projective techniques have massive potential for evaluation. Their usage is not limited to psychologists; but they can be employed widely by teachers as a stimulus for creative thinking, expression of feeling, association, construction and choice of ordering. As an evaluative device, incomplete sentences can be employed just after an innovation has been piloted or some new unit has been implemented to gain feedback. For example, 'The thing I liked best about this unit was . . .' or, 'I never knew that . . .' A separate strategy might involve showing respondents pictures and asking them to talk about the content of the picture.

Incomplete sentences

The researcher provides each subject with a worksheet containing a number of incomplete sentences or phrases. Subjects can then complete each unfinished sentence in writing or the researcher may call upon them to finish each one aloud. Another variation may be to write down their answers and then break into groups for discussion. Incomplete sentences as a projective device serve two purposes: either they can act as a *diagnostic tool* or they can function as an *evaluative feedback tool.* Wording is crucial, depending on which function is intended. As a diagnostic tool the teacher should develop stems which evoke the desired information. For example, 'In my community . . .' or 'I am afraid of . . .' or 'I am happiest when . . . '

The following are examples of some incompleted sentences:

1. I get upset when the teacher . . . .
2. In class I feel happiest when . . . .
3. If I were the teacher I would like to . . . .
4. Secretly I wish I was . . . .
5. What I want most out of school is . . . .
6. In a group I am . . . .
7. My biggest problem at the moment is . . . .
8. In my teaching career I have accomplished . . . .
9. Many of my school friends are . . . .
10. The trouble with this unit is . . . .
11. I wish the principal would . . . .

. . . .

LIFE/CAREER HISTORY TECHNIQUE

Here lies the body of Cecil Moore
Dropped by four bullets from a forty-four
No less, no more.

This 19th-century inscription on a tombstone in America's Old West serves as testimony not only to the cheapness with which life was valued but also to the wonderful humour of such men. Gravestone inscriptions are just one example of the archival material available for serious researchers and often archives can be found that have educational connections.

The life history (or career history) method presents us with a tool that makes it possible to study the experiences and definitions held by an individual, a group, or an organization, as interpreted by the informant, group or organization (Denzin, 1970:220). Certain anthropologists employ the term *life history interviewing* in referring to this technique when seeking rich life narratives. Goetz and LeCompte (1984) suggest that in educational and curriculum research life histories may be unnecessary for most purposes, but the allied concept of *career histories* may provide valuable accounts of the narrative and professional lives of informants. This technique may be triangulated with key informant interviews and case histories to provide a fuller ethnography. The life history technique includes all sorts of materials — diaries, letters, documents, archives, etc. — which are useful in illuminating the life story of the person being studied.

The life history method has been rigorously applied by Ivor Goodson (Goodson, 1981; 1983) in curriculum inquiry. Goodson collected life histories of key innovators and advocates of curriculum subjects. He supplemented his material with syllabus review, letters and minutes of meetings in order to establish how particular subjects appeared on the timetables of schools.

A central assumption of the life history is that an actor's life be studied from the role perspective of the person involved. For example, Wolcott's study of *The Man in the Principal's Office* (1973) discussed an account of the protagonist, an elementary school principal, from the time his career began until the time the research work was completed. Another study (Fuchs, 1969) charted the careers of a group of novice teachers in inner-city schools through interview methodology. Teacher differences and similarities in the execution of duties may be highlighted dramatically through the life history technique. Howard Becker (Becker, 1966:v–vi) describes it as

> Not conventional social science data . . . nor is it conventional autobiography . . . it is certainly not fiction. As opposed to these more imaginative and humanistic forms, the life history is more down to earth . . . less concerned with artistic values than with a faithful rendering of the subject's experiences and interpretation of the world he lives in.

Denzin reminds us that life history materials include any records or documents, including case histories, public records, and so on, that throw light on the subject of the investigation. These might range from court records to letters and diaries.

The task of the researcher is to determine the subject's own story as he or she defines it. The life history must present a selective and subjective account of the subject's experiences as he or she defines them, thus the objectivity of the respondent's data becomes central data for any final report.

Types of life history

Three types of life history exist: *complete* life history, *topical* life history and *edited* life history.

Complete life history covers the sweep of the subject's life or career. An outstanding early example of the genre is Clifford Shaw's (1931) *The Natural History of a Delinquent Career,* which he followed with *Brothers in Crime* (1938). Perhaps the most famous study of this type is that by Thomas and Znaniecki (1927) *The Polish Peasant in Europe and America.* For educators, Wolcott's (1973) *The Man in the Principal's Office* is of immediate interest. The complete life history has three features: (1) the person's own life story; (2) the social and cultural milieu in which he or she and others respond; and (3) the sequence of events.

Topical life history shares many features of the complete history but it delimits the investigation to a particular theme, topic or period of the subject's life, exploring this thoroughly.

Edited life history may be either complete or topical. Its key feature is the interspersing of comments and explanations by someone other than the principal subject.

The two basic forms of records for life histories are public archival records and private archival records. The difference between the two is that the former are prepared for an audience while the latter are not.

Typical public archival records
Webb et al. (1966) cite four kinds of public records:

1. Actuarial records — birth, death, marital records etc.
2. Political-judicial — court records, voting records.
3. Government statistics on crime, education, etc.
4. Mass media — letters to editors, video and audio records, etc.

Typical private archival records

1. *Autobiographies.* These are the most common form of personal life document. The sustaining feature of the autobiography is that it gives the insider's account — often an account which has never been fully disclosed or acknowledged publicly.
2. *Diaries.* There has been a renewed interest in the use of diaries in

both teaching and research; for example the use of diaries in action research (Nixon, 1981). In a diary the author may express beliefs and emotions that are held in private. Diaries can be further classified as intimate journals, the memoir or the log.

3. *Letters.* Unlike the diary, the letter has an interactive audience that includes the sender and the receiver. In analysing letters the researcher must constantly interpret the message from the receiver's and sender's viewpoints. Historians have made good use of letters as a data source. With the rise of the specialist field of curriculum history as a form of curriculum inquiry, the letter should receive greater attention as a data source.

4. *Survey instruments: interview schedules, questionnaires, checklists and verbatim accounts.* The data source for life histories may also include published material, such as questionnaires and interview schedules, to discover the motivating values held by researchers; verbatim reports, artistic products and interview data may also be included.

The image of a mosaic is useful in thinking about the conduct and character of the life history — how do the pieces fit together to tell us the complete version? The life or career history can serve to inform us about the appropriateness of theories advanced about a problem in curriculum building, for example. It can, at least, demonstrate that a negative or null example exists, forcing us to reject some theories. It can provide us with insights into the hidden territory of institutional life.

Becker (1966) argues that the life history, more than any other research technique except perhaps for participant observation, can enable one to see and understand the concept of *process.*

The life history method is akin to participant observation in the sense that instead of studying an entire organization, the researcher selects critical informants who have a critical role in piecing together the mosaic or story which is the subject of the inquiry. For some inquiries, archival records and interviews with key participants may be the only sources and avenues open for researching a problem — a good example is of 'teacher drop out' to alternative careers which might only be studied fruitfully by recourse to official employment records and interviews with teachers who have left their careers in teaching. This is a real-life practical problem being faced daily by the profession, and skillfully conducted career histories might help to identify the key variables requiring remediation if drop-out rates among teachers are not to rise.

For teachers and administrators the life history method has not been used much but it could be employed to examine the successes and failings, say, of an exemplary teacher, principal or academic so that more general theory could be developed about successful practice. Perhaps this method will produce a new series of personal documents by practitioners which will help us in both the above ways and in ways we have not yet anticipated. One exception to the lack of use is the collection of papers by Ball and Goodson (1985) focusing upon the career histories of teachers.

PHYSICAL TRACES

In any cultural setting three types of foci are present: what the actors know, what they actually do, and what objects they make. These might be called cultural knowledge, cultural behaviour and cultural artefacts. It is mainly with the last of these three categories that physical traces are concerned.

According to Webb et al. (1966) physical traces are of two types: erosion measures and accretion measures. An *erosion measure* is where some degree of wear and tear on objects exists, such as the 'dog-earedness' of pages of textbooks that is indicative of heavy usage, or the deterioration of audio-visual equipment like blackboards. On the other hand, there are *accretion measures* which count as the deposits which are left behind in a setting. These then are additions rather than erosions or deletions. For example, the number of colour crayon pictures left behind by the infant class at the end of term; the books and student paraphernalia that build up and are uncollected in locker areas; student projects, etc.

Analysis of physical traces amounts to the least obtrusive or reactive of methods and, as Goetz and Le Compte remark (Goetz and LeCompte, 1984:154), it is also one of the least used research methodologies. The author noted (McKernan, 1978) the amount of political graffiti found on school desks to be an indicator of political socialization reflecting political allegiances in Northern Irish secondary schools. This was similar to a study by Kinsey et al. (1953:673) of graffiti inscribed in toilets, where significant differences emerged in the analysis of erotic inscriptions between men's and ladies' toilets.

It is crucial to be able to separate the *witting testimony* from the *unwitting testimony* in the examination of pysical trace evidence. For example, examination of gravestones in early Britain reveal that many were artisans (witting) but the unwitting testimony was that they were also very literate, evidenced by the eloquent inscriptions.

An interesting study of non-attendance at school and the amount of broken glass littering the school grounds was found by one researcher (LeCompte, 1969). When the glass was removed and local shops shifted from selling bottles to tins, school attendance increased.

Some guidelines for examination of physical traces

Goetz and LeCompte (1984) suggest four steps in the study of artefacts: location, identification, analysis and evaluation. First, most artefacts are located in the cultural mapping phase of a project, where a record is made of all objects in the setting. Second, artefacts have to be identified — for example, documents must be labelled, copied, etc. so that such records are available for further cross-referenced analysis. What is the shape, colour, size of the artefact? Identification can be made by other actors in the research setting, such as principals or teachers, who are asked to provide a detailed inventory. Third, artefacts are analysed — who produced the object? If not produced locally, how was it acquired? When was the artefact used and who by? Was it read, used manually or what? Finally, some interpretive asides are made to evaluate the artefact. What judgements are accorded the artefact by actors in the setting? Is it a good textbook?

Each of the above stages needs to be thoroughly addressed by the curriculum action researcher examining artefacts as physical traces. Artefacts may be located through the use of auxiliary records, such as school record files or suppliers' invoices kept on file in the office; or they may be dramatically present, such as the life-size figures of Christ hanging from a cross found frequently in Roman Catholic schools.

A further set of questions arises when one moves beyond single measures and attempts to aggregate artefacts in a setting. For example, how many religious objects are found in the principal's office of a denominational school? What level of religiosity is there between the principal's office and staffroom or classroom? An index can be constructed to give a mathematical proportion that can act as an overall measure of religiosity for denominational schools. A careful sampling procedure needs to be followed when creating cultural artefact inventories. One thing is certain, there is a paucity of studies focusing on artefacts.

The use of physical trace evidence may have particular rewards for the teacher-as-evaluator. Through the examination of equipment, textbooks etc. one can determine what pieces of equipment or which books are used most and least, indicating preferences.

5 Discourse Analysis and Problem-Solving Research Methods

> You must lie upon the daisies and discourse in novel phrases of your complicated state of mind. The meaning doesn't matter if it's only idle chatter of a transcendental kind.
>
> Sir William Schwenck Gilbert (1836–1911)

DILEMMA ANALYSIS

Dilemma analysis was developed by Winter (1982; 1989) as a technique which would assist in the massive problems of the interpretation of qualitative action research data. Winter is concerned that while action research has inherited something in the way of a number of research *techniques* for gathering data, such as the interview, case study, triangulation, diary, etc., there is not yet a fully sufficient action research *methodology* in existence for the *interpretation* of data once we have it in our possession. In short, after transcribing a half-hour interview running to a dozen pages, what categories, theories or modes of analysis can be used to make it intelligible? Or, to put the question differently, how can one carry out an interpretive analysis of a restricted data set? That action research projects face dilemmas has been documented (Elliott, 1985b).

Winter (1982:166–173) suggests three stages in the process of analysing interview data in connection with the problems of teaching practice: (1) the nature of the specific action research task, (2) the theoretical basis of the method, and (3) the procedural sequence in 'doing' dilemma analysis.

1. Nature of the specific action research task

In Winter's case, the action research task focused upon his role as a supervisor/researcher of teaching practice supervision in order to *create an account of the teaching practice situation which would be faithful to the views of students, teachers, pupils and fellow supervisors.* The research task was to create an account of a research problem which would be regarded by others as authentic and valid.

2. Theoretical basis of dilemma analysis

Winter argues that basing any interpretation directly on social theory, e.g. neo-Marxist or symbolic interactionist explanations, *creates an interpretation which is imposed by the researcher.* Winter suggests that this problem may be overcome by working with formal as opposed to substantive theory, in so far as while substantive theory may guide the collection of data, formal theory assists in interpreting data appropriate for that method. The formal theory guiding dilemma analysis is the concept of *contradiction*, i.e. that institutions have conflicts of interests, that members are split and divided, and all of this is beset by *dilemmas.* Winter states:

> It became intelligible to analyse the interview transcripts *not* in terms of particular opinions, but in terms of the *issues* about which various opinions were held. This method is called 'Dilemma Analysis' precisely to emphasise the systematic complexity of the situations within which those concerned have to adopt (provisionally at least) a strategy. (Winter, 1982:168)

3. Procedures in conducting dilemma analysis

Once the interviews are complete — in Winter's case open-ended interviews and written statements from 22 students, 16 supervisors, 11 teachers and 50 pupils on the experience of teaching practice — then the data are analysed in terms of a number of *dilemmas, tensions, or contradictions* classified by Winter as *ambiguities, judgements and problems.* Winter admits that while a little vague, these categories try to embrace the following distinctions. Some tensions are background awareness of inevitable complexities of the situation, tolerated because they are not directly linked with courses of *action.* These are referred to as 'ambiguities'; 'judgements' and 'problems' refer to required courses of action. 'Judgements' are those actions seen not as 'wrong' but complex and interesting, and which require a requisite skilfulness. 'Problems' are those courses of action where the tensions and ambiguities seem to undermine the validity and rationality of the action required.

The next step is to organize *perspective documents,* where each of the above categories — ambiguities, judgements and problems — is presented from the perspective of each of the actors, e.g. teachers, pupils or supervisors. This is the essence of the process and involves:

1. formulating the dilemmas the actors were presented with in the interview;
2. choosing as a starting point the most elaborated formulation of

any given dilemma from among the various episodes in the interview scripts;
3. formulating the dilemma so that it is counterbalanced by an equally held view; and
4. building up the *perspective* for each role by *adding* together the various dilemmas formulated.

At the next stage in the process these assembled *perspective documents* were checked with the students, supervisors and teachers involved so as to formulate an overall perspective which would transcend individual beliefs.

The analysis is thus a 'mapping' of individual perspectives. Winter argues that by basing the analysis on formal rather than substantive theory, the appearance of the document is not academic but characterized by honest summary of practitioners' own views.

Case example of dilemma analysis

From a script, four areas of tension, complexity and contradiction were identified:

1. *The complexity of the student role:*
   - The student should be in control of the children.
   - The student should generate enthusiasm among the children.
2. *The complexity of the student-teacher relationship:*
   - The teacher is required to give advice and make resources available.
   - The student is required to know how to take advantage of these.

These two examples are then subject to the threefold division of ambiguities/judgements/problems to create a 'teachers' perspective document' (after Winter, 1982:171). What follows is an annotated account, adapted from Winter (1982), to highlight the nature of the activity of dilemma analysis.

The teachers' perspective document

A: AMBIGUITIES

1. The nature of teaching
(a) On the one hand, teaching is an art, depending on instinctive feelings and reactions, which a person may have or develop but which *cannot* directly be taught.

On the other hand teaching is a science, depending on detailed, skilful techniques which *can* directly be taught.

(b) On the one hand, teaching consists of developing and managing a personal relationship with pupils.

On the other hand, teaching consists of explaining and organizing pupils' work.

2. *The relationship between teacher and pupils*
(a) On the one hand, students may bring a welcome, even if rather artificial, novelty and stimulus to a class.

On the other hand, students may bring an unwelcome, temporary disruption to a class.

B: JUDGEMENTS

1. *Concerning how to help students (student-teachers)*
(a) Teachers help students by combining (or often having to choose between) the following: material resources and emotional support; criticism and advice; examples of teaching technique for students to observe and emulate; freedom for students to try things out and learn from their mistakes.

(b) On the one hand, teachers have superior experience, expertise and knowledge of the children (and so can give *direct* advice).

On the other hand, teachers and students are individuals and a teaching style is a highly personal matter (so that any advice must be *adapted* by the student).

C: PROBLEMS

1. *Concerning the gap between teaching practice and real teaching*
Teaching practice (TP) is a short-term performance emphasizing variety of media and aids, display of detailed planning and painstaking effort by the student, and the production by pupils of attractive, visible material.

BUT

Real teaching requires the mastery of a long-term routine, capacity for effective improvization, economy of effort, the fulfilling of general pastoral responsibilities and the communication to pupils of skills and information.

2. *Concerning the gap between college courses and real teaching*
In college courses students learn about theories of education by being taught them by theoretically oriented lecturers.

BUT

The craft of real teaching is learned in schools by observing practitioners at work and by experience of a wide range of practical classroom situations.

Edited from a fuller account provided by Winter, 1982: 171–172.

Winter's method of 'dilemma analysis' bears some resemblance to Elliott's method of 'triangulation' in providing perspectives from all the actors in a social setting. Winter has also provided a practical book (Winter, 1989) in which he argues that dilemma analysis helps us to learn from our own experiences, and he gives several examples of the technique in use. Elliott (1985b) cautions the action researcher about certain problems relating to interpretation of data: the researcher should not control participants' interpretations of events through some theoretical input; nor should he or she be naive to the extent of believing that sophisticated theory will emerge from the reflections of actors who have not had considerable experience of, or access to, theories other than their own.

Dilemma analysis appears to be very systematic and rigorous, but unfortunately it is time-consuming as well. When one considers the massive task involved in creating 'teacher perspectives' and then in creating 'student-teacher, pupil and supervisor perspectives', one begins to appreciate the importance of time as a constraint in the conduct of action research. Dilemma analysis does address difficulties in thematic induction, content analysis and theoretical exemplification. As Winter points out, it is not without its problems, but he has begun to provide empirical findings on the effectiveness of this strategy which should be the subject of increasing interest and research in the future (Winter, 1989).

CONSTRAINTS ANALYSIS

The method of analysing general constraints is a ranking technique for determining the relative importance of teacher, school and communal barriers to, or constraints on doing action research. The instrument was developed in connection with a three-nation study (McKernan, 1989) in which empirical evidence was collected from a variety of action research projects in the USA, UK and Ireland. Practitioners interested in taking a first step in locating those impediments to improving the justice and rationality of their curriculum tasks, are encouraged to use and adapt this instrument.

For purposes of this strategy, action research is defined as inquiry by practitioners to understand and/or solve pressing practical problems in order to improve the curriculum and the rationality and justice of their curriculum working conditions.

Directions

The constraints survey contains a list of 12 barriers to the effective use of action research. Your task in using the instrument is to place these barriers in order of their importance as constraints on action. Study the list carefully, then place the number '1' beside the constraint that is most important to you as an impediment to doing action research; place the number '2' beside the factor that is second most important, and so on. The constraint that is least important should be ranked '12'. The source is McKernan's (McKernan, 1989) international study of curriculum action research (p. 45).

Constraints survey

Study the list with care and rank in order of their importance as constraints on your work. Most important ranked '1', least important ranked '12'.

- Obtaining consent/support to research
  curriculum problems   _____

- Disapproval of principal (or other
  administrators)   _____

- Disapproval of fellow teachers/colleagues   _____

- Disapproval of students   _____

- Students' examinations   _____

- Personal beliefs governing the role of the
  teacher (belief that teacher role is to teach and
  external staff do 'research')   _____

- Lack of resources (equipment, finances, etc.)   _____

- Personal lack of research skills and
  research knowledge to do action research   _____

- School organization (e.g. timetabling etc.)   _____

- Lack of time to do research   _____

- Language of educational research (difficulty
  in understanding/terminology is off-putting)   _____

- Professional constraints (contract, teacher
  union policy, professional association, legal
  factors etc.)   _____

- Other: specify . . . .

  . . . .   _____

CONTENT ANALYSIS

Content analysis is concerned with inquiring into the *deep meaning* and structure of a message or communication. The message may be contained in a written document, a commmunications broadcast, film, video, or in actual human behaviour observed. The goal is to uncover hidden themes, concepts and indicators of the message content. Developments in qualitative field methodology such as 'theoretical sampling' (Glaser and Strauss, 1967), 'conceptual mapping' and 'curriculum mapping' (Weinstein, 1986) may assist in the procedure for studying the message in curriculum and the time devoted to tasks.

The initial developments were of a quantitative process for the application of content analysis (Kerlinger, 1986). For example, frequency counts, histograms of recurring phenomena, etc. Kerlinger (1986:477) defines content analysis as a method of studying communications in a systematic, objective and quantitative manner for the purpose of measuring variables. A 'scientific' orientation. But the reader ought to be aware that content analysis is much more than a device for measuring — it is also a device for *observing a communication.* In viewing content analysis in this light we take it out of the analytical/methodological rag bag and place it into the same class as interviews, stream of behaviour chronicles, etc. Content analysis is basically unobtrusive and non-reactive.

The procedure

In its simplest form, some working categories are set up and the occurrences of category units are observed, counted and noted. This is the key problem — setting up good categories to filter the message through. Once the data of a message are available then a coder can work his or her way through the message, assigning a numerical code to particular categories as they occur.

Some work in curriculum has concentrated on analyses of textbooks (Child et al., 1946; Mulryan, 1984). In a study of third grade readers published since 1930, Child, Potter and Levine (1946) (see Kerlinger, 1986) found that three-quarters of the content of the readers equalled a sum of 914 stories. The basic unit examined was the 'theme', defined as a situation confronting a person, the response behaviour and the consequences of the behaviour by the person. A total of 3,409 themes were identified from the total base of stories, or an average of four themes per story. Next, a category system was set up including *characters, behaviour, circumstances, consequences* and *type of story.* These categories were further broken down into sub-categories.

Content analysis of textbooks is becoming a rich field for

curriculum research. Curriculum research in Ireland conducted by Mulryan (1984) examined primary school mathematics texts for children, indicating inadequate vocabulary in many standard texts which present learning difficulties. Mulryan used three main indicators: word signifiers (general, technical and special vocabulary), notational signs (numerals/notations) and graphic symbols (pictorial symbols, diagrams). Counting and sampling procedures were used of these categories on each of three widely used maths textbooks. Results showed that more new words were introduced in the first three grades of maths books than in grades one to six in English readers for the same pupils. Maths was clearly not in synchronization with the English curriculum.

Content analysis of female roles in library books

A study by Barnard (Barnard, 1966 in Brandt, 1972) focused on the occupational roles of women as displayed in children's books in the library. The total number of books for grades one to three on the open access shelves of the library were examined. Of 911 books examined, 204 were selected for further analysis on the basis of several criteria: (1) published since 1944, (2) counted as realistic fiction rather than fantasy, (3) featured a US setting, and (4) discussed female roles significantly. The main variables under measurement scrutiny were: type and frequency of female roles.

Results
Of the 204 books only two illustrated 'working mothers' and both instances portrayed women in a negative light, e.g. 'My mother and daddy both work so there is no one at home to take care of me.' The results are tabulated in Table 5.1 overleaf.

Procedures for doing content analysis

1. *Define the universe of the content* — the text, message, communication, etc. For example, let us say that our research problem concerns the examination of mathematics books for third grade. Begin by examining a sample of the books used. Get another researcher to look at the same books and try to estimate the level of inter-observer agreement. If the rate of agreement between the two observers is low, say less than 70 per cent, then discuss the categories being used to trap or catch concepts, and recode or refine these. Select a new sample of protocols and begin the analysis anew.
2. *Write careful definitions of key categories being coded.* Decide on the level of analysis: words, themes, characters, items, space-time measures, etc.
3. *Analyse the data and code categories.* Quantify. One needs to

Table 5.1   *Distribution of female roles in 204 books*

Homemaker	160
Teacher:	26
married	1
unmarried	18
no designation	7
Grandmother (domestic or idle)	15
Idle or indefinite	12
Sales clerk	7
Babysitter	4
Circus woman	4
Maid	4
Nurse	4
Other: librarian, waitress, seamstress, movie star, railroad leverman, etc.	40

Source: Barnard (1966). Unpublished study reported in Brandt, R. M. (1972) *Studying Behavior in Natural Settings.* New York: Holt, Rinehart and Winston, pp. 343–345. Used with permission.

assign numerical codes to categories in the content analysis universe. One mode is to use *nominal* categories, e.g. boy/girl or permissive/non-permissive, and quantification would merely be a matter of counting the frequency at which these categories occur in the universe. A second level of measurement would be *ordinal,* e.g. through ranking in some hierarchical order. A third level would be through *ratings,* e.g. for creativity.

4. *Quantify and do counts.* Conduct word counts and frequencies of data. Content analysis has been used primarily in communications-type research, e.g. propaganda studies, yet it would be an ideal tool for the analysis of curriculum problems such as gender and race stereotyping in school texts.

DOCUMENT ANALYSIS

A rich source of evidence for the research practitioner can be found in documents, such as texts, newspapers, minutes of meetings, articles, letters, diaries, memos or scripts — indeed any written account may be considered a document. Hook (Hook, 1985:213) argues that 'the use of documents has been a neglected source of information about schools and classrooms'. Documents provide the researcher with facts pertaining to the subject and serve to illuminate the purposes, rationale and background history of the topic, event or subject of the investigation. Documentary analysis may well be used at the exploratory stage of a project to glean the goals and rationale of the curriculum. It would seem inescapable in certain subjects, e.g. historical work or contemporary social issues. The aim of document analysis is to lay bare the facts of the inquiry.

In certain inquiries document analysis may be the only way of proceeding — such as in the investigation of long-deceased persons. It is often carried out as a prelude to further inquiry, like interviewing or participant observation. By engaging in document analysis pupils learn how to examine *primary sources of evidence.*

Documents are also non-reactive. That is, the researcher does not affect the situation as he or she would in an interview or other form of interpersonal inquiry.

Using the newspaper in documentary inquiry

Newspapers are a readily available and rich source of evidence. A good deal of newspaper content is of a social and personal nature and can be used in humanistic programmes. The researcher can also master some skills in using a document which is regarded by many as the single most important source of continuing education throughout adult life. The following are some ways in which the newspaper can be used in the classroom:

1. Participants identify a pressing community problem and design a plan to tackle this problem. Let them try out their plan and report back.
2. Compare tabloid and standard newspaper accounts of the same issues.
3. Study the employment pages, searching for jobs and requisite skills.
4. Examine editorial comments of different papers on the same issue.
5. Identify conflicts of values and controversial issues.
6. Describe the philosophy of a single editorial cartoonist over an extended period of time.
7. Compare and contrast local with national and international problems.
8. Get students to write a letter to the editor.
9. Trace fluctuations in money market exchange rates.
10. Identify facts, opinions, values in news articles.

Some advantages of document analysis

1. Data collected establishes the facts retrospectively.
2. Information may be more reliable and credible than that obtained from questionnaires, interviews, etc.
3. Documents are condensed and easy to use.
4. Documents are often readily available.

5. Documents are often inexpensive.

Some caveats

Document analysis contains the following disadvantages:

1. The accounts may be biased or based on propaganda.
2. The records may be inaccurate.
3. The document may reflect the author's memory of events.
4. The categories may be inappropriate to the inquiry.
5. Obtaining some documents can be quite time-consuming.
6. Some documents may be 'confidential'.

Personal documents

Gordon Allport (Allport, 1942) has discussed the use of personal documents in psychological research and defines this as 'any self revealing record that intentionally or unintentionally yields information regarding the structure, dynamics and functioning of the author's mental life'. The forms of documents according Allport's account are: autobiography, questionnaire, interview, verbatim records, diaries, letters, artistic and projective documents, e.g. poems or essays, and so on.

Allport suggests that individuals compile these for a number of reasons: special pleading, exhibitionism, desire for order, literary delight, personal perspective, relief from tension, monetary gain, assignment, therapy, social re-incorporation, scientific interest, public service, and a desire for literary reputation and immortality. A classic is Thomas and Znaniecki's *The Polish Peasant in Europe and America,* which established the use of documents in research by using court records, autobiographies, letters, newspaper accounts and public records.

Curriculum action research

A practitioner may also engage in document analysis if she or he wishes to research some aspect of the curriculum. For example, if a teacher wishes to conduct a programme of action research to improve his or her evaluation of pupils, he or she may examine:

- past examination papers
- minutes of assessment committee reports
- official school reports on assessment and evaluation
- government documents setting out policy
- samples of pupils' work
- sample tests from publishers
- standardized tests
- pupil assessment records and school files

- official curriculum guides

From this information the teacher begins to build up a 'manifesto' or picture of the background and context of his or her topic. This portrait can be illuminative in suggesting which questions still require answering and which questions have not yet been asked. Parlett and Hamilton (1972) cite the use of document analysis along with observation, interviews and questionnaires/tests as the chief methods for conducting 'illuminative evaluation'.

It should be borne in mind that the final report or case study of an action research project is itself a document that will be read and discussed by other practitioners. The same care that went into the gathering of original documents and their subsequent analysis must be carried through in the preparation of the report document.

PERSONAL TIME ANALYSIS

Recent research (McKernan, 1989) has indicated that *lack of time to do research* was rated the most important constraint by action researchers from a list of 12 obstacles. The analysis of the use of one's private or personal time might shed some light on this problem. How we use our personal time is a reflection of our interests, attitudes, and most importantly our values. Personal time is also 'discretionary' time. Glatthorn (1985b) has provided a useful technique for studying how we manage our time through looking at: what choices we make and what areas of growth we consider important in our lives — the areas of growth being physical, social, intellectual and spiritual.

Procedures

1. The teacher should make out a sheet for each day of the week for pupils. 'Uniqueness' refers to anything that made this day special, e.g. visitors, weather, joys, etc.
2. Keep a daily log for all the 'discretionary' time — this is the time left over when obligated time, such as school attendance, sleeping, eating and bathing, is eliminated. Record in half-hour segments all other activities, noting the time of day and nature of the activity in the column labelled *time and activity.*
3. For each activity check its *decision focus.* This is a crucial aspect of personal time analysis. *Obligated time* is time spent on activities that other people wanted you to do, or that you did out of a sense of obligation. *Free time* is time spent on activities that you chose freely, i.e. you did them because you wanted to.
4. For each activity examine the *person focus.* If the activity was aimed at yourself, tick the *self* column. If the activity was

concerned with assisting, or providing for others, tick the *others* column.

5. Next tick *time focus. Goal directed* activities are those that are engaged in in pursuit of some future goal or objective. *Being directed* activities are those undertaken because they are good in their own right or intrinsically worth while, e.g. playing.

6. Finally, tick the *growth focus* column by noting whether the activity was likely to produce growth in any one of the four areas of growth concern: physical, social, intellectual, spiritual or none.

7. Work out the following indices as follows. First, count the total number of half-hours you had available for the *entire week*; do this by adding the total number of activities for each day. Then work out:

   • *Free choice index* (FCI) — Divide the total number of discretionary half-hours into the total number of *free choice* half-hours.

   • *Self-focus index* (SFI) — Work this out by dividing the total number of half-hours in the day into the total *self* half-hours.

   • *Being directed index* (BDI) — Divide the total number of half-hours into the total *being* half-hours.

   Work out four growth focus indices: physical, social, intellectual and spiritual.

Personal time analysis

8. Write an analysis of your personal time-use in the light of the following questions:

   • Does your *free choice index* (FCI) indicate or suggest that you are in charge of your own time?

   • Does your self-focus index (SFI) reveal what you consider to be an optimal balance between yourself and others?

   • Does your *being directed index* (BDI) suggest a desirable balance between goal orientation or direction, and 'being direction' or orientation?

   • How satisfied are you with each of your *growth focus indices* (GFI) in the four aspects of your life?

9. Examine the composite picture suggested by the first three indices and see if any of the following five stereotypes fit you at all:

Stereotype	FCI	SFI	BDI
1. *Child*	Low	High	High
2. *Martyr*	Low	Low	Low
3. *Striver*	High	High	Low
4. *Hedonist*	High	High	High
5. *Happy servant*	High	Low	High

10. Write about yourself, summing up what you have learned about using your personal time from this exercise.

Personal time analysis worksheet

Day _____ Date _____ Uniqueness _____

Time & activity	Decision focus Oblig.	Free	Person focus Self	Other	Time focus Goal	Being	Growth focus Phy	Soc	Int	Spir	No
1											
2											
3											
4											
5											
6											
7											
8											
9											
10											
11											
12											
13											
14											
15											
16											
17											
18											
Total											

Note: The author is very grateful to Professor Allan Glatthorn, School of Education, East Carolina University, for the personal time analysis exercise.

SOCIOMETRIC ANALYSIS

Sociometry consists of a number of techniques for measuring emotional distance and for determining the pupil's position within the *social structure* of the class setting. The sociometric approach is conducted by examining and analysing the choices and rejections made by each member with respect to the other members in a social group. Thus sociometry is invaluable for measuring and illuminating the complexities of classroom behaviour and group dynamics — thus it is an ideal tool for classroom action research. Many teachers are plagued with the practical problems of pupil misbehaviour, indiscipline, noise, etc. Sociometry may provide data which can help analyse such problems and group relationships in the classroom.

The *sociometric technique* was first developed by J. L. Moreno (1934) with his seminal work *Who Shall Survive?* The approach has been refined and described by other researchers (Kerlinger, 1986; Thorndike and Hagen, 1969: Gronlund, 1981; Hopkins, 1985). It is in the 'scientific' tradition of classroom research.

Sociometry refers to a variety of methods of gathering and analysing data on the choice, communication and interaction patterns of people in groups. It is defined as the study and measurement of social choice (Kerlinger, 1986:499). It seeks to inquire into the attractions and repulsions of members of a group. One of its results is that it will highlight those pupils who are 'social isolates' and thus identify pupils at risk. As it seeks to uncover both pleasant and unpleasant dispositions it can be effectively used by teacher action researchers in curriculum settings. For example, pupil preference for particular classroom curriculum activities, mode of grouping etc.

The sociometric procedure

The responses obtained in a sociometric study have direction — either positive value, neutral or negative value. The main effect is that it is an ego-involving activity in its own right. Perhaps the chief benefit is through the evaluation of the social acceptance of pupils by pupils and the charting of social relationships within the setting. A typical sociometric instrument used to measure seating arrangements, choice of work and playmates, and group choices is set out on p. 157.

It is important that the pupils know one another and have spent some time together as a group. The teacher should also note the names of any pupils who are absent at the time the instrument is completed. If the teacher presents this not as a 'test' but as a confidential inquiry which will lead to improved classroom life, then the relationship between research and action may be better appreciated by the pupils.

Administration
The teacher gives each pupil a form containing the questions, such as that in *Sociometric instrument* shown below. The pupils are instructed to name their five best friends; those with whom they would like to study and work; those who they would like to accompany them if they are transferred to another class or school, etc. As a diagnostic tool the results can be used to set up more effective working groups. The most important aspect of the process is *choice*. Here are further sample questions which could be used:

1. With whom would you care to work (play, sit, etc.)?
2. Who are your three best friends?
3. Which two members of this class do you like best?
4. Whom would you like to work with on an important school project?
5. Which two students would you pick to share a room with at summer camp?
6. Who should lead the group?
7. Who would you choose to represent the class on student council?
8. Which four individuals are most important in your life?

An alternative approach is to ask pupils to use a scale to rate members of their group according to various questions, e.g. 'Here is a list of your classmates. Rate each one according to whether you would like to do homework with them, etc. Use the following scale:

$$3 \quad 2 \quad 1 \quad 0 \quad -1 \quad -2 \quad -3$$

The rating -3 indicates that you would very much *dislike* doing homework with this person, while the number 3 means you would very much *like* to do homework with this pupil.'

Sociometric instrument

Name _____   Teacher _____

Class _____   Date _____

Since this is the start of a new term we shall be working on new projects. To help in making arrangements, please answer the questions below by writing down: the names of the pupils you would like to work with; be on projects with; play with etc. You can write down the name of any pupil in the class, even if they are absent today.

Make your choices thoughtfully. This information is private and will not be given to anyone else. There are some rules:

1. Choose five pupils in order of importance to you (number 1 is the most important, number 2 the second most important etc.).
2. Pupils may be named for more than one question.
3. Only the teacher will see your choices.

Build the sociogram, matrix and index from a list of pupils represented by the numbers I–V.

I=Agnes   IV=Dom
II=Bill   V=Eve
III=Carol

Pupil choices form

1. I choose the following five pupils from this class to sit near me:

    1. _____ (my first choice)

    2. _____ (my second-best choice)

    3. _____ (my third-best choice)

    4. _____ (my fourth-best choice)

    5. _____ (my fifth-best choice)

2. If I had to work with five pupils from this class, I would choose the following (place in order of importance, e.g. 1=first choice, 5=least important):

    1. _____ (my first choice)

    2. _____

    3. _____

    4. _____

    5. _____ (my fifth-best choice)

3. If I had to play with five pupils in this class I would choose:

    1. _____ (my first choice)

    2. _____

    3. _____

    4. _____

    5. _____ (my fifth-best choice)

4. If I had to serve on a school committee with five pupils from this class I would choose:

   1. _____ (my first choice)

   2. _____

   3. _____

   4. _____

   5. _____ (my fifth-best choice)

5. If I found myself in a difficult (dangerous) situation I would choose the following pupils to be with me:

   1. _____ (my first choice)

   2. _____

   3. _____

   4. _____

   5. _____ (my fifth-best choice)

THE END

THANK YOU FOR YOUR HELP

Analysis of sociometric data

Three different types of analysis are available: sociometric indices; sociograms and sociometric matrices. After gathering the questionnaire instruments, the next step is to render an interpretation of the results. While the answers provide valuable data regarding social choices in the classroom, the full value of the sociometric research will not be known until the sociogram is drawn and a matrix is constructed.

First, chart the *sociogram.* The following is an example for a group of individuals, with commonly used symbols indicated on it. (I=pupil no. 1, II=pupil no. 2, etc.)

Sociogram

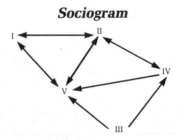

Second, calculate the *sociometric index* as follows:

When: C = centre of choice, or ego.
Let: Ciy = $\sum$Cy (number choosing individual y)
$\overline{N-1}$ (number in group minus one)

Ciy = the choice of the individual person y.
$\sum$Cy = the sum of the choices in column y.
N = the number of pupils in the group minus one (this formula of N − 1 is used because clearly one cannot count oneself).
Let us examine pupil V as

   CiV = ¼ or an index of 1.00
and pupil I as
   CiI = ²⁄4 = .50

How well or poorly the pupil has chosen is revealed then by the sociometric index.

Interpret: Clearly pupil V is the 'star', receiving four choices. Pupils I, II and V form a 'clique' in that they all choose each other. Pupil III is an 'isolate' or 'neglectee'.

   Finally, construct the *sociometric matrix*:

1. List names on the X axis along with a number for that pupil.
2. Along the Y axis place the numbers of the pupils chosen (in this case there are five pupils in the group).

Sociometric matrix

	Pupil	I	II	III	IV	V
		Columns = y				
Rows = x	I	0	1	0	0	1
	II	1	0	0	1	1
	III	0	0	0	1	1
	IV	0	1	0	0	1
	V	1	1	0	0	0
Sum of choices		2	3	0	1	4

1=Choice
0=Not chosen
C=Matrix of choices

Interpret: Pupil I has chosen II and V
Pupil II has chosen I, IV and V
Pupil III has chosen IV and V
Pupil IV has chosen II and V
Pupil V has chosen I and II

Note: It is suggested that with young pupils it might be best to limit choices to two or three as these pupils find it difficult to discriminate in the ranking of many pupil choices. Some teachers may wish to ask pupils to name those rejected as this will allow social rejectees to be identified.

Advantages and disadvantages of sociometry

Advantages	*Disadvantages*
1. Simple to plot and calculate pupil choices.	1. May serve to heighten awareness of the social rejectees
2. Enables identification of social relationships.	2. Test does not indicate why individuals are chosen or rejected.
3. May become a class activity.	3. Not stable with children under ten years.
4. Permits remedial work.	
5. Observations are measures.	
6. Useful for classification of students and groups.	

Common practical problems demanding action research responses will evolve around such issues as sorting or grouping pupils in the classroom. Using sociometric techniques the teacher can arrange groups on the basis of peer popularity, scholastic ability, achievement motivation and desire to learn.

Common notations found in sociograms

Key: A ──────▶ B   D ── ── ──▶ E
      (A chooses B)   (D rejects E)

1. *Isolate:* An individual not selected by anyone

2. *Mutual pair:* Where A chooses B and B chooses A A ◀──────▶ B

3. *Triad:* Where three pupils choose one another

4. *Chain:* Where pupils connect by mutual choice

5. *Rejectee*: Pupil receiving negative choices

EPISODE ANALYSIS

Episode analysis refers to a process of breaking down classroom discourse and events into more manageable bits for the purpose of analysis. In this respect it resembles *stream-of-behaviour chronicles*. The term is offered by this writer as a method for combining the properties of these techniques into a common unit for the analysis of discourse. The principal use of episode analysis is in direct observation of action and in its subsequent analysis, so it straddles both the observation of action and data analysis dimensions of action research. The aim is to establish coherent units and to examine relationships among and between these units, or 'episodes', of classroom action. Thus, an episode may be defined as a brief micro-unit of human behaviour, whether verbal or non-verbal, that is integral to, yet separable from, the continuous chain of classroom events (McKernan, 1978).

One mode of proceeeding is to divide social interaction into units that have integral boundaries. Of course there are many logical modes of classifying units: sentences, words, paragraphs and so forth. Yet it is clear that an episode begins with an expression which triggers a response — be it verbal or non-verbal behaviour — culminating in a goal or completion of discourse. After the seminal work of B. O. Smith et al. (1970) concerned with the logic of teaching, these units will be referred to as *episodes*. An important principle is that an 'episode' always involves more than one actor — it is interactive. When utterances or other behaviour are contributed by only one actor then the type of unit is referred to as a *monologue.*

To use episode analysis to analyse classroom action and as a tool in action research, one wants more than to simply chop up the bits of a 40-minute lesson. Episodes need to be *logical* in the sense that they facilitate examination of those aspects of verbal behaviour relevant to an analysis of the logical dimensions of teaching. They must be neutral, i.e. they would take the same form whether they were part of a political science class or a mathematics lesson. They must also contain two further qualities: adequate time-sampling frames and reliability. Episodes must not be selected based upon poor sampling of typical behaviour — they must be typical not atypical, which means they must take place over a good portion of the teaching-learning time-scale. Finally, they must be reliable. This implies that different observers collecting episodes would be able to locate and identify the same units with the same properties and boundaries as others working independently of each other.

Units of discourse

Two types have been mentioned: the episode, amounting to a multi-speaker unit, and the monologue, or single-speaker unit. Division of classroom discourse into these units completes a segment or unit of verbal interaction. Where one unit terminates, the next unit or episode begins. Episodes pass through three stages: first, an *initiation,* or opening phase which contains remarks like statements, assertions, questions and so on — these may also be referred to as *entries.* Second, there is a *continuance* phase in which the unit is developed. Finally, there is a *terminal* or *closure* stage.

Example of an episode of classroom discourse

Episode 1	*Teacher:* Who was the first man to circum-navigate the globe? (entry)
	Pupil 1: Was it Columbus? (continuance)
	Teacher: No, that is not correct. (closure)

Episode 2	*Teacher:* Does anyone know the answer? (entry)

The entry is by the teacher who asks a question. There is a continuance in terms of pupil 1's response, and the teacher brings termination or closure of the episode with the response 'No, that is not correct.' The teacher's new entry for episode 2 is given with the question 'Does anyone know the answer?'

A good example of a *monologue* is given with the teacher's continuance of the entry in episode 2:

Monologue 1	*Teacher:* I cannot believe that no pupil knows the correct answer. At this particular period in history several European powers were seeking to expand their empires. This remained the pattern for many years until we arrive at the period we have been studying for the past three lessons.

The above is an example of teacher uninterrupted talk, a *monologue.* Monologues do not have stages, they are rather expositions characteristic of didactic discourse in which teachers lecture, move to discussion, and return to exposition.

Classification of discourse

It is possible to categorize classroom entries into the following categories:

1. *Defining* — where the meaning of terms is requested. 'What does the word 'astronaut' mean?'
2. *Describing* — to represent by words or drawing. 'The touchdown was scored in this way . . .'
3. *Designating* — to identify by naming. 'What do you call a word used to modify a verb?'
4. *Stating* — declaring or asserting.
5. *Reporting* — revealing what a book or document states.
6. *Substituting* — requesting pupil to make symbolic operation in maths.
7. *Evaluating* — rendering judgements by estimating the worth of an object, mode of behaving, or some end-state of existence deemed desirable.
8. *Opining* — soliciting opinions. 'Was he right?'
9. *Classifying* — placing objects, persons, etc. by type, sort, class. 'What kind of triangle is this?'
10. *Comparing/contrasting* — requesting comparions, similarities or differences.
11. *Conditional inferring* — 'When it snows the streets are slippery and therefore dangerous.' The consequences (streets are dangerous) being inferred from the antecedent condition of 'when it is snowing'.
12. *Explaining* — when reasons are offered to account for some phenomenon.
13. *Managing* — entries which direct or orchestrate classroom activities and keep the stream of action moving.

The above category system developed by B.O. Smith and colleagues in 1970 for studying the logical properties of teaching, preceded the massive amount of work done by interaction analysts of classroom behaviour (Simon and Boyer, 1975). It differs from the many other category systems such as Flanders (1970) in that it lets us in on some of the *logical properties* related to teaching, rather than simply classifying entries as one or another form of teacher talk or pupil talk. Flanders-like interaction analysis protocols do not inform us about the content of the message, only about whether it is teacher or pupil talk. Verbatim accounts do not enter into this type of analysis. Thus, the Smith et al. (1970) scheme seems to hang on to the advantages of *narrative observation* by recording narrative accounts as well as classifying these according to the 13 logical properties outlined above.

It is rather an unfortunate turn of history that at the time of Smith's pioneering work on classroom discourse (Smith et al., 1967; 1970) video recording technology was not available. Audio taping was, of course, available but the technique is notoriously difficult and onerous to complete since transcripts have to be written up for analysis. Completed transcriptions on the Smith model had to be put on ditto paper with codes to ensure anonymity. The flow of discussion was then broken down into utterances, which were typed as paragraphs. An utterance is the verbal record of one speaker, at one point or another, with another speaker. Utterances were then numbered, with teacher utterances labelled 'T' and pupil utterances with the name of the pupil or 'B' for males and 'G' for females. Simple frequency counts were then made of the types of utterances to get some handle on the distribution of the various logical properties.

Episode analysis is an ideal way in which to examine field notes, videotape and other qualitative data closely. In the author's study of political socialization in Northern Irish classrooms, episode analysis was used to locate significant indicators of pupils' values:

Episode 1	*'Peace' as a preferred student ideal or value*
Teacher:	'Sean, what do you dislike about Northern Ireland?'
Pupil:	'I don't like the shooting and bombing and other things. I wish there was peace again.'
Teacher:	'Oh.'

Episode 2	*'Beauty' as an idealized value*
Teacher:	'William, what do you like about Northern Ireland?'
Pupil:	'I love it because it has beautiful scenery — it's lovely with the rivers, beaches and mountains.'

Source McKernan, 1978: 172

ACTION INQUIRY SEMINAR

The seminar is a very appropriate method for conducting action inquiry, given that the seminar is a small, self-directed and democratically oriented strategy for learning. Indeed, the seminar is the main method of teaching and learning used in many Western nations' universities — particularly at postgraduate level.[1] The

---

1. Early German universities made extensive use of the seminar method as the main strategy for education. The view was taken that the seminar is a vital way of gaining not only knowledge, but the canons of inquiry for gathering further knowledge.

seminar may also permit the cultivation of an educational encounter between inside action researchers (first order researchers) and supportive outsiders (second order action researchers). Frequent meetings of the action inquiry group can help to break down problems faced mutually and interchangeably by these parties.

Other features of the action inquiry seminar are:

1. Group collaboration and sharing as distinct from authority/ expert models of learning.
2. Documentary evidence presented — tabling of case or position reports and working papers as the basis for ideas and sharing.
3. Identification, sharing and reflective analysis of positions, cases and results of experiments.
4. First and second order action research agents present: frontline action inquirers and a facilitator (second order agent) who chairs, encourages and facilitates.
5. A critique — group adopts a critical stance towards the topic under examination and group discussion.
6. A commitment to the inquiry as opposed to the authority role of education and learning.

Procedures

The action research seminar should be held in a small group — say five to a dozen participants. Seminars should meet regularly — on a weekly or bi-monthly basis. Individuals should be given alternating responsibility for leading the discussion around topics they feel comfortable with. Duration can range from less than an hour to several hours. The author has found that the seminar is an ideal method for learning about a topic before large-scale field experimentation is undertaken.[2] In 1973–74, Professor Malcolm Skilbeck led a university-wide seminar for staff and doctoral students interested in 'cultural and community education' in Northern Ireland: the seminar helped each individual to develop knowledge and skills about the topic which became invaluable in the later development and implementation of a school-based curriculum improvement project in social and cultural studies. The seminar brought together a considerable pool of expertise and skills which were shared collectively by the group and which laid foundational thinking for the action project which followed. The seminar is best utilized in areas where there is a lack of first-hand models or research literature. The Northern Irish roundtable

2. Seminar on Cultural Studies in Northern Ireland, Education Centre, University of Ulster at Coleraine, 1973–74. The author led a seminar on American experiments in intergroup education using action research methodology seen as possible models for Irish experience.

curriculum seminar is a good case in point. We had little knowledge of how other systems could use curriculum development processes to reduce intergroup conflict and promote mutual understanding and tolerance. Normally each member of the group prepares a position paper and other members are expected to read around the topic and to reflect and discuss ideas. Without a strong commitment to this group cohesiveness the seminar is likely to break down.

It is best to organize seminars around *problems in curriculum.* This is another reason why the action research focus is ideal for the seminar. The group can absorb members' contributions to how problems can be explored and illustrated.

Case report

The following minutes are from the Seminar in Cultural and Community Education for 10 October 1974. In discussion a number of issues and problems were identified:

1. The nature of an interventionist strategy and the contrast between social work and 'working with the social'; dispositional problems and possible relationship between unhappiness and intervention in schools.
2. The need for and the particular features of an appropriate perspective from which to undertake relevant empirical inquiries.
3. The problems of 'team research' specfically building a supportive climate and establishing congenial work styles.
4. Problem-solving techniques, value analysis and other ways of facilitating interpersonal relationships through intervention in schooling.
5. The uses of kits of materials, suggestions for teachers, workshops etc. for teachers specifically dealing with local history and culture.
6. The project field officer as a partial means of meeting the need to develop communications.

The action inquiry seminar should be group-directed, yet some form of organizational chairperson or facilitator is required. This person should not be seen as the leader but as an equal with the added responsibility of chairing. The role here is not unlike that of the *neutral chairperson* outlined elsewhere in this book (pp 183–88). The aim is essentially that of forwarding human understanding of the issue in question.

Presentations can be of several kinds: a short synopsis of what has been read can be presented in a summary form. Second, a critical view can be adopted towards a position or line of implementation. It is immensely helpful to provide copies of presentations *in advance* to other group members. Finally, members may table 'working papers' which are for group eyes only and which collectively document the thoughts of members for discussion.

Advantages and disadvantages of the seminar

Advantages

1. Democratic in style.
2. Cooperative group deliberation on a common problem or idea.
3. Useful as a mode of professional inservice education/learning.
4. Members make active inputs in the form of reports.
5. Individual members can take facilitator/chair role.
6. Agenda may be group-determined.
7. Useful references, literature-search can be accumulated as result of inquiry.

Disadvantages

1. Demands small groups — unsuitable for large group sessions.
2. Not appropriate for information/knowledge mastery.
3. Group participants need to be familiar with an inquiry/ reflective mode of learning — some may experience discomfort with the model.
4. Not suitable for grading students.

BRAINSTORMING

Brainstorming is a group problem-solving activity, widely used for creative thinking, that aims to elicit a wide variety of possible ideas, or solutions, to a novel situation or problem. The key aspect of brainstorming is that it engages an individual's creative imagination. As an action research strategy it helps elicit alternatives in the form of value choices and subsequent examination of these choices and their consequences for behaviour and action. The school working party or deliberative workshop is an ideal setting for brainstorming as an action research exercise.

Many new curriculum units force pupils to solve problems, whether these are scientific, aesthetic, moral, social, etc. It is argued that pupils have to learn to deal with problems; virtually anything in life that is important is also likely to be problematic, and things that are not problematic are often unimportant. Thus problem solving is a lifeskill. Problem solving, particularly creative modes, is at the core of the action research process.

The basic aim of *brainstorming* is to solve problems by piling up the widest range of ideas and alternatives. Thus the problem put to pupils ought to be one which elicits a number of possible 'answers' or solutions. Any number of problems can be tackled through group brainstorming: How can we improve this course next year? What will we name this new product? How do we solve the noise problem in the room? What use can we put five room-dividers to? It is an active, rather than passive, pupil strategy and is particularly useful when facing new problems or content.

Brainstorming emerged out of think-tank sessions pioneered by Alex Osborn (Osborn, 1953). As the title suggests, the activity calls for the storming of an idea or problem by many brains. It is a truism to say that more opportunities could be provided for pupils and teachers to put forward their ideas. Don't just read this section, experiment with brainstorming — it promotes open-minded inquiry, learning in a democratic group structure.

Rules

Certain rules must be observed in brainstorming sessions. It is a good idea to write these rules on a blackboard and display them in the setting. It is important to try to involve every pupil in the activity.

Rule 1: Criticism and evaluation are not permitted during the 'thinking' session. The notion here is to suspend any evaluative judgement until all ideas are tabled and noted. The reasoning is that individuals will become more concerned with defending their ideas than with thinking up more and better ones. Evaluation will act as a censor. By deferring judgement at this stage, more responses will be provoked from group members.

Rule 2: Encourage a free-exchange of ideas. The wilder and more exotic the inputs the better. It is often easier to tame a wild idea than to try to pep up a bland suggestion. Welcome both practical and impractical ideas as these may spark new offerings from other group participants which may not have been evoked in a more conventional discussion.

Rule 3: Quantity of ideas is desired. The more suggestions and alternatives offered the better, since the greater is the likelihood of choosing a sound solution from the final list. It is easier to edit a long list than to build one up. The author recalls a brainstorming session in which 117 ideas were offered on how to use documents to teach history. Of course, many of the contributions were trivial, but in the final analysis some 30 or so were approved by the workshop group for use.

Rule 4: Combination and adaptation of ideas is sought. Encourage group participants to build on others' suggestions and to modify, adapt and use these for improved solutions. There are very few original thinkers, and thus one progresses by degrees of innovation and modification of what has gone before.

Preparing for brainstorming

The teacher needs to be familiar with the rules and procedures of implementing brainstorming. If a teacher has a problem he or she wishes to use, then a pilot trial session should be carried out with colleagues before it is used in the classroom. Be especially clear in explaining the problem to the participants so that the situation or problem is not ambiguous. As Dewey remarked, a problem well defined is half-way solved. The teacher could develop his or her own list and when the session begins to slow down and the responses fall off, he or she could then interject his or her own ideas and give the session a new burst of energy. The teacher may ask certain idea-spurring questions: How might we put this to another use? How could we adapt it? What could we substitute here? What about an alternative layout?

Procedures for brainstorming: implementing the strategy

As with the rules, there are a number of steps to be observed in getting started and engaging the creative energies of a group of individuals. In retrospect, the author has found that for successful ideas-producing sessions, the participants must engage in the activity in a spirit of enthusiasm and belief. Unless this spirit or ethos prevails it will be tough-going.

Process
1. *Explain the problem clearly.* The teacher must carefully explain the idea or problem to be tackled. Then the teacher, or group leader, calls for suggestions. It is usual to permit, say, five to ten minutes for pupils to brainstorm, though there will be an initial period of thought and consequent silence.
2. *Record ideas visually.* The group leader needs to keep a careful public record of the suggestions offered. This is best done by taking ideas, one at a time, and writing them on an overhead projector transparency or on the blackboard. Alternatively, the facilitator, or leader, may appoint a recording secretary, though this will have the disadvantage of withdrawing that person from the participating group.

   Recording ideas is crucial as it testifies to the group thought productivity. This must be done efficiently as often many pupils will want to make suggestions simultaneously, and the physical impossibility of taking all of these ideas at once may serve to put some pupils off. Also, it is important to number ideas and keep the list for future reference.
3. *Discussion of ideas and suggestions.* The average session will normally only last a few minutes — this is a fine example of how little pupils are used to working reflectively and creatively. The

facilitator will then direct the group to examine the list, deciding upon which suggestions are most appropriate and promising.

A glance at the list will reveal a number of categories, or possible classifications. It may be useful to break these down into like groups of ideas, thus producing several smaller lists.

It is now time to evaluate the ideas. One way of doing this is to get pupils to think of the consequences of employing each suggestion.

Another way of approaching discussion is to ask the group to select the best three or four suggestions and then to break the whole class group into smaller working groups of between four and six members, with each group taking one of the suggested alternatives as a topic for further inquiry. The work can thus proceed in depth and the small groups can report back on their own internal discussions. Often the discussion will lead to further suggestions and new inquiries may be opened up. It is in the give and take of the discussion session that the problem is more clearly defined, the alternative ways of solving it are proposed, and the consequences are evaluated. Thus, several important steps of scientific problem-solving are present: the problem is defined, suggestions are offered (hypotheses), consequences are explored, conclusions are reached, decisions about action are taken, further action and reflection on the action ensues.

GROUP DISCUSSION

Group discussion can be used as an important action research technique in the classroom, lecture theatre, workshop, or any other relevant educational venue. Since action research has discourse at its core and since discussion, rather than the written word, is the chief means of communicating throughout life, it is thus a very potent tool. In this section the focus is on developing members' roles for engaging in effective group discussion in the classroom. Studies have shown that in adult life a person is at least three times more likely to exchange meaningful information with others by speaking than by writing. Adults require speaking and listening skills for three main purposes: *occupational, citizenship,* and *social and personal maintenance.* While the thrust of these remarks is directed at the practising teacher, group discussion can be used in diverse community, leisure, occupational and other settings.

Discussion may take place in a dyadic or Socratic group; in small groups, of say 3 to 15 pupils; or in whole class groups — though the latter is the most difficult to manage and sustain in schools. There are important roles to be played by both the group facilitator, who adopts the role of chairperson, and the group members, who must learn something of group dynamics.

Developing participation: some caveats

Discussions are not easy to lead. Participants are not used to making such direct contributions. This is due to a number of factors:

1. Discussants need a knowledge base to discuss a topic; often teachers do not respect this point and rush into topics which pupils know little about.
2. This may mean collecting 'evidence' to feed into a discussion.
3. Participants are often shy out of fear of public embarrassment.
4. Chairpersons need to tolerate long silences and not always be willing to 'tell pupils'.
5. Participants have a responsibility for contributing to any inquiry.
6. Pupils often define knowledge as mastery of facts and come to view discussion as 'bull sessions', and, therefore, a waste of time.

Physical resources

Discussion can be aided by paying attention to the physical surroundings: furniture, size of group, setting, etc. The idea is to make discussants feel comfortable. It is preferable for participants to be face to face. This is important as physical arrangements influence communication patterns, allowing for direct interaction. This will also mean that the teacher may have to emancipate his or herself from the traditional position of staying at the front of the group. It is more in keeping with participation and collaborative inquiry to position the teacher within the circle of participants.

Triggers for discussion

1. Packs of materials, pictures, films, videos, newspapers and other 'evidence' may be used to spark off reaction to a topic.
2. The 'confrontational comment' strategy can be used to trigger a reaction.
3. Use of outside guest speakers, panels, interviews, etc. to function as a lead in, or trigger, to a field or area of inquiry.

Role of teacher

The teacher becomes a chairperson, or group facilitator, ensuring that an issue is explored, summarizing contributions, raising questions, and so on. In this section an important set of guidelines for running group discussion work is offered. The role of the chairperson is to enhance understanding of the issues being discussed. These rules or guidelines should be interpreted as 'hypotheses', that is, not as correct solutions to the problems thrown up by discussion work, but as ideas worth experimenting with in the true spirit of inquiry, which at base is the foundation of our approach to learning.

Rules for group discussion

1. The chairperson is responsible for defining and clarifying the problem or issue to be discussed. In doing this, the chair submits to the responsiblity of establishing the limits or boundaries of the discussion.
2. The chairperson's view is equal to others, not dominant. The chair is a manager of inquiry.
3. The chair ought to serve as a model for the promotion of the scientific method of critical and reflective problem solving.
4. The chair should not dominate discussion but be a good listener.
5. The chair should tolerate pauses/silence in the group.
6. Adequate time should be given to pupils to develop their points.
7. The chairperson should protect individual points of view and divergence, without necessarily accepting them.
8. Pupils should not be coerced into participation — though full participation is sought.
9. The chair should not seek consensus of opinion, but elicit a variety of honestly held views.
10. The chairperson, as well as the participants, is responsible for introducing new evidence and ideas into the discussion. Evidence, or materials, people, etc. should be introduced to:
    *   provide a new perspective or act as a stimulus;
    *   facilitate development of a point already tabled;
    *   represent a new set of concepts that may be helpful to understanding;
    *   challenge complacent participants;
    *   challenge consensus.

    The notion is one of extending the range of ideas and giving the group access to these views.
11. The chairperson should organize a setting that is conducive to discussion.
12. It is a responsibility of the chairperson to clarify issues from time to time during the course of the discussion, and to give a summary of the major points and views presented at the end of the session.

    A short agenda for giving a summary would be:
    *   a restatement of the key ideas;
    *   a review of the factual and value issues;
    *   a list of the constraints and problems;
    *   a review of the issues so far unresolved and requiring further inquiry.
13. The chairperson should seize opportunities to develop values awareness skills.

Role of the participants

Participants must endeavour to work hard so that the group achieves its objectives. A group will develop cohesiveness when the members realize they are a team. The chair must teach the principles for inquiry and group behaviour: asking questions, clarifying issues or seeking clarification, raising issues, regard for evidence, self-reflection, making inferences and generalizations.

A self-evaluation process

It is hoped that chairpersons taking on an expanded interest in the use of group discussion will seek to examine the effects of this work through self-evaluation. One can improve by evaluating one's performance.

Some questions about chairpersonship
1. To what extent do you feed evidence and ideas into the group?
2. How much interruption is effected by the chair?
3. Are you pressing for a particular moral stance within the group?
4. Do you interrupt silences?
5. Do you ask questions to which you already know the answer?
6. Do you press for consensus ('I think we all agree')?
7. Do you reprimand group members?
8. Do you summarize positions at relevant points?
9. Are you reliable regarding time-keeping?
10. Do you watch for continuity in moving from issue to issue?
11. Do you offer evaluative comments on pupil inputs?
12. Do you listen attentively to all contributions?
13. Do you keep notes on comments?
14. Do you dominate, or tend to make the largest contribution?
15. How do you deal with dogmatics?
16. How do you deal with bullying?
17. Do you work to develop understanding?
18. Are you 'an authority' or 'in authority' in your approach?
19. Do pupils understand the rules of participation?

Evaluating pupil contributions

- Who leads?
- Who talks to whom?
- Which pupils are dogmatic/open-minded in their views?
- Did all pupils contribute?
- Were pupils restless? Did all pupils listen to one another?
- Who did not understand?

Concluding comments on group discussion

In conclusion, it may be restated that effective discussion work will hinge on the creation of a trusting climate on the one hand, and the acceptance of a set of rules which govern discussion on the other. The teacher will be most effective if his or her role as chairperson is clearly defined for the group. Effective chairing means abandoning any pretence of being an expert on the issues, or being seen by pupils as an 'authority', but rather acting 'in authority' in the sense of promoting inquiry and working within rules for group understanding. In short, operating under inquiry/discovery as distinct from authoritative instruction. The presentation here has had group discussion as a classroom action research pedagogical strategy aimed at *pupils*. The premisses and general tone of these remarks is applicable to all deliberating groups whether they are pupils, teachers, or others.

Other models

1. *Dyadic group*: This group has two members and may be considered a 'one-on-one' scenario. Participants can change roles, e.g. act as listener or discussion leader. After each member has spoken for several minutes this can be followed with open discussion by both.
2. *Socratic group*: With this model the group leader poses questions for various small groups to consider. The groups then deliberate and form a position, then report back publicly. This open discussion may offer new avenues for action research or further inquiry. Procedures involve the creation of groups with four to six members. Pose a question for each group and allow them to mull it over for five minutes. The movement from the whole class group to smaller cells allows for a group dynamic to ensue. Socratic groups are motivated to discussion because of the 'rehearsal' in the small group. The group facilitator can move from group to group to offer advice and support; clarify questions; and identify sources of evidence.

THE PROBLEM SURVEY

This pedagogical strategy involves a census, or survey, of issues and problems identified by participants. The technique opens up an area of study and permits cooperative planning and enquiry by teachers and pupils working in a partnership. It thus serves a democratic function by allowing students to have a role in planning/researching their own curriculum. At the initial stage of an action research project, once a practical problem has been identified, the problem survey map help in the search for possible planning and solution formulation.

Problem survey as an instructional technique

The teacher-researcher may be aware that a certain problem is causing concern among pupils and he or she may therefore suggest this problem or topic as the subject of further planning and inquiry. The problem survey engages pupils in *inquiry learning* and motivates them to explore topics of interest and relevance to their lives. The survey will provide answers to the problems posed and will serve to diagnose these needs for the teacher.

Procedures

The teacher might begin by posing a question for the class to explore. The question is written on the blackboard or overhead projector. For example, 'What would you like to know about tests?' Then the teacher must wait. After a period of silence pupils will begin to respond. If they fail to respond, then the question is likely to be of little interest to the group, and the teacher must start anew with a fresh query. As pupils respond, the teacher should record their comments and questions on the blackboard. The teacher makes no comment at this stage of the inquiry, acting simply as a recorder. He or she can probe pupils in order to record, precisely, their problem.

After a number of responses have been recorded, say, eight or ten, the teacher may look to the group expectantly for more; if these are not forthcoming, he or she can read the question aloud again, and may elicit some more responses. After several silences, the pupils will probably have exhausted their queries. The teacher then duplicates the list, with a copy for each pupil, and announces that it can be added to at any time.

The problem question

This is the most critical factor in the inquiry. If the question does not have appeal or relevance then there will be few responses. There are certain *rules* to bear in mind:

1. *The question asked must ensure that all answers are 'right'.* If this premiss is not respected then certain pupils will feel excluded — believing that the teacher is after one particular line of thought, or searching out those pupils who share his or her belief system.

   Some questions are not suitable — for example, 'What are the facts surrounding the outbreak of World War II?' — since the question will not evoke pupils' feelings or affect, but rather solicit empirically verifiable facts from textbooks. This is not to say that history can only be taught at the factual level.

   The question must also ensure that many answers are permitted and acceptable. Indeed, a tenet of inquiry learning is that knowledge is only provisional, inquiry always moves knowledge further, and that the process of inquiry always throws up new questions. Especially in curriculum research, we have much to learn about the topics which make up the curriculum, e.g. subjects, core programmes, integration etc.

2. *All pupils must be able to participate in the survey.* The questions should not be such that only the 'bright' pupils can get involved. The goal is total participation. The teacher must work to reassure pupils that answers are sought from all of them, thereby convincing those students who have, for one reason or another, been devalued or put down in the past. Pupils-as-researchers is the aim.

3. *Phrase the question simply, in language understandable to pupils.* Too often a teacher will use words that pupils do not understand, and while it is, in itself, a good thing to get pupils to learn new meanings, this should, however, be avoided when using a problem survey as it breaks the survey's inquiry and continuity.

4. *The question should be specific.* Broad questions are discouraged as they would result in the inquiry having great breadth, but lacking depth — for example, 'What do you want to know about relationships?' would dredge up a wide range of responses that would render it impossible to plan a series of lessons on the responses.

5. *Pupils must be interested in the topic or problem question.* The foregoing have suggested that the teacher should initiate the questions to be explored; this has been suggested as a strategy only if pupils are unwilling to do so. One might also allow pupils to identify questions of interest and concern to themselves. Indeed, two radical American educators, Neil Postman and Charles Weingartner (1969), have suggested in their book *Teaching as a Subversive Activity* that the entire curriculum ought to be based upon answering the questions of pupils through inquiry learning. Of course, the questions asked would have to be worth seeking answers to, not only from the teacher's viewpoint but more importantly from the pupils'. It is important to recount that the philosophy of inquiry learning dictates that pupils play a central, but not necessarily exclusive, role in defining the inquiry questions. In a very real sense, the problem of curriculum is the problem of finding answers to the question 'What is worth knowing?'

6. *The teacher must demonstrate an interest in the answers.* The work must not be seen as just another time-filling exercise. There ought to be a spirit of application — that is, that something will be done about the problem once the answers have been determined. At base, this is the idea of 'action research' — inquiry carried out to solve some pressing problem by those affected by the problem.

It would speak volumes for trust and caring in curriculum were teachers actually to use pupils' work to reshape curriculum. Perhaps a good deal of the motivation, trust and respect could be restored to the teacher–pupil relationship by adopting this strategy.

Some teacher guidelines

1. *The teacher should not change the question.* If desirable responses are not forthcoming the teacher must not change the problem question, but should stick to the one at hand.
2. *The teacher must keep a record of pupil responses.* Be sure to record exactly what the pupils say. Do not attempt to rephrase the pupils' comments by stating 'Dont you mean . . .'
3. *The teacher should not evaluate the quality of responses, nor encourage pupils to do so.* This rule is similar to the one which does not permit evaluation during a brainstorming session. The idea is to gain a maximum responsiveness and to bring out all the alternatives.
4. *The teacher should not identify responses with pupils' names.* A form of labelling may result from attempts to link particular responses to pupils — in fact, pupils may feel that that response will be permanently associated with themselves.

Some sample problem survey questions

- What would you like to know about dating?
- What would you like to know about AIDS?
- What seems to worry you most?
- What is a community?
- What do you want to know about history?
- What don't you know about race?
- What would you like to know about research?

Taking the question about race, and putting it to a group of adolescents might produce a list of questions such as:

- How many races are there?
- What causes skin colours?
- Why are whites called Caucasians?
- Why are blacks sometimes discriminated against?

Once a number of questions on a topic have been set out, the teacher can then begin the task of attempting to interpret their meaning and look for patterns. Do the questions suggest racial fear, animosity, hatred, etc? Second, working groups can then be assigned the task of finding out more about the topic to report back to the whole class at a later date. Organization and division of labour in the conduct of such inquiry work is highly important. Perhaps each group should appoint a spokesperson to keep an accurate record of the group's research work. Certainly, the actual research work should be shared out among group members. Third, individual students can take on responsibility for pursuing research unassisted. Such work could form the basis of a 'project' or 'essay' to be submitted at a later date, or possibly as part of an examination.

Whichever strategy is adopted, be sure that certain standards are observed: that pupils acknowledge sources of information in writing and reporting, that hypotheses are clearly stated, that work is neat, etc.These standards can also be put in the form of questions:

1. Will these inquiries, and the answers to these questions, increase the will of learners to learn?
2. Can alternative modes of answering the questions be found?
3. Will the answers provide joy and excitement for learners?
4. Will the answers better prepare the pupils for living?

What should be noticed is that such questions are divergent and therefore consciousness-expanding in that they generate more questions. This is the proper role of inquiry and the beauty of it is that once started, it is difficult to know where one may end up. Inquiry learning through a problem survey will also tend to take a learner across subject boundaries and may not restrict him or her to one field of academic knowledge — it is thus interdisciplinary or integrated study. We should note that pupils will have to spend some considerable time in answering questions, and that time must be found if the activity is to prove rewarding. Needless to say, question answering and question asking go hand in hand. The problem survey is a tool whereby many educational objectives can be realized, including the teaching of research skills, problem solving and critical thinking.

SMALL GROUPS: THE DELIBERATIVE WORKING PARTY

Inquiry learning of any kind, including action research, goes hand in hand with small group work. In the recent past there has been growing interest in cooperative group work in schools; this has taken place mainly in social and personal education, and some new teaching techniques have been thrown up by this development (Cowie and Rudduck, 1989). For learning to be effective, an environment of trust and support needs to be nurtured so that pupils feel free to share feelings, views, values and ideas.

In this section small group work is discussed in relation to both student groups and action inquiry groups. Action research has been characterized by the small, intimate team or group approach. Two basic types of groups are discussed here: *primary work groups* and *secondary support groups.* While it is true that there can be good rapport and cohesiveness in the whole class group of, say, 30 pupils, the amount of input allowed each pupil is severly limited. Small groups have certain advantages over whole group organization.

Rationale

1. Pupils gain support from classmates through group activity — they are intimate, dynamic and cohesive units.
2. Small groups present a more efficient division of labour for tackling a range of inquiries and problems.
3. Pupils receive evaluative feedback from group members as well as the teacher — in the whole group evaluation is isolated to the teacher.
4. Small groups enable a teacher to treat pupils more flexibly by opening up options.
5. Small groups provide social relationships and motivation for learning through the establishment of cooperative norms and sharing.
6. Small groups allow pupils to continue an inquiry, at the personal level, which was intitiated in the teacher-led whole group.
7. Small groups allow one to reflect upon work done in the whole group.

Introductory activities

To get started, the teacher should explain carefully the introduction of the new work group arrangements. A few non-threatening exercises requiring group work should be tried at this stage — brainstorming, discussion, etc. The teacher must emphasize that a considerable period of the term's work will be done in these groups and for the pupils to succeed they will need to have the support and cooperation of all group members.

A firm contract, or commitment, is required within the small group. There is no correct number, but optimum results can be expected in groups of between four and eight pupils. It may also prove productive to assign particular tasks to group members to keep for, say, a month or a term — tasks such as chairperson, rapporteur, etc. These, of course, need to be negotiated within the group.

The teacher needs to conduct a careful analysis of his or her pupils. Some data can be gathered by means such as sociograms, test scores, sex, age, aptitude, etc. Decisions will have to be made as to whether a pupil will stay with one group on a permanent basis or be a transitory member of several groups. Pupils probably need the stability of a permanent group for their continuous learning and mastery of work, but they should also have access to other groups for special interest projects as they work through the curriculum. By asking pupils several questions a teacher can quickly establish a network of cooperating pupils. For example, sociometric analysis may proceed by giving out a list of all the pupils and asking each one to indicate five pupils on the list whom he or she would most like to work with; five who are best friends; and five who he or she would like to be accompanied by if transfer to a new class was immanent. It should be stressed that it is not always best to select your best friends for group work since the forming of groups allows the opportunity of making new friends and working relationships. Using such sociograms, the teacher can find out about pupil acceptance from classmates. A second strategy may be to allow pupils to complete a short self-report type questionnaire so that the teacher will have sound data upon which to assign pupils to groups.

The primary work group

For an extended period of time — a term or calendar school year — each pupil might be a member of a *primary work group.* While the main purpose will be to work towards the achievement of the core mastery objectives set by the teacher, the group members should be encouraged to declare their own objectives and to give support to one another in their attainment. In point of fact, it is the job of each group member to assist other group members to work towards objectives collaboratively. This may work out as sharing the task of 'peer tutoring', in which members instruct/help others to understand concepts, facts or important principles that may be found difficult at the individual level. It is important to allow this cooperative assistance without pre-empting individual initiative. The group should have a facilitator, chairperson, or leader — for want of a better term — whose task is to facilitate the work of the group.

Tasks for group members

- To get to know one another.
- To establish their own identity.
- To provide assistance and support to others in the group.
- To try out new behaviours.
- To become aware of the attitudes and values of group members.
- To be clearer about their own effect on other group members.
- To gain skill at research and inquiry work within the group.
- To develop their speaking, listening, writing and reading skills.

Thus, the process of group dynamics throws up important humanistic objectives by virtue of its existence and these need to be monitored by the teacher. The teacher can work to achieve the above objectives by permitting a heterogeneous group membership that enables pupils to learn from other pupils who are quite different from themselves. Thus, groups ideally should contain both boys and girls, and pupils who have different aptitudes, levels of achievement, interests etc.

The teacher needs to set out some simple rules for group work, such as the following: that all pupils communicate freely within the group; that 'clowns' will have to learn new, more acceptable behaviour; that pupils work towards developing commitment to the task at hand.

Teachers will, of course, require some training and more than a little experience to become highly skilled at facilitating group work. Some interesting publications by Button (1974; 1981), Simon, Howe and Kirschenbaum (1972), Glasser (1969), and Cowie and Rudduck (1989) offer specific guidelines and sample teaching strategies helpful to those contemplating group work. It should be stressed that group work ought to be a natural follow-up to the rigorous group work conducted in many elementary and primary schools, and should be seen as a core part of second level schooling.

Secondary support groups

In addition to retaining membership in the primary work group, pupils should also be permitted to join special *secondary support groups* that perform the following functions:

1. They allow pupils to meet in a group to solve an immediate, one-off type project or problem of special interest to the group members.
2. They may be convened simply as 'assist' groups, where members learn to support and listen to one another. These groups are particularly helpful in creating value awareness.
3. The teacher may form a secondary group whenever he or she feels that the class will benefit from a special group assignment — these may arise quite spontaneously as a need arises. For example, if the teacher feels the pupils are thinking quite narrowly on a topic he or she may set up a role-play situation to explore a problem. How does the newly employed teacher feel about teaching the less able classes? Role playing the conflict may help members learn about the feelings of the teacher.
4. From time to time the teacher might find pupils quite naturally forming their own groups to work on assignments, as they learn how to work more cooperatively and democratically.

All pupils should have the opportunity to work with others. Group work provides for this 'close encounter' of the personal kind. Pupils need to have experience of some measure of success in group work.

NEUTRAL CHAIRPERSON

One of the most exciting experimental pedagogical strategies developed to conduct research into a defined line of teaching was that of the *neutral chairperson*, as elucidated by Lawrence Stenhouse through the Humanities Curriculum Project that he pioneered in Britain between 1967 and 1972 and disseminated widely after that date. The strategy is included here as it marked a watershed for promoting the notion of the *teacher as researcher*. The critical feature of this experimental pedagogy was its concern to work out a *process model* of curriculum practice, as opposed to the traditional 'objectives' model of design. Stenhouse argued that the teacher could work according to certain *procedural principles* which are educational in their own right, as distinct from pursuing some ends or objectives as a target.

The Humanities Project was concerned with the broad aim of developing an understanding of social situations and human acts, and of the controversial issues they raise (Schools Council, 1970) among adolescents; the teacher operated a style of discussion-based teaching where the pupils examined critical 'evidence' as it reflected upon issues, under the agenda of a teacher-neutral-chairperson who submitted his or her work to the criterion of neutrality.

The major thrust of the project's work was in exploring the authority of teachers and schools — particularly the relationship between teachers and pupils in learning groups based upon discussion methodology (Stenhouse, 1971; 1975). Thus, the discussion-based group examined evidence as it worked *under the chairpersonship of a teacher submitting to parliamentary procedures, and the criterion of neutrality.*

Neutral chairpersonship and teacher/pupil curriculum research

The strategy has import in this book because it provides a set of procedures for researching teaching, and for setting out an alternative pedagogy. The concept of a teacher working as a neutral chairperson was Stenhouse's idea of a hypothesis which project teachers were invited to test. Certainly, it was one of the most exciting ideas to have emerged from the British curriculum development movement. It was suggested that there may be public concern about teachers using classrooms as platforms to air their prejudices and promote their own moral biases — thus the most rational option was neutrality, i.e. not using their authority position to dominate and limit discussion.

At least two implications of the project's aim are worth underlining: first, it conceived of both *teachers and pupils as learners;* and secondly, *understanding can never totally be achieved*

— only deepened. Understanding as an aim results from the process of exploring what counts as a valid understanding by the group — the group must take on board the exploration of the very nature of understanding itself.

The Humanities Curriculum Project was based upon the following five premises:

1. That controversial value issues should be handled by teachers and pupils in curriculum.
2. That the teacher needs to temper his or her position on value issues by adopting the criterion of procedural neutrality, i.e. teachers regard it as a responsibility not to use their authority position to promote their value beliefs.
3. That discussion should be the main teaching strategy.
4. That divergence of opinion should be supported.
5. That the teacher, as a chairperson, should have responsibility for quality and standards in learning through inquiry.

The project published packs of materials which served as the basis for discussion on such diverse areas as war, relations between the sexes, the family, the law, poverty, education, people and work, living in cities, and race relations. Further, and most importantly, the project provided a training procedure for teaching through discussion by using procedural neutrality as the guiding chairperson principle.

It is important to appreciate that neutrality here does not mean 'value-free' teaching. It recognizes that education is not value-free but that the teacher should be committed to *educational values*, such as rationality, concern for evidence and sensitivity to others rather than publicizing his or her own views.

Outline of the experimental strategy of neutral chairperson

Given that discussion was seen as the strategy, there was the demand that teachers be committed to certain procedural values governing inquiry learning. And moreover, that teachers took on the responsibility *to monitor their teaching carefully so as to improve the quality of chairpersonship*. That is, on controversial issues, which cannot by their definition be settled by recourse to data, the teacher should remain neutral and not pose as the source of information or expert views on the matter being discussed. Moreover, the goal is to involve the students in the inquiry, not to put the teacher up as an authority on the subject. It was felt that student research would not be adequate as the basis for a full and searching discussion — for example, it was noted that even high-powered university seminars often collapse due to student papers being deemed inadequate. Accordingly, the notion of access to *evidence* was seen as crucial in researching issues — evidence here meaning any material which is used for its relevance to the issue under discussion, rather than for its own sake. The project published starter packs of evidence and encouraged students and teachers to do research.

Role of the chairperson

The teacher, functioning as a chairperson, has a number of responsibilities: to know the materials, to provide evidence, to keep the discussion on a coherent track etc. One key feature of this role is to open up as wide a range of alternatives on an issue as possible. The chair must also pay attention to classroom processes as they affect understanding. In developing his or her skill as a chairperson, the teacher needs to be a keen observer of group processes. Questions to be answered are: Who does the talking? Which students lead? Does the chair involve everyone?

The major task of neutral chairpersonship is *to create the conditions conducive to taking responsibility for the development of understanding of the issue being discussed.* The chair needs to learn ways of helping students to take on responsibility for their own learning. The chair is a facilitator. Some of the tasks are:

1. Promoting an enquiry-research perspective among group members.
2. Setting a favourable context for discussion — groups of not more than ten in number sitting in a semi-circle format.
3. Promoting a good group identity.
4. Clarifying the nature of the issue under discussion.
5. Protecting pupil divergence of expression.
6. Keeping under review the contributions of members.
7. Introducing new 'evidence'.
8. Ensuring that high standards which support quality work are observed.
9. Maintaining continuity between discussions.
10. Ensuring that procedural rules are observed.
11. Rounding off discussions with a summary which organizes positions and understandings.

The teacher as a chairperson is responsible for the conditions of the inquiry, its coherence, and finally its standards of judgement. Of interest to classroom action researchers is the *teaching of procedural principles to students for conducting inquiry work.* For example, students need to learn to listen to points being made, contributions should be respected, etc.

Key procedural principles

The chair needs to conduct work so that opportunities are given to increase pupils' understanding of the issues. Paramount in this endeavour is the need to explain the project aim to students and for them to be committed to it. The following are key procedural principles:

1. *Principle of continuity and sequence.* Discussion work should not be a fragmented series of contributions; thus the group should have a chair with an agenda, and perhaps minutes of the proceedings should be taken to carry ideas forward.
2. *Principle of an open inquiry.* Here the chair endeavours to open up to the group a wide range of resources and sources which feed the inquiry: persons, texts, handouts, films, etc. These help to present views not considered by the group.
3. *Principle that the chair generate critical standards to judge work by.* Resources need to be evaluated independently by the group *vis-à-vis* their interpretation and authority. The chair may ask questions too — it is vital that he or she is seen as a learner.
4. *Principle that the chair ensures needs of the group are served.* The chairperson needs to help all members to make contributions and express their views freely.

Successful chairpersons seem to be able to:

1. Help the group to set limits to the discussion.
2. Query sources and resources.
3. Summarize arguments.
4. Keep a record of the proceedings.[3]
5. Ensure that group members build on each other's ideas.
6. Through careful questioning provide an intellectual model for self-reflection and critique.

A training procedure for discussion work

These principles will be useful to all action researchers who use discussion work in classrooms.

1. Do you tolerate silences and pauses, or do you interrupt silence?
2. Do you use your position as chair to press students to adopt a moral position on an issue?
3. Do you ask questions to which you already have the answer?

3. This aspect of the chairperson's role has major implications for classroom action research. For example, the keeping of documents, tape recordings and video tapes of discussion work can be seen *inter alia* as a data base for research work into the effectiveness of the facilitating chairperson in refining and using competently this role of neutral chairpersonship.

4. Do you interrupt pupils?
5. Do you act consistently according to procedural rules?
6. Do you look for consensus of opinion, e.g. 'Do we all agree with this?'
7. Do you encourage and praise student contributions?
8. Do you provide evidence?
9. Are you really neutral on value issues?
10. What is the chairperson's hidden agenda?
11. Do you try to press for a position which you support?
12. Do you try to involve all members?
13. Do you keep time?
14. Do you set an agenda and stick to it?
15. Do you follow up inquiries with suggestions for future research?
16. Do you tape record discussions and monitor particular pupils?
17. Are you a consistent and reliable chairperson?

Research and respect for thorough inquiry is highly valued in the neutral chairpersonship role. The chair should attempt to teach pupils the modes of inquiry and canons of research appropriate to the study of disciplines, e.g. careful statement of problems, formulation of hunches and hypotheses for testing, data collection strategies, concern to analyse and evaluate data, and the forming of general and specific conclusions.

The adoption of neutrality as a criterion may not suit all teachers but it is offered as an alternative style of dealing with contentious and highly emotive value issues. It has positive and negative sides. On the negative side one might seriously question the adoption of this role regarding issues such as racism or poverty, where teachers are expected not to be neutral. On the positive side the role allows an atheist to search for evidence to help a fundamentalist Christian pupil to put his or her views in their strongest light. The teacher can make inputs without taking sides or showing approval for issues, thus encouraging a critical attitude to research material, evidence etc.

In conclusion, the adoption of neutrality does not mean that the teacher does not have values — only that he or she is not going to use his or her authority position to inculcate pupils; rather the teacher wishes to work towards pupil autonomy and emancipation by ensuring that all issues are handled with a critical attitude to evidence. It seems to this author that Stenhouse is making is a plea for teaching which has its roots deep in moral philosophy. The project has been indicted with the criticism of asking teachers to remain neutral on value issues, yet if we look carefully at what Stenhouse and his colleagues have said, we find that they are often more aware of the distinction than their critics. It is, briefly, the distinction between 'substantive' and 'procedural or methodological' values. The project advocates a strategy which asks pupils to review evidence under the chairpersonship of a teacher who represents *educative values* and critical standards, but who maintains neutrality on the substantive values under discussion. The position is akin to that of Richard Peters' (Peters, 1966) ideas of principles of procedure — i.e. that we try to teach pupils rational procedures for arriving at substantive positions.

The Humanities Curriculum Project has been said to be the only curriculum development project which has offered practitioners an *alternative pedagogy* of learning through discussion and inquiry methodology, while asking teachers to take responsibility for self-evaluation and research into their work. It set the scene for much of the new 'teacher-researcher' work coming out of curriculum projects in the West. Jean Rudduck, a colleague of Lawrence Stenhouse on the HCP central team, later edited a book (Rudduck, 1979) produced by a group of HCP trial teachers, advocating the teacher self-monitor notion. This idea of the teacher and pupils becoming researchers into their own actions was pushed yet further by John Elliott and Clem Adelman with the Ford Teaching Project.

6 Critical-Reflective and Evaluative Research Methods

> He that judges without informing himself to the utmost that he is capable cannot acquit himself of judging amiss.[1]

TRIANGULATION

Triangulation is used in several senses by sociologists and curriculum action research workers. Denzin (1970) conceived 'triangulation' as the advocation of combinations of research methodologies; for example, participant observation is seen as combining direct observation with survey interviews, document analysis, etc. Campbell and Fiske (1959) and Webb et al. (1966) argue that triangulation is the use of multiple methods in the study of the same object. Yet this interpretation differs slightly from that employed by contemporary action researchers (Elliott, 1978b) who favour a sense of triangulation which combines the perspectives of various actors within a research setting. Indeed, Denzin (1970:301) cites four types of triangulation involving varieties of *data: investigator* (multiple versus single researchers), *theory* (single versus multiple perspectives of the same problem), and finally, *methodological* (within method triangulation and between method triangulation). For example, 'theoretical sampling' is an example of the latter type of triangulation.

Triangulation and action research

Triangulation (Elliott and Adelman, 1976; Elliott, 1978b) is a procedure for organizing different types of evidence into a more coherent frame of reference or relationship so that they can be compared and contrasted. Elliott (1978b) discusses triangulation as 'a theory of method for self-evaluation within a democratic-professional system of classroom accountability'.

The basic ideas underlying triangulation were worked out in the experience of the Ford Teaching Project (Elliott, 1977; Elliott and Partington, 1975). This was a two-year action research project, based in East Anglia, which sought to use teachers as researchers to discover general rules relating to the use of inquiry-discovery modes of teaching in elementary and secondary classrooms, and to suggest and test general hypotheses about how teaching problems could be resolved. By asking teachers to self-monitor their activities,

---

1. John Locke (1690) *An Essay Concerning Human Understanding.*

triangulation was introduced. Elliott comments:

> Triangulation involves gathering accounts of a teaching situation from three quite different points of view: those of the teacher, the students, and a participant observer. Who gathers the accounts, how they are elicited, and who compares them depend largely on the context. The process of gathering accounts from three distinct standpoints has an epistemological justification. Each point in the triangle stands in a unique epistemological position with respect to access to relevant data about a teaching situation. The person in the best position to gain access via introspection to the intentions and aims in the situation is the teacher. The students are in the best position to explain how the teacher's actions influence the way they respond in the situation. The participant observer is in the best position to collect data about the observable features of the interaction between teacher and students. By comparing an account with the accounts from the two other standpoints, a person at one point of the triangle has an opportunity to test and perhaps revise it on the basis of more sufficient data.
>
> (Elliott, 1977:10)

In addition to 'triangulation', the Ford Teaching Project used other research methods to investigate teaching problems in schools including: questionnaires, outside observers, interviewing pupils, keeping field notes, audio/video and tape slide recording of classrooms, participant observation, and case studies of classrooms.

Procedures for triangulation

The project staff functioned as 'participant observers' and the accounts were collected for the personal study of project teachers. However, teachers were encouraged to share their data, particularly with pupils, so that triangulation could open up a dialogue between outside observer and teacher-researcher, and foster inquiry skills among pupils. The following are procedures for triangulation:

1. *Post-lesson interview: observer and teacher-researcher.* The technique involved firstly a post-lesson interview between the outside observer and classroom teacher, before showing the taped class to students. The purpose of this interview was to identify the sort of data that needed to be collected from pupils if the teacher was to be able to compare two versions, or accounts, of the same event. It also enabled points of divergence in the teachers' and the observers' accounts of the same action to be seen.
2. *Post-lesson interview: observer and small sample of students.* The observers interviewed a small group of pupils from the taped lesson, with the teacher's permission. The interview was taped.

The observer then sought permission from pupils to show this tape to the teacher. The observers told pupils before the interview that they were only after honest accounts and that pupils would retain control over the teacher's access to the tapes.

3. *Final dialogue between observer and teacher using the observer-student tape as data.* If permission is granted by students to allow the teacher access to the observer-student tape, then there is a post-conference discussion between the observer and the teacher-researcher about the various perspectives offered by the observer and the students.

The triangle is now complete. The provision of the three-sided accounts is a very momentous occasion for participants as often it will be the first time that a practitioner has come face to face with evidence of a factual nature concerning his or her practice. Equally interesting, is the fact that often pupils do not see the objectives that teachers hold in the way that teachers see them — teachers may thus be able to adjust their teaching practice accordingly.

Yet the procedure is not without stress and anxiety — particularly for classroom teachers (Elliott, 1977:11). Teachers frequently cited the collection of student data (step 2 in the procedure) as that part of the process that aroused the greatest anxiety for them in the Ford Teaching Project.

Stages in self-monitoring

The process of monitoring one's performance is central to the conduct of action research, no matter what the method of data collection. The following three stages are suggested:

1. The identification of those actions which are performed *willingly or directly*, rather than indirectly, via the consequence of a prior action such as asking a question.
2. Making an evaluation of these *directly willed* actions.
3. Assessing culpability for the consequences of actions — for example, the extent to which a person is responsible or accountable and can be 'blamed' for his or her actions.

Some guidelines

In taking the three perspectives into account, the action researcher should make an effort to note precisely where the three accounts (that of the student, the teacher and the observer) *agree*, and *disagree,* but especially where they tend to *differ*. When reports diverge, evidence contained in field notes can be checked against tapes and transcripts of the action. Discussions could be mounted specifically on points of disagreement, preferably under the chairing of a neutral and independent person. Triangulation is also an excellent foundation for building up thorough case reccrds and case studies of the action. Data gathered by the action researcher through interview and subvention are directly fed back to the 'researched' and even third-party audiences (the pupils), who offer critical comment on the data. A wide number of regressions are permitted but at some point the action researcher must decide when to make the results public (Adelman and Walker, 1975).

Triangulationnrequires that the researcher becomes familiar with the day-to-day reality of the setting and participants. The researcher mustsee cause and effect; spot the cycles of action, response and new action; and comprehend relationships, beliefs and above all practices. While one is using a number of perspectives (teacher, pupil and researcher) one is also carrying out three tasks: observing in depth; making further inquiries; and finally explaining from the data, actors, theories and research methodology used.

QUADRANGULATION

Quadrangulation is both a method for collecting data as well as a mode of monitoring evidence so that it can be viewed through various research spectacles by key actors in the setting. It is a four-sided evaluation process in a naturalistic setting. Quadrangulation is a highly obtrusive technique, developed by the writer and sharing some common features with 'illuminative evaluation' (Parlett and Hamilton, 1972) and 'triangulation' as used by Elliott (1978b; 1981), in which the research act is made up of constructing accounts of action from a variety of angles and from various participants (observer/teacher/pupils) and then comparing these accounts. That is, by comparing an experiment in teaching through the account as given by a participant observer in the classroom, the teacher and the pupils.

It is of interest to note that Elliott's usage differs from that originally posited by social researchers (Denzin, 1970) of 'methodological triangulation', which amounts to examining a problem by bringing various *research methods* to bear upon it — for example interviewing, case study, observation etc. Some years back, Trow (1957) put forward that social researchers ought to give up their arguments regarding the superiority of one method over another. Trow suggested that no single method is superior; each has its own strengths or advantages, and weaknesses or disadvantages. This has been recognized in this book and the author has attempted to list these advantages and disadvantages where possible. Similarly in educational and curriculum research, one must recognize that particular problems are suited to particular research techniques and the notion of methodological triangulation should be embraced.

Quadrangulation is a systematic approach to observation in the research setting. In addition to the use of various methods for collecting data, it refers to several other varieties of 'triangulation'.

Types of triangulation

Triangulation may occur at one of four levels: first, there can be *conceptual/theoretical* triangulation — seeing a project from different models or perspectives; second, there can be triangulation of *information/data* collected in various settings; third, *researcher or investigator* triangulation can be conducted by using different inquirers; and fourthly, there can be *methodological* triangulation — carried out through collecting data by multiple research methods, e.g. participant observation with field notes, questionnaires and documentary analysis.

The more rigorous the evaluation through multiple investigators, databases, methods and theories, the more reliable the observations and results. It is argued that since each research method reveals the uniqueness of a setting or problem, then multiple methods ought to be the norm to exhume this richness (Denzin, 1970:26–27). In this the writer concurs with Webb et al. (1966) that it is no longer feasible to employ single method research designs. What the present writer has been searching for is *triangulation within a single methodology.*

The nature of quadrangulation

It may be fruitful at this point to discuss precisely how *quadrangulation* is actually conducted in an action research setting. Let us imagine that a teacher is willing to examine the handling of controversial moral issues in a social studies class. He or she agrees to allow an outside observer/facilitator to collaborate and monitor the action. The practitioner thus is about to begin *a four-stage research study.* Quadrangulation can be thought of as a four-sided box, or quadrangle, as is found in the architectural design of many ancient European universities: the first side, or wall, represents the external-researcher and the teacher-researcher as they study a video account of the action; the second side involves the external researcher and the pupil-researchers as they discuss the action without their teacher; the third side represents when the video is played for other practitioners in the school or project, with the teacher-researcher explaining what has happened and what he or she has been learning about solving his or her curriculum problem; finally, the quadrangle is complete with the fourth wall, when all of the data — videotape, field notes, memoranda, project course guidelines, documents and so on — are tabled and this entire 'case data' is discussed. The purpose is to make a thorough appraisal of the problem, bringing all those with a role into the evaluation process.

The following shows how it works.

Procedures for quadrangulation

Stage 1: External researcher with the teacher-researcher — video-recording the action. The external facilitator arrives and takes up an unobtrusive position in the classroom; he or she is equipped with a video camera on which a full record of the behaviour of teacher and students is recorded. At the end of the lesson, or sometime later in the day, the researcher plays the videotape back with the teacher present. Together, they go over and examine the action.

Key incidents are discussed, but not in a supervisory or threatening fashion — more a curious detached comment in an exploratory manner to understand what is happening. The video may enable insights and reflective asides to surface on the teacher's part — for example, he or she may not have allowed all pupils with a view on a contentious issue to say their piece, moving quickly away from the 'danger zone'. He or she may make mental notes to try X or Y the next time this arises. The first cycle or side of the research quadrangle is now complete.

Stage 2: External researcher with the participants — video record of an exploratory interview and play-by-play account of the action. The external researcher then selects four to six pupils from the class and takes them to a quiet area where they can be interviewed about the lesson. This interview is videotaped and will serve as a highly useful data set for the classroom teacher at a later stage. Basically, the idea is to gather pupils' accounts, insights, difficulties and reactions to what the teacher was doing, how the lesson developed, etc. The external researcher is very supportive and evaluative of pupil comments. The external researcher needs to request pupil permission to play this tape back for the benefit of the teacher, this principle of trust and negotiation being an important principle which must be respected in human relations research. This should be done in such a way that the pupils are told that 'the teacher will be able to learn, and improve his or her work'.

Shortly after this interview takes place, the tape of the interview is played back to the teacher-researcher. It would be highly desirable to employ a VTR machine with 'freeze frame' capabilities so that important behaviours and events can be examined in some depth. The teacher and outside facilitator try to arrive at some general understandings and plans for further action; they need to learn what has resulted and what they now can do about it. The second stage in the research process is complete.

Stage 3: Teacher-researcher with project team/school faculty members. At this stage the videotape of the lesson and the video of the interview with the pupils is played for the benefit of other subject specialists, staff members, members of the curriculum team, etc. The major purpose is to allow insights and perspectives from these different actors to filter through the evaluation screen. The notion of the group is one of a supportive/facilitative group who expect to learn from one another and who respect one another's professional comment. This is a critical-reflective and discursive stage which accords with the concept of curriculum-making as hypothesis testing, and with the idea that all teaching is in a sense a testing of hypotheses and hunches.

The teacher-researcher should endeavour to allow all present to comment and criticise the action. It is also vital to make a permanent record of this session to use as 'evidence' later.

Stage 4: Analysis of the total case data — planning the way forward. At this fourth and final stage of the action reflection cycle, the external researcher and teacher-researcher pool all of the data collected, including all documents, tapes, videotapes, memos, field notes, teachers comments etc. The data should then be put into perspective. This is the time for the writing up of a case study as an important cycle of action inquiry, experiment, reflection and decision making has finished. The pooling of all this data helps with reliability checks in validating ideas and evidence.

The process is now complete: (1) teacher and observer, (2) observer and pupils, (3) teacher and staff, (4) observer-teacher and data analysis. The way forward is to learn by doing — by getting one's feet wet in the research waters. Essential here is that the outsider and insider are supportive and collaborative. Together they can help the teacher to improve his or her craft in an interactive research relationship. Perhaps at some stage in the future teachers will be able to conduct action research individually, but for now it would seem prudent to give them all the support they need, and this means the collaborative research dyadic relationship between outside facilitator and teacher-researcher.

The study of action and of classrooms is the best way to improve curriculum and develop good curriculum theory. As Stenhouse (1975:143) commented:

> All well-founded curriculum research and development whether the work of an individual teacher, of a school, of a group working in a teachers' centre or a group working within the coordinated framework of a national project, is based on the study of classrooms. It thus rests on the work of teachers.

The thesis being worked out here argues that it is not enough to have curriculum research, i.e. that teachers' work be studied. It argues rather that it is important that teachers become the researchers of their own practice by adopting an inquiry stance to their work.

Before concluding, it should be noted that *quadrangulation* is not simply four perspectives from within one research method (use of video in observation by different actors), but rather that it 'triangulates' methods, perspectives, actors, data and theories. The basic idea is to bring various methodologies and perspectives to bear on a problem so that the best data and decision choices are available for solving practical curriculum problems. Traditionally, the best-known techniques for classroom research were those of interaction analysis protocols; the advent of naturalistic observation and field methods has made this an experimental field. The video is a tool which captures what is said and done, permitting reliability checks to be made on observations. Combined with sensitive interviewing and participant observation, the potential for quadrangulation in action research is unlimited.

COLLEGIAL REVIEW

Collegial review is the practice of gaining reports from colleagues through the use of either structured observation instruments, such as *interaction analysis protocols*, or through methods of *quadrangulation,* or peer holistic observation.

There is little doubt that peer review can play a powerful role in the improvement of instruction and curriculum. The improvement of instruction is often the number one priority of most school districts. Note that one is not talking about self-evaluation here but *peer evaluation*, in which performances are appraised by contemporary colleagues. The bottom line is *reflexivity* — to get teachers to think about and reflect upon their practice. The evaluation of performance sheet on p. 198 below suggests 13 skills which might be used as criteria for evaluating classroom teaching.

Note that the thrust of such an initiative is not on *inspection* of teaching, it is rather on *appraisal for improvement*, by creditable colleagues. Perhaps one way in which collegial review can be started at school level is for colleagues to form development teams. Glatthorn (1977) has suggested that collegial development arises because:

1. Teachers wish to see the school's aims achieved.
2. Teachers are concerned about their own personal agendas.
3. Teachers' concern for self-growth can be linked to a plan for collegial review and development.
4. Teachers working together can help one another to grow as professionals.
5. Teachers can be helped by school administrators to develop teams.

6. Teachers are able to appraise their progress.

The present writer would agree with Glatthorn's premisses and add that teachers are in the best position to study the effects of their practice. Yet certain exceptions may present themselves:

1. Student or induction-year teachers may benefit from the help of a trained supervisor.
2. Experienced teachers who are having difficulty with practice may benefit from the help of a skilled supervisor.
3. All teachers might benefit from periodic review by trained observers (and student evaluations).

Collegial review: getting started at school level

1. Identify a few colleagues with whom you would like to work.
2. Meet with the group and discuss how you can help one another.
3. Put your plan into action, allowing for review by peers.
4. Appoint a secretary who will report to the staff and principal on the progress of the group.

Of course, it is accepted that honesty will govern all reporting and that observations will not be reported outside the collegial group (except in favourable terms). It is an issue of some controversiality whether the group uses ratings (evaluations). Some observers, such as Glatthorn (1977), argue that any type of rating interferes with the helping relationship which he feels is at the centre of collegial development. The present author takes a different viewpoint, arguing that one cannot escape the responsibility of offering value judgements or evaluations in classroom research. No play on words will detract a professional from making professional evaluative judgements. When observing a colleague, prepare yourself in the following ways:

1. Decide what it is that you wish to observe — such as a particular teaching skill, strategy or behaviour.
2. Keep a record of what you see either through videotape or field notes, observation schedule etc.
3. Get a good seat so that you can see all of the action.
4. Be sure to have a conference with the teacher in a private space soon after the observation. The main purpose is to give the data to your colleague so that he or she learns from your observations. Your observations, if regarded as contentious, can be triangulated with videotape for authenticity and validity of comment.

It is vital to be *honest* yet *tactful* in giving your own opinions of the class observed. If the lesson was successful then you have no problem. If the lesson had some weaknesses, then emphasize the good points but say 'I am concerned about one or two things which the pupils struggled with, but I admired the way you performed X or Z.' If the lesson was extremely weak and you wish to preserve the professional relationship, then you must be tactful by saying something like 'You did have problems with X or Y, and I wonder how those things strike you?' Remember, at base, more is at stake than this conference or a particular skill — what matters is the building of a mutual work ethic that suggests teachers can grow from collegial review. Make the development of collegiality an overarching goal.

Evaluation of performance: peer review

Teacher _____ Visit _____

School _____ Date _____

Class _____ Lesson _____

Overall summated grade _____ Experience of lesson _____

Instructions: (1) Circle one grade (1–5) for each item.
(2) Summate the scores and record grade (58–65=A; 50–57=B; 42–49=C; 34–41=D; below 34 = non-master)

CRITERIA FOR MASTER TEACHER

1. Skill in: *Planning the lesson.*
   5   4   3   2   1   0

2. Skill in: *Implementation of the lesson plan.*
   5   4   3   2   1   0

3. Skill in: *Handling equipment and materials.*
   5   4   3   2   1   0

4. Skill in: *Gaining pupils' interest and attention at outset.*
   5   4   3   2   1   0

5. Skill in: *Explaining, narrating, directing, gesturing.*
   5   4   3   2   1   0

6. Skill in: *Controlling pupils.*
   5   4   3   2   1   0

7. Quality of: *Voice and speech habits.*
   5   4   3   2   1   0

8. Skill in: *Gaining active pupil participation in lesson.*
   5   4   3   2   1   0

9. Skill in: *Developing appropriate pupil responses.*
   5   4   3   2   1   0

Items 10–13 assessed following lesson in conference with teacher.

10. Skill in: *Controlling timing and pace.*
      5   4   3   2   1   0

11. Skill in: *Displaying interest, enthusiasm, liveliness.*
      5   4   3   2   1   0

12. Skill in: *Recognizing and dealing with pupil difficulties.*
      5   4   3   2   1   0

13. Skill in: *Self-evaluation and monitoring of performance.*
      5   4   3   2   1   0

LECTURE FEEDBACK

This technique may prove useful as a device for college and university tutors/professors, though a similar instrument can be used by teachers at elementary and secondary schools. The questions are loosely structured to gain maximum feedback around several probes, or key areas of concern. Students should be encouraged to comment honestly and in some depth. A copy of the questions should be reproduced for students to complete.

Please comment on the lecture you have just heard.

1. Please say what you believe to be the aims or objectives of the lecture you have just attended.
2. How successful was the lecturer in achieving these implied goals?
3. What negative aspects of the lecture can you comment upon?
4. What would you say were the positive aspects of the lecture/ lecturer?
5. How could the presentation be improved?
6. Any other comments?

Lecture rating form

Lecturer _____   Date _____

RATING								REMARKS
		5	4	3	2	1		
Audibility Clearly audible							Almost inaudible	

	RATING							REMARKS
		5	4	3	2	1		
Quality of delivery	Lively paced						Dull, poor pace	
Intelligibility	Easy to follow						Difficult to follow	
Speed	Right						Too fast or too slow	
AV resources	Clear, neat						Poor, illegible	
Preparation & organization	Thorough						Weak/poorly organized	
Irritating mannerisms & distractions	None						Cause marked distraction	

Note: Under 'Remarks' section please insert any comments which will guide the lecturer. Please use other side if necessary.

LESSON PROFILES

The lesson profile captures and illustrates, in a segmented style, the continuity of actors' behaviour, tasks, etc. during the course of the lesson. Thus, it provides a shorthand version of the major clustering of classroom events and actions performed — or other curricular setting, such as staff meeting, workshop, etc. — and the actors involved, over a period of time. Lesson profiles are not to be confused with *pupil profiling,* which is more concerned with recording the attributes, traits and achievements of pupils by means of some record card. The lesson profile, on the other hand, tries to illustrate who does what and when during the class period. Some good examples of lesson profiles are offered by Cohen and Manion (1977) and Walker and Adelman (1975).

Lesson profiles can serve several purposes. First, they can be used by an observer to condense the action in order to understand, in shorthand, what is happening here and now. Thus they can become a field note or record of the observations in the field setting. Second, they can serve as part of a scheme of general lesson recollection to inform staff meetings, curriculum projects, etc. Third, they help the teacher to understand better how time can be used effectively. Fourth, they can initiate pre-service teachers into the rigour of lesson planning during their teacher education training programme, acting as exemplars of what teachers of various subjects actually do in classrooms. Finally, they can provide feedback for the practitioner.

Example 1: Lesson profile

	0–5 mins.	6–15 mins.	16–25 mins.	26–40 mins.
Pupil behaviour:	Hanging up coats; talking; get books.	Listening to directions; ask questions; start exercise.	Continue work; move to small groups.	Complete tasks; answer teacher.
Teacher behaviour:	Cleans desk; gives directions for exercise; hands out workbooks.	Introduces task; gives clarifying instructions; assigns pupils to small group; walkabout.	Walkabout; help individual pupils with exercises.	Asks questions; clears away books; home-work.
Materials and and resources:	Blackboard; chalk; pencils; workbooks.		Logsheets for recording data.	Workbooks; pencils.

Adapted from Elliott (1981). Lesson profiles may be entered into journals, field notes, etc. at appropriate places.

Teaching modes for analysis of episodes in profiling

For the purposes of using our lesson profile four modes of teaching are identified:

- Mode 1: *Directive teaching.* This is basically an expository mode of instruction. It is best characterized by transmission of knowledge, skills, etc.

- Mode 2: *Question-answer style.* This is 'one on one' teaching in which the teacher raises questions and takes answers from pupils one at a time.
- Mode 3: *Discussion — small or whole group.* The teacher adopts the role of chairperson — leading and facilitating pupil discourse. Interaction is not one-way, but free and open to all participants.
- Mode 4: *Independent work.* Pupils work individually on problems/worksheets — this may be written or a study.

Example 2: Lesson profile

Time	Action: teaching mode and pupil behaviour
5 mins.	Episode 1 (Mode 1) — Introductory remarks. Teacher conveys purpose.
5 mins.	Episode 2 (Mode 2) — Evidence/fact sheets/resources introduced. Discussion centred around question and answers.
15 mins.	Episode 3 (Mode 3) — Pupils work in small groups on problems. Buzz groups/role-play etc. Pupils actively participate.
5 mins.	Episode 4 (Mode 2) — Question/answer session following group work.
10 mins.	Episode 5 (Mode 4) — Pupils work independently on problems/projects relating to previous episodes.
5 mins.	Episode 6 (Mode 1) — Teacher assigns homework on topic.

Total 45 minutes: 6 episodes.

STUDENT COURSE/TEACHER EVALUATION

A major function of evaluation is to provide information in the form of feedback to the teacher, lecturer or tutor so that he or she may revise and thus improve the course offered to the student. The purpose of the student course evaluation form discussed in this section is to provide an informal device for gathering *systematic* data on teaching. The form addresses a number of general features applicable to the teacher-learner relationship: purposes, content, structure, methods, and evaluation procedures.

Course evaluation serves a variety of purposes such as helping with curriculum improvement, identifying student concerns, interests etc. Generally, the aim is to determine what instructional changes are needed in terms of materials, teaching styles, workloads, etc.

Course evaluation provides student appraisal of not only the course and its content, but also the teacher, and his or her effectiveness or lack of it. Thus, course evaluation invites student appraisal of teaching performance. In this instance, a seven-point *rating scale* is operationalized as the research instrument.

Course evaluation instrument

Course _____ Instructor _____

Department _____ School _____
Student level
College undergraduate _____ Graduate _____

Instructions: Please answer the questions using the numerical scale below (7 being the highest rating and 1 the lowest rating) by circling the number that comes closest to your appraisal.

---

1. Please rate the overall appropriateness of the aims/objectives of the course.   1 2 3 4 5 6 7

2. Please rate the quality of course structure/ organization.   1 2 3 4 5 6 7

3. Please rate the extent to which the course goals were achieved.   1 2 3 4 5 6 7

4. Please rate the quality of teacher-student relationship.   1 2 3 4 5 6 7

5. Please rate the level of concern of the teacher with student mastery of course objectives.   1 2 3 4 5 6 7

6. Please rate the overall quality of the teacher.   1 2 3 4 5 6 7

7. Please rate the extent to which the course contributed to an increase of knowledge/ skills in this subject.   1 2 3 4 5 6 7

8. Please rate the effectiveness of the teaching strategies/methods used.   1 2 3 4 5 6 7

9. Please rate the extent to which course the course contributed to the development of critical/reflective thinking.   1 2 3 4 5 6 7

10. Please rate the course quality overall.   1 2 3 4 5 6 7

11. Please rate the level of satisfaction with reading materials.   1 2 3 4 5 6 7

12. Please rate the grading standard (1=easy 7= difficult).   1 2 3 4 5 6 7

13. Please indicate the number of out-of-class hours spent on coursework per week (1=1 or less; 2=2; 3= 3/4; 4=5/6; 5=6/7; 6=7/9; 7=more than 10 hours).   1 2 3 4 5 6 7

14. Please rate the overall difficulty of the course (easy=1; difficult =7).   1 2 3 4 5 6 7

15. Indicate the extent of your willingness to recommend this course to other students.   1 2 3 4 5 6 7

16. Please rate the effectiveness of the lectures.   1 2 3 4 5 6 7

17. Please rate the effectiveness of class discussions.   1 2 3 4 5 6 7

18. Please indicate the grade you expect to receive (1=fail; 2/3=D; 4/5=C; 6=B; 7= A).   1 2 3 4 5 6 7

19. Please rate the success of the teacher presentations.   1 2 3 4 5 6 7

20. Please rate the value of out-of-class inquiries and assignments.   1 2 3 4 5 6 7

21. Please rate the teacher's skill in gaining student interest.   1 2 3 4 5 6 7

22. Please rate the teacher's skill in directing, narrating and explaining.   1 2 3 4 5 6 7

23. Please rate the teacher's quality of voice projection (audibility).   1 2 3 4 5 6 7

24. Please rate the teacher's skill in developing student participation.   1 2 3 4 5 6 7

25. Please rate the teacher's enthusiasm and liveliness during class.   1 2 3 4 5 6 7

26. Please rate the teacher's ability to spot and deal with student difficulties.   1 2 3 4 5 6 7

Comments

27. Please indicate ways in which this course could be improved

_____

_____

28. Please make any additional comments here

_____

_____

_____

Since taking up his present position as a university lecturer, the present writer has introduced a number of new courses and desired to know what students felt about these innovations. Thus his primary motivation in constructing this evaluation feedback instrument was to *gain information and student affect-appraisal* on a wide variety of variables affecting the implementation of college-level courses — although the instrument has been modified for general use by teachers at all levels of education.

Teachers can develop their own objectives, depending on their priorities, but whatever shape the formal appraisal instrument takes it becomes one's 'professional development plan' by which both the students and the teacher evaluate the teacher and the course.

By carefully tabulating student responses on the one to seven scale and arriving at mean scores for each variable (and the total number of variables) one can calculate a teaching index. By making adjustments to particular aspects of one's teaching (for example quality of presentations) one can improve performance and have the aid of successive group mean scores as an indicator of quality. For example, if a mean score for item 10 was 3.8 for 1988 and after reflection and revision of this behaviour the score was increased to 6.5 for 1989, then one might reasonably conclude that some improvement was evident in 'course quality overall'.

A salutary warning: practitioners can avoid collecting data on their performance and therefore not benefit from feedback; they may receive it involuntarily from students; or they might set out to research their practice — the latter is the professional response.

Pupil evaluation instrument

Directions: This form will allow you to provide your teacher with some information on how well he or she explains, clarifies and presents ideas in the classroom. The key thing to bear in mind is *explaining* and helping *you* to see things clearly. Think carefully about each statement and then place an 'X' on the line which best states how *you feel.*

Statements	How often is this statement true of your teacher?				
	Always	Most of time	Half of time	Some-times	Never
1. The teacher uses words which the class understands.	____	____	____	____	____
2. The teacher takes time to define new terms/words.	____	____	____	____	____
3. The teacher relates new ideas with ideas we already know.	____	____	____	____	____
4. The teacher explains ideas at an even pace — not too fast, not too slow.	____	____	____	____	____
5. The teacher's explanations are understandable and clear.	____	____	____	____	____
6. The teacher sticks to the point of the subject (does not drift).	____	____	____	____	____
7. The teacher explains the goals of the lesson — where we are heading and what we are expected to know/learn.	____	____	____	____	____
8. The teacher helps us connect ideas with our own life experiences.	____	____	____	____	____
9. The teacher provides examples of the ideas being explained.	____	____	____	____	____
10. The teacher summarizes and explains the main points at the end of a lesson.	____	____	____	____	____

Thanks to Professor Allan A. Glatthorn, East Carolina University.

CURRICULUM CRITICISM

By *curriculum criticism* is meant the art of 'critiquing' — i.e. critically disclosing the quality of a curriculum through literary devices such as metaphor, thick description, alliteration, etc. with a view to developing deep appreciation and personal understanding. As a single exercise, curriculum criticism does not solve practical curriculum problems, it allows one to view them through the bifocal spectacles of description and critical interpretation. It is a way of 'seeing' a curriculum; of viewing the innovation close up, as if one were eavesdropping on some curriculum moment in a dramaturgical manner.

The present writer's initial thinking about curriculum criticism was flavoured by early encounters with portrayal-type evaluators such as David Jenkins, a colleague at the University of Ulster. While working as a social/peace studies project officer, the writer was subjected to an 'illuminative-responsive' type of evaluation directed by Jenkins which included Stephen Kemmis, the evaluator/action researcher. The evaluation report was subsequently to receive critical praise as *Chocolate, Cream, Soldiers* (Jenkins et al., 1980; Burgess, 1984). The work of Elliot Eisner is instructive here; chiefly his model of evaluation as literary criticism and connoisseurship (Eisner, 1980), which places a premium on meaning and the interpretation of qualities as opposed to outcomes and the measurement of traits.

Curriculum criticism finds similarities with ethnographic styles of evaluation, case study methodology and illuminative evaluation principles (Parlett and Hamilton, 1972). Criticism requires practitioners who are capable of making knowledgeable and informed statements and judgements about curriculum intentions and resultant activities. Indeed, it might be regarded as responding to the activities which actually occur as the focus of the exercise rather than what was intended to happen. To engage in *curriculum criticism*, several qualities are required.

Requirements of the curriculum critic

1. The ability to distinguish important from trivial curriculum issues and events.
2. The ability to see events and subtle occurrences within a larger socio-cultural school context (it is not enough to say that kids are 'cutting classes', playing 'hooky' or going a.w.o.l. — they may be cutting classes due to fear of violence and bullying, which itself deserves detailed comment).
3. The ability to 'see' to appreciate, rather than 'look' to describe.
4. The criterion of long service and experience of curriculum, theory and research, and how these impact on practice.
5. The ability to write well — to use descriptive, factual and interpretive critical language in discussion and report form.
6. The ability to understand the hidden curriculum, pupils as persons, and all others who interact in curricular settings.
7. The ability to illuminate and disclose educational encounters in compelling and telling appraisals.
8. The ability to examine textual documents and underline all the adjectives, nouns, value judgements and factual statements — the ability to understand composition.

Curriculum criticism is at once *descriptive;* through a careful rendering of programme problems, potential, etc.; *interpretive,* in that it aims at deeper understanding; and *evaluative,* in so far as it judges and assesses worth. Criticism presupposes that the role of the teacher is that of the artist. The teacher as critic-evaluator tries to become personally knowledgeable about the curriculum — a 'connoisseur' — and when he or she makes public his or her disclosures and appreciations then this constitutes the act of *curriculum criticism.*

Criticism, then, amounts to skilfully crafted 'snapshots', vignettes, cameos, portrayals and caricatures of events and activities. Such criticisms are made on the basis of certain premisses:

1. That the evaluation is *independent.* By this is meant that the critic should be allowed reasonable access to the project's activities, files, etc. and that any critique be negotiated with actors in the setting.
2. That the report is characterized by a *methodological eclecticism:* illuminative principles may be used alongside participant observation aided by video technology etc.
3. That the critique will be *evaluative-judgemental.* It will serve to make judgements as opposed simply to collecting the judgements of others. The critic can never be value-neutral.
4. That the report will be *responsive.* It will pursue issues and events rather than set out to check antecedent intentions such as preordinate instructional objectives.
5. It is usually in the *literary critic*'s style — short, sharp, pointed and colourful, reading like a thriller. Jenkins used cameos of characters in the project to sharpen the portrayal.

In *Chocolate, Cream, Soldiers*, Jenkins comments:

> One paradox of startling irony emerged from the project's occasional excursions into iconography (alluding to a diagram showing the project sheltering itself under an umbrella while violence rains down). How do its members (teachers) see themselves? What affective stance is associated with belonging? From early Skilbeck [referring to the Director, Malcolm Skilbeck] days the project's image of itself was high profile, high risk ['I am very conscious that in some quarters it will be regarded as dynamite. But why should the devil have a corner on the explosives market?).

Referring to the evaluation team's final report, *Chocolate, Cream Soldiers*, McKernan retorted:

> I read the evaluators as saying that values clarification does not offer sufficient theoretical rigour to count as a significant model for curriculum development. I think it does. I believe that the fault does not lie with the model, but rather with the teachers for not implementing it properly and generating new values education

strategies. Perhaps the central team did not make the model clear to the project teachers ... but I think the teachers are the key to curriculum effectiveness on this count.

Something of the critical-metaphorical character of the evaluator, David Jenkins, is captured by the following comment, taken from the same report in a section titled 'Arguing from the evidence'. Here the evaluator demonstrates the power of observation; not only observation of the curriculum in the school, but the cultural surround:

> Your friendly neighbourhood evaluator is sitting at the back of a class in one of the strongly Republican ghettoes of Derry City. Walls near the school are daubed with slogans 'Smash the H-Blocks (prisons)', 'Informers Will Be Shot'. The school itself is bullet scarred ... but in the classroom the atmosphere is one of disciplined order: even the desks look newly scrubbed for the parade ground. Pedagogically, the style is friendly and open. (Jenkins et al., 1980:43)

The following point is made by the Department of Education for Northern Ireland:

> If people realize how liberal the SCSP (Schools Cultural Studies Project) is, Paisley [Ian Paisley is the Member of Parliament for Antrim and principal spokesperson for the Loyalist point of view in NI] and the Democratic Unionist Party will be down on our heads like a ton of bricks.

Jenkins believed in the use of metaphor, cameos and verbatim accounts as vehicles for offering interpretive asides on the project, its personnel, the trial schools and the general cultural milieu in which the innovation operated. Such an evaluation report as *Chocolate, Cream, Soldiers* is eminently readable. The title is illustrative of Jenkins' philosophy of literary evaluation — the *chocolate* symbolized the funding agents, in this case Rowntree Macintosh, the UK sweet giant; the *cream* represented an approach through the ideas and involvement of the curriculum cognoscenti in the UK and Ireland; while *soldiers* stood as a glaring reminder of the 'Troubles' and the war in Ulster.

Curriculum criticism is thus a specialized form of literary criticism that is broadly qualitative in character and empirical in the best sense, rooted as the comments are in actual empirical happenings; and that is open-ended and non-dogmatic. It doesn't attempt to prove a case or hypothesis, but to improve understanding of a case.

Criticism explores the constraints and injustices which serve to distort ideology in institutions. It is reflective of the aims and purposes of human actions and programmes. Professional judgement and reflexivity are at the heart of criticism. Perhaps all student teachers and certainly all 'professional evaluators' ought to take mandatory courses in literary criticism.

DISCOURSE EVALUATION

Discourse evaluation is a method of evaluation consisting of a number of procedures for obtaining *conversational* or *narrative* accounts of teaching and the problems of curriculum implementation. The purpose is to advance practitioner understanding and thus allow practical decisions to be made by practitioners governing their work. This approach argues that the main sources of evaluation are the participants and their utterances in human discourse, and not aspects of the surroundings which are external to the main actors.

The essence of being human is to engage in social action and to have a dialogue with others and with the self. This is not the prerogative of the chosen few philosophers, but of all, and it should result in illumination of understanding and permit practical orientations. Evaluation ought to begin from the lives of those involved in educational problems and practice. The goal of evaluation of a discursive nature is enlightenment and emancipation through self-empowerment. The aim is to create a forum so that co-inquirers can talk and listen in ways not typically provided for in usual evaluation styles.

Ethnographers interested in collaborative research (Florio-Ruane, 1986; Buchman, 1983) advocate conversation as an alternative to argumentation when researchers and educators meet, suggesting the staging of 'forums' whereby researchers and teachers can examine their claims about knowledge, writing, etc. The *discourse* approach offers a way to transcend status differences between researchers, administrators and teachers. Besides, conversation, like inquiry, goes in unpredictable directions. In a discourse approach, theory is put on the 'back-burner' and forced to share a platform with practitioners' ideas, knowledge and ideology. Conversation as a research methodology is very likely to yield stories and tales as data. Every practitioner has 'a story' to tell but decison makers are often not interested in hearing these tales. Discourse evaluation makes the telling of these accounts possible.

However, even at the theoretical level, social scientists in the distant and recent past (Lewin, 1948; Schon, 1983) have argued that it is imperative to use practitioners' knowledge in theorizing and model-building when explaining their work.

A basic goal of 'discourse evaluation' is to provide participant understanding and to remove, if possible, the constraints on action.

Yet understanding, as a concept, is elusive and has defied the analytic lenses of generations of philosophers. Habermas (1976:3) suggests:

> a minimal meaning indicates that two subjects understand a linguistic expression in the same way; its maximal meaning is that between the two there exists an accord concerning the rightness of an utterance in relation to a mutually recognized normative background. In addition, two participants in communication can come to an understanding about something in the world, and they can make their intentions understandable to one another.

Thus, it would seem to be classified within the new *critical-emancipatory* field of action research. More often than not, pupils and teachers are eliminated from serious evaluation work in which they can provide data to make decisions about practice. The evaluation of pupils, programmes and, indeed, teacher performance is often conducted from afar, by outsiders, and the data is not shared in a humanistic manner with participants so that they can learn from the inquiry. Discourse evaluation is concerned to encourage understanding through human dialogue. The establishment of the message, rather than the identification of appropriate behaviours is the underlying aim.

Participants become joint co-inquirers in the evaluation process. There are some precedents for this type of evaluation work in the experiments conducted by John Elliott and Clem Adelman (1976) under the aegis of the Ford Teaching Project in Britain, which established 'triangulation' as an interesting partnership style of action research into inquiry/discovery methods of teaching.

Until this point there has been an implied belief that evaluation is too difficult or technical an enterprise for teachers and pupils to lead — that it should be left to trained 'experts' in social scientific disciplines. This is an arrogant view which must not be allowed to go unchallenged in future. Teachers, administrators, pupils and parents are better placed than outside researchers to benefit from doing action research as a form of curriculum evaluation.

Some critical theorists argue the primacy of 'understanding' as the goal of inquiry, action research, evaluation and so forth. But it should be recognized that the term 'understanding' is problematic, even for philosophers and epsitemologists, who do not always agree on the definition of understanding.

Conceptions of understanding

Understanding can be used in at least half a dozen different senses:

1. I fully understand what you say.

2. I think that I understand what you have said.
3. I do not fully (only partially) understand your meaning.
4. I understand what you say, but you are wrong.
5. I do not understand what you have said.
6. I misunderstood what you said.

Understanding, as a concept, has two related aspects or senses: *understanding 1* in which a *psychological* understanding is evident when one says 'I now understand' where one previously has said 'I do not understand' — this amounts to understanding as an event, or experience; and *understanding 2* where formal criteria are laid down for deciding upon the claim. *Understanding 1* equals understanding versus not understanding, and *understanding 2* is used in the sense of understanding versus misunderstanding. As professionals interested in understanding as a goal, *understanding 1* is the most important as far as action research or dialogue is concerned. The most important point is for all participants to have the psychological experience of understanding which is characterized by the *will and desire to inquire for the purpose of understanding.*

The all-important question remains, 'How do we know that one understands?' One answer is that the person is able to explain the ideas or concepts involved in the discourse by giving a demonstrated account in a sentence while evincing a desire and enthusiasm. The person who is the partner in the process should question his or her partner by saying 'Tell me more about X . . . ' or 'What did it feel like?' etc.

The second sense of understanding, which has been labelled *understanding 2*, is the laying down of formal criteria for establishing the claim of understanding. What constitutes having understood a book, painting, rule etc? Here the *content* of what counts as understanding becomes important. Thus the six questions above are linked with whether an account is understanding truly. Yet the fact remains that one can understand something, and yet that something is wrong (see number 4 above), indicating that someone has an understanding in the sense of 'grasping the meaning'. Yet, any meaningful proposition is open to falsification. The fact that I understand 'y' does not entail the truthfulness of 'y' as valid. Thus understanding is a problematic aspect; take a poem for example, can it be said that there is one correct understanding of Byron's *Don Juan*?

The discourse evaluation procedure

The purposes of discourse evaluation are several:

1. To record and describe the conversation or dialogue as the

primary data for evaluative decision-making.
2. To describe individuals, their values, perspectives, etc.
3. To be useable in practical deliberations and applications, giving practitioners a handle on, and control over, some situation or behaviours.
4. To provide a style for classroom and curriculum evaluation.

Discourse evaluation should begin by seeking to uncover the assumptions, intentions, goals and declared purposes of programmes, and should seek to explain why such values ought to be seen as a rationale or defensible set of purposes. Reciprocal questioning and reformulating of goals is certainly imperative in systems undergoing massive social and cultural change.

Let us say that in an action research project the second order action researcher (facilitator) asks the question 'What are some of the rules in this classroom?' The teacher might answer that the pupils should not interfere with each others' learning, or that they should queue in an orderly fashion when entering or exiting from the classroom. The purpose of asking such questions is to establish the values and platform of premises which support the teacher's (and school's) philosophy and sense of purpose in education.

Practitioners are often closed off from important decision alternatives and rational curriculum problem solving. For any significant staff enlightenment and *a fortiori* staff development of an intellectual nature to occur, then staff must be open to all the data and reasons for adopting one particular policy or action. By using discourse, the teacher and student use evidence, reasons etc. to develop rational arguments and policies. For Habermas (1972) pure discourse is equivalent to 'the ideal speech situation', by which he means that such a scenario is characterized by an *absence of constraints* on one's thinking, except for that of the *force of the better argument.* When this is applied to research for better action and improved understanding, Habermas argues that participants must have equal opportunities to take on dialogue roles and the concomitant freedom to summon evidence, make points, and so forth. Elliott has argued (1980) that these conditions of discourse approximate to the 'liberal democratic' values of freedom, equality and justice. It would follow that administrators must accord such basic values to both teachers and pupils otherwise they would be constraining their opportunity to engage in understanding. Discourse causes understanding.

Sources of evidence: data in discourse evaluation

1. A first task is to clarify the 'value perspective' and 'action stance' that are held by the practitioner who is experiencing a genuine problem for action research. This ensures a practitioner

understanding of issues and concerns, and may entail the scheduling of deliberative group meetings so that conversations can be held.

2. Research can only be validated by dialogue between and among practitioners using educational action research. By making dialogue possible it then becomes a tool for self-knowledge and self-awareness.

3. By concentrating on discourse, the research/evaluation process itself becomes a discursive and an educational process, and may be exploited as a genuine source of teacher re-education.

4. The second major task is to identify sources of constraint on successful action — this can be done through a situation analysis.

5. The collection of discourse data — records of action (videos, tape recordings, etc.) — is a valuable source of documentary evidence since these can verify who said what, when and how. Thus such records are valid and reliable. Interpretation is vital as it will enable one to answer the question 'What is the meaning of this event or act?' Further, 'Do we agree with this interpretation?' One of the best ways of checking interpretations is to interview participants.

6. The evaluator should seek to collect any *documentary evidence* which outlines rules, values, aims or intentions.

7. The careful collection and keeping of reliable records of behaviour. That is, the researcher must be committed to establishing an accurate base of data from which to have a genuine dialogue, which, when unconstrained, will result in understanding. Field notes and logs, diaries and other verbatim accounts are invaluable.

8. Once a secure data archive base has been built up one might conduct 'fidelity analysis'. This is the process of checking observed and overt behaviour against the declared intentions, objectives and goals. Does one get what was intended? It is important to expose and consider educational intentions and then check these against implementation.

9. Criticism is a pillar of the discourse evaluation process. One need not accept rules or patterns of behaviour because they serve tradition or the whims of authority; they must be justified and grounded in a rationale. For example, students should rightfully challenge why they must complete 150 hours of classroom-based student teaching to qualify for their teaching certificate — the onus is then upon the teacher educators to satisfy this request through warranted reason. Thus, the interactive dimension is based upon a conversation between students and authorities. When the challenges made by programme members extend beyond the boundaries of the

institution and look for discourse about external constraints on human actions, then one can say that genuine *critical emancipatory action research* is operative.

10. Conversation is aimed at increasing the political as well as the professional autonomy of the practitioner. Few evaluation models have taken on board a heavily weighted procedure for *critical interpretations and actors' perspectives.*

    Perhaps the truest form of discourse evaluation occurs when everyone with an educational stake in the problem is talking with every one of the actors with a view to eliminating constraints on action, ensuring personal understanding of the dialogue, and perhaps least with arriving at some practical solution.

11. It seems that a code or set of rules/principles of procedure is required which states that:
    - practitioners are free to engage in dialogue to promote self- and mutual understanding of their practices — implicit is the asking of challenging and critically searching questions of practice;
    - the key critical incidents which constrain the participant or actors in the educational setting are identified;
    - time and resources are set aside to allow for professional development through periodic cycles of *discourse evaluation.*

    This idea of a *code of practice* is in keeping with the thrust of the argument for professional criteria[1] and the self-autonomous behaviour of teachers.

The notion of discourse evaluation has important implications for staff development, given that the process itself is a form of education in its own right. Moreover, as Carr and Kemmis (1986) suggest, those who subscribe to this critical view accept much of the thinking that informs the 'practical' model of curriculum thought. Both accept the idea that practitioners must be committed to self-critical reflection on their educational aims and values. It would appear that a *free and open dialogue* is a necessary condition not only for discourse evaluation, but for true understanding and good action research.

---

1. See the discussion in Chapter 2 relating to education as a profession. It is argued that all professions require a code of ethics for the governance of their behaviour.

CRITICAL TRIALLING

The technique of *critical trialling*[1] refers to the ongoing monitoring of a curriculum project during its *development* stage; or it can be used to monitor a course of action during its *implementation* phase. The twin notions of *critique* and *trialling* further indicate that the purpose of this activity is to gather informed data about the appropriateness, impact, effectiveness, etc. of an innovation while it is being *field tested* through *trials,* so that the innovatory project, innovation or action response may be improved.

Critical trialling allows for the practitioner to gather and critique, for the first time, empirical evidence about the usefulness of the innovatory practice. Such data may be used as part of a larger curriculum evaluation at a later date. A primary belief of trialling is that no innovation should be used uncritically, or without being subjected to tests of validity. Trialling should be a necessary stage for all educational practice, and not just another technique to be employed by those action research minded personnel.

Critical trialling refers to a general research strategy and does not constitute a fixed set of procedures; case study may be used as well as interviews, questionnaires, etc. There are several general points which should be borne in mind in relation to the conduct of critical trials.

Principles of procedure

1. Every innovative course of action should be installed and given *ample time* to settle down. Quite often an innovation is not given sufficient time to prove itself before being discarded by cynical practitioners.
2. The researchers ought to be sensitive to impact and take-up effects by allowing for *more than one trial of the innovation.* Often a set of materials needs to be revised several times before it is 'right' for the audience.
3. Evidence should be gathered from *all actors affected by the innovatory process.* This would suggest a naturalistic or descriptive evaluative style of reportage in which students, administrators, teachers and others would have the right to discuss and critique the innovatory action. Illuminative evaluation or case study format would seem highly appropriate.
4. 'Mark-up' copies of the trial materials should be provided so that practitioners can pencil in their comments or suggestions for improvement. A form at the end of each unit requesting feedback

1. This technique is loosely associated with the idea of *trialling*, as developed by Davis (1981), but differs in that it goes beyond the scope of application to trial curriculum materials alone to include human actions and other innovatory practices.

on specific worksheets, fact sheets, resources, etc. is highly useful and a 'ready-reckoner' for teacher evaluation.
5. Confidentiality should be respected as a working principle and the release of any information should be negotiated.

Format for critical trialling

Trialling ought to indicate the strengths and weaknesses of a set of trial materials or innovative practices. If the innovative action is represented by a *set of trial course materials,* then the following approach is offered as a suggested approach to trialling.

Setting/milieu/target audience
First of all, it would seem vital to be clear about the purposes of the trial materials. What are the goals of the new programme? What subject teachers will be involved? Which group of students will be involved? How much time will be devoted to the programme? This is simply instructional background evidence, but crucial to understanding how an innovatory practice is proceeding.

Trialling adopts several concepts held dear by the *illuminative evaluation-learning milieu.* It offers illumination in that the primary concern is to render up a rich description and interpretation of the action. It would stand unambiguously within the naturalistic or case study tradition of community studies.

Trialling attempts to provide an *interim evaluation report.* How is the programme operating? What roles are played by various actors? What are the main advantages and disadvantages? What recurring problems surface in implementation?

A principal argument in favour of doing critical trialling studies is that an innovatory programme or action research project initiative *cannot be separated from the instructional programme and behavioural setting* with which it becomes entwined. The innovation is not outside or external to the system; it is not self-contained but distinctly influences the learning milieu of which it is a vital part.

Doing critical trialling

Description of the action project programme
1. State the title of the trial project.
2. State the target audience.
3. What is the aim/purpose of the programme?
4. How did the project come about?

Rationale/philosophy
Every unit or course should be grounded in sound reasons or a convincing rationale for its usage. This may be contained in project

papers, an official course of study outline, or curriculum guidelines, but it counts as a manifesto exalting the usage of the innovation. Thus, a careful study of project background papers and documentary evidence is required.

The researcher needs to acertain whether there is a written rationale or not. Has the document been circulated to all users of the action, practice, programme etc? What is the *clarity* of the rationale? Is it understood in the same sense by all? Is any justification offered for its implementation?

Detailed description of the programme materials (products)

The researcher must become thoroughly familiar with the materials and practice, and describe these. Does the trial programme have an *internal logic*? By this is meant does the project have a set of ideas, principles, or key concepts which run through the programme like a thread, giving it structure, sequence and continuity of thought?

1. Describe the contents of teacher and pupil materials.
2. Describe the format of the materials (loose sheets, book, pamphlet).
3. Describe directions for usage.
4. Draw a time-line chart indicating course or programme units and their expected dates of mastery.
5. Is there a table of specifications?
6. Are assessment instruments developed?
7. Describe recommended resources required.

Logic of programme

How does the innovation hang together? Is there a coherent internal logic? Are there any contradictions? What mode of organization is preferred — subject, integration of themes, issues etc? Is there a core curriculum? What are the boundaries or limits of the programme? What pedagogical style is preferred — teacher directive or non-directive? Is the inquiry/discovery method used? Is there clear fidelity between objectives and assessment procedures?

Project implementation

1. How are the materials used in action? Are the materials designed for whole class teaching, small group work or individualized instruction and inquiry?
2. Rate the readability of materials by the target student group?
3. Rate the practicality of the materials in use.
4. What weightings are given to knowledge objectives as opposed to skills, dispositions, etc?
5. What constraints are evident on *implementing the action*?

Assessment/evaluation
1. What tests or instruments are available?
2. Has any other evaluator commented on the action?
3. Build up perspectives and arguments for and against using the materials.
4. How do the materials compare with other exemplars for the same area of curriculum?
5. What level of interest is there among students and staff for the project action? Describe this and provide verbatim narrative accounts.
6. What does the 'hidden curriculum' look like in this case?
7. What are the *key critical incidents* during implementation?
8. What aspects need improvement?
9. What aspects are successful?

Research methods

A wide range of techniques/methods for doing critical trialling are available and ought to be used wherever possible, thus building in the 'triangulation' perspective for action research — i.e. seeing issues from various vantage points using different research methods to fix positions. The following methods can be used:

1. *Observation* would seem inescapable and part and parcel of the teacher-researcher brief. Observations can be structured through the use of checklists, ratings, interaction analysis protocols or be more fluid as in the case of anecdotal comments, diary or log journal keeping, writing field notes, etc. Observations may also be had from fellow teachers. external consultants, evaluators, supervisors and so on, who may have special training in observational techniques.
2. *Interviews* with participants, including students, teachers and administrators. Interviews may be structured or unstructured, and conducted individually with actors or through *group interviews.* Interview data can provide the 'missing bits' and yield questions for further enquiry.
3. *Documents* contain background information on the project. Examine any proposals, committee minutes, texts, newspaper stories, official course of study guidelines, etc. referring to the innovatory practice.
4. *Teacher or user annotation* of the materials. Give a spare copy for teachers to include comments to be returned. Send a copy of the programme or units to parents for comments.
5. *Tests* — these may be informal teacher-constructed formative mastery instruments or more formal standardized tests. Test data is useful for trialling.

6. *Student comments through questionnaires/interview schedules* — it may be useful to analyse opinionnaires and attitude measurement instruments if the appropriate questions have been asked of students. These may render a general sense of student affect towards the innovation.

7. *Ethnography techniques* — keeping field notes during the course of the innovation by the researcher may prove valuable for trialling. This may be done by keeping a journal in which anecdotal data, factual evidence and observations are recorded and later interpreted by the researcher. Diaries, logs, dialogue journals and field notes will admirably serve this purpose. One attempts to tell a story by collecting evidence from the day-to-day life of the project in action.

8. *User workshops and project meetings* — a forum may be held on a regular basis for gathering project feedback from a number of users, including teachers and students. The meeting, or critical discursive workshop, should be conducted in an honest and authentic search for project improvement. Video accounts may greatly enrich the deliberations under discussion. Workshops should be formally conducted with a chairperson and recording secretary. These allow for evaluative comment, debriefing and problem analysis. The key to success here is to try to establish an atmosphere in which participants may distance themselves from any sense of 'personal failure' by discussing their own participation in objective and frank modes. The workshop or discussion group may be helped if an experienced evaluator is able to lead the discussion by targeting key issues and problems.

Final word on research methodology

Research in curriculum must involve the active participation of reflective practitioners in the study of classrooms and schools, and recognize that a tradition of teachers as researchers is the basis not only of staff development but of curriculum improvement. Yet these sentiments shall only amount to empty platitudes if practitioners do not possess the skills or the will to engage in the conduct of curriculum action research. Research, through sound methodology, becomes the basis for teaching and for learning.

PART 3

Analysis and Issues in Action Research

The final part of this work is devoted to answering a number of crucial questions: How might one set about analysing educational action research data once it has been collected? Can critical communities of discourse concerned with the establishment of networks of support agents be formed and maintained? How can these critical communities or networks disseminate the findings of their research? Finally, can a code of practice, a set of ethical guidelines, be formulated and agreed to govern the conduct of action research in educational settings?

Chapter 7 explores a variety of procedures and techniques for the analysis and interpretation of action research data.

Chapter 8 tackles the thorny issues of establishing networks or communities of action researchers, and offers strategic advice on their maintenance. The dissemination and writing of action research reports is described and the sensitive territory of ethics is discussed.

7 Analysing Action Research Data

> Educational practices provide the data, the subject matter, which form the problems of inquiry . . . A constant flow of less formal reports on special school affairs and results is needed . . . it seems to me that the contribution that might come from classroom teachers is a comparatively neglected field; or to change the metaphor, an almost unworked mine.
>
> John Dewey (1929) *The Sources of a Science of Education*

CYCLES OF INQUIRY

The analytic function of research is crucial in terms of making sound inferences and judgements which lead to improved practice and understanding. One often hears the comment 'Now that I have the data collected what do I do next?' In this book action research has been described in terms of cyclical human activities or cycles. Some key questions relate to the *amount of time in each cycle, data collection methods, duration of cycles, activities of monitoring* and finally, *analytic activity.* Time is a crucial variable not only in learning, but in doing action research. A key question is: How long does a cycle take? There is no direct answer since a particular line of action may be abandoned due to inadequate analysis of the problem. Since school timetables are drawn up around 'terms' with subsequent periods of vacation, these then would seem natural units. With a 13-week term a cycle may be divided up into a number of events, each containing a particular analytic episode (see Table 7.1 on p. 224).

Action research is a tradition which is still in a state of becoming an acceptable research paradigm. Winter (1982) has made the point that despite the fact that a number of techniques are presently available for use by practitioners of action research for the *creation* of data, there is not, as yet, a sufficient methodology for the *interpretation* of data. That is, we have diaries, observation schedules, interviews, triangulation and so on, but we need to be shown *how to interpret* this collected information. The purpose of this chapter is to offer some guidelines and perspectives on the process of analysing research data. Analysis is not a separate stage in research work — it begins with the practical deliberation that accompanies the pre-fieldwork stage and continues as one collects information and writes up the research report. Rather than doing analysis immediately after field work and data collection, there is a

Table 7.1 *Cycles of inquiry, monitoring and analysis*

CYCLE 1 . . .

WEEK	EVENT	MONITORING	TIME	ANALYSIS
1	Define problem	Keep diary; video record	2 lessons per week	Staff meeting 30 mins; agenda writing
2–4	Needs assessment; hypotheses; develop plan of action	Record lessons; keep diary; short action		Staff meeting; write reports; memos
5–8	Implement plan	Record lessons; keep diary	2 lessons per week	Staff meeting; analyse video; discuss diary; analyse data;
8–9	Evaluate plan in action	Interviews; Video record; diary	2 lessons per week	Quadrangulate team; discuss; reflect; code key issues
10–11	Decide on plan	Record lessons; diary		Reflective group deliberation
12	Implement revised action plan	Record lessons		Discuss action reports
13	Execute steps as per above in weeks 1–11			
14	Write a case study based on case data, case records etc. — maximum of 5,000 words — for team meeting next term			

CYCLE 2 . . .

Note: Hold team meetings at the end of each week or at least bi-monthly. Keep a minute of decisions made and write up the 'case study' constant comparative analysis going on during action research. There are at least four stages of analysis: *processing data, mapping the data, interpreting the evidence*, and *presentation of the results.*

It should be borne in mind that fuller treatments for the analysis and interpretation of research data are available[1], and that analysis will differ depending on whether the study is quantitative or qualitative in nature. There has been a major increase in the literature concerning qualitative data analysis in particular, yet only a few studies focus directly on educational or curriculum problems (Bogdan and Biklen, 1982; Goetz and LeCompte, 1984). The emphasis in this treatment is on the teacher-researcher, who ordinarily will not have extensive training in the use of quantitative-type statistical studies. It is crucial to be able to see what information and data one has and how one might proceed to interpret and understand these from the teacher-practitioner vantage point. One important point should be underlined at the outset — one should not wait until one has hundreds or even thousands of pages of field notes etc. before beginning analysis.

GETTING STARTED

Becker (1958), Glaser and Strauss (1967), and Schatzman and Strauss (1973) provide qualitative modes of analysis; while Goetz and LeCompte (1984), Hook (1985), Hopkins (1985), and Woods (1986) directly relate ethnographic analysis to educational problems and offer various frameworks for analysing qualitative research data. Data comes in many guises: observations, verbal behaviour, non-verbal behaviour, artefacts, documentation, etc. Goetz and LeCompte (1984) discuss modes of analysing qualitative educational data and suggest that one needs to know how to retrieve data, what to do with them, and what they all mean. They go on to develop modes of analysis which they call 'theorizing' and which consist of discovering or manipulating abstract categories and patterns of relationship among these categories (Goetz and LeCompte, 1984:167). When one is 'theorizing' one is perceiving, comparing, aggregating, ordering and generally finding connections in the data. Theorizing also includes speculating or making good guesses based on reflexive activity. Speculating is thus ruminating in the same manner as that engaged in by makers of formal hypotheses.

One needs to get a good conceptual framework on this information base. Hopkins (1985:108) suggests four steps in fieldwork methodology, summarizing the Becker and Glaser-Strauss format (see Table 7.2).

1. See Webb et al. (1966) for reactive data methodologies. For social-anthropological/case study data see Goetz, J.L. and LeCompte, D. (1984); also, Bogdan and Biklen (1982). For measurement-minded treatments confer Borg and Gall (1983) and Borg (1981).

STAGES OF DATA ANALYSIS

For Becker (1958:653) there are four distinct stages to doing, processing and reporting field research: first, the selection and definition of problems, concepts and indices; second, the check on the frequency and distribution of phenomena (data); third, the incorporation of individual findings into a model of the organization under study; fourthly and finally, problems of presentation of the evidence and proof. Similarly, Glaser and Strauss (1967:105) describe the *constant comparative method* as the device for analysis of data:

> We shall describe in four stages the constant comparative method; 1. comparing incidents applicable to each category, 2. integrating categories and their properties, 3. delimiting the theory, and 4. writing the theory.

One can note the similarities in both Becker's and Glaser and Strauss' notions of data treatment. Both use a four-category classification: *problem and concept definition, data frequency checking, integration/validation of data, presentation of results/evidence.*

Table 7.2 *Stages of fieldwork — data analysis*

Action research	Becker	Glaser & Strauss
• Defining problems/ concepts	Selection & definition of concepts	Comparing of incidents for each category
• Checking data frequencies	Frequency & distribution of concepts	Integrating phenomena
• Validation of ideas/concepts	Model-building	Delimiting theory
• Presenting proof	Presentation of evidence/proof	Writing grounded theory

Hopkins (1985) presents a four-stage process of data analysis:

1. *Data collection.* Information collection and generation of hypotheses.
2. *Validation.* Data and hypotheses are validated principally through the use of 'saturation' (case where no additional properties are being found) or through 'triangulation' (where various actors or methods are cross-checked for validity).

3. *Interpretation.* Checking data by reference to the existing stock of theory, or by reference to practitioner folk knowledge and judgement.
4. *Action.* The taking of action to improve a situation and the further monitoring of this action through action research.

One might state that the simple four-stage model of Hopkins is simplistic in the extreme, for rarely does research fall neatly into such a distinct set of sequentially ordered stages.

CONDUCTING DATA ANALYSIS: SOME GUIDELINES

It seems that the most essential factor is the *reflexivity* of the researcher; the ability to think and reflect critically about what he or she has and what he or she still requires. In accordance with Becker's scheme outlined above, this author suggests the following model of the research analysis process.

Stage one: Processing the evidence — Editing, coding and conceptual and theoretical sampling

Editing data
Now that the fieldwork is completed the processing of data commences. This is particularly true for surveys, although one can argue that in qualitative studies a certain amount of editing and analysis goes on during the fieldwork stage of data collection. However, for purposes of clarity let us assume that the researcher holds off on editing until the case data are complete. First, check that you have all the questionnaires, interview schedules etc., being sure to chase up missing cases and values where possible. Editorial work is mundane yet it is essential that care be taken to ensure that mistakes and errors do not creep in, so that tight analysis will be possible later. For example, one must make sure that coded values are entered for all items; the present writer recalls doing computer analysis of questionnaire data to discover cells appearing in the printed tables with values that were not coded, thus aborting the analysis completely until these gremlins were removed. Completeness is the key concept at this stage.

Second, check that you are interpreting each response *uniformly.* That is, every item should be treated with the same criteria of interpretation. This is especially important when one comes to the assignation of numerical codes or values to the data.

Coding
When one is involved in processing data which will be put into quantifiable form later, it is useful to assign codes to the responses to

help with analysis. The purpose of coding is to classify evidence and place the data into neat categories so that patterns may be coherently established. Coding is used in the analysis of survey data as well as qualitative data, such as *content analysis* of communication messages, textbooks, documents etc.

A good practice is to set up a *coding frame* which outlines a set of codes for each question asked. Responses to the item are then assigned codes. Imagine a survey of pupils in which respondents were asked about their feelings/attitudes to changing schools.

Q.1: How did you feel about changing school?

    'I liked it very much'   . . . Assign code '3'
    'I mostly liked it'   . . . Assign code '2'
    'It didn't matter to me'   . . . Assign code '1'
    'I didn't like it at all'   . . . Assign code '0'

These codes can be set up in advance as this is a forced-choice or closed-ended type question in which the respondent must select one of the four responses provided.

Coding becomes more arbitrary when an *open-ended* question is asked. In this case the researcher must search through all of the responses given and come up with a small number of categories which encompass the range of responses provided.

Q.2: What worried you most about changing schools?

    'Worried that I would not see my friends as much'   . . . Code '1'
    'Worried about the new teachers'   . . . Code '2'
    'Worried about bullies'   . . . Code '3'
    'Worried about the size of the school — I'd get lost' . . . Code '4'

Sampling: conceptual and theoretical
Here the concern is to immerse oneself in the data by comparing and contrasting findings, and by ordering themes and components. In short, by letting the data speak for itself. For not only is it vital to examine the new data, but to do this creatively and reflexively so that valuable concepts emerge to inform powerful theory. This is, in essence, what is meant by Glaser and Strauss' (1967) idea of 'grounded theory'. The key activity is that of 'scanning' the data, i.e. checking to see what one has got. For instance, in one field study of problems associated with the education of Irish 'Traveller' (gypsy/ itinerant) children, the author (McKernan, 1973) noticed the importance attached to certain cultural themes such as 'scholarship' and medical taboos. For example, the researcher was regarded as a 'scholar' because he could read and write — indeed, to arrive at being a 'scholar' often signalled the end of formal education, as the

time had then come for more serious and productive work, such as the trading of scrap metal or horses. Scholars can write letters to relatives in Scotland or England, thus keeping kinship networks informed.

Often cultural themes emerge but only begin to make any theoretical sense when linked with other relationships and themes. During the first stage of data analysis the field notes are read carefully, allowing key concepts to be identified. Another example cited in the above was that of refusing to receive medical blankets donated by a local hospital since this is associated with the concept of 'death' and 'dying' and is therefore taboo for Travellers. The researcher witnessed blankets left on the side of the road by well-meaning doctors who failed to realize this cultural belief. It was ironic that despite the fact that these people lived in tents and cardboard shacks and begged for a living, they would refuse warm blankets in the face of a bitter Irish winter. Such is the strength of group beliefs.

Stage two: Mapping the data by noting the frequency of recurrence of issues, themes and units

During the second stage of data analysis it is important to get some purchase on the frequency of occurrence of specific units or cultural themes, and to try to chart or 'map' these relationships. For example, during fieldwork in Northern Ireland in connection with the development of a social-peace studies programme for secondary schools, the author noted similarities among and between culturally diverse groups of Catholic and Protestant boys (McKernan, 1978). The author's field notes and interview data revealed clothing as a symbol of cultural identity and group allegiance. One tactic employed was to tabulate recurrences of themes in a components chart in order to see relationships in cultural themes more clearly. Table 7.3 provides an example of such a cultural components analysis.

Table 7.3 *Distinctive type of clothing worn by schoolboys in Catholic and Protestant schools in Northern Ireland*

Type	Catholic	Protestant
Heavy high-top bootboy boots	Very common	Very common
Hats	No occurrence	No occurrence

Scarves	(Andy Capp sort) Very common	(Football-type) Very common
School blazer	Does not occur	Very common
School sweater	Does not occur	Common
Denim jacket	Common	Does not occur
Denim jeans (above ankle)	Common	Does not occur
Black topcoat (six-button)	Common	Does not occur
Tattoos*	Common	Common

(McKernan, 1978:188)
* While not clothing, they are symbols which are worn as 'gear'.

Thus, a good part of analysis at this second stage is concerned with mapping out distributions, and with constructing tables and frequencies. The notion is that a 'statistical description' rather than a strict 'analysis' would be more appropriate here. Note that this stage is not concerned with *inference*, but with describing. By making counts and carefully recording these details, a form of systematic quantification of themes can be developed. The use of percentages and simple descriptive tables will suffice for even the most sophisticated studies. Of course, if one has access to a computer using social science software packages, such as SPSS, then simple frequency counts as well as advanced multi-variate analyses are available at the press of a button.

Stage three: Interpretation of data/model-building

When one moves beyond description and tries to make some statement about what various responses *mean* and to suggest relationships among data, then one is conducting an *interpretation of data*. Data analysis depends upon conceptual dredging and theory-building. In the study above, several findings emerged through the analysis of clothing: Catholic and Protestant boys shared similar values — a fact later substantiated by analysis of a value survey in which the rank order of certain terminal and instrumental values demonstrated a high concordance of agreement (McKernan, 1982b). Here one tries to get the larger picture in focus by assembling the various indicators and themes into a more self-explanatory set of relationships — a model of the research data. Theories do not develop as a result of slavish adherence to implementing the research process in a linear fashion, but rather are the result of continuous looking at the collected data, posing questions and seeing how these hang together. One can literally be swamped by the sea of data. Although brilliant ideas may surface here and there, usually little coherence persists. It may be helpful to put the notes away for a while, then to come back to them with fresh insights and see patterns that were missed before — then the researcher can decide whether the notes represent the empirics of the field experience. This seems to be the problem with and experience of model-building — for this author at least. Yet a final stage remains: that of organizing the proof or evidence in a coherent fashion and writing the study.

Stage four: Presentation of results — reporting evidence/ conclusions

After the analysis has been completed then the researcher must assemble the major findings and present them for others. This is the subject of the final chapter of this book and a brief comment will suffice here. The presentation will depend upon the audience of the study. A report written for one's colleagues at school will not be written in the style of a report destined for an audience of policy makers or social scientists. The researcher must pay paramount attention to the audience. This will also mean paying attention to the *language of reporting*. Clear exposition is the rule. One must ensure conclusions are fair and based upon careful selection of concepts and indicators. The real test is to reconstruct an adequate explanation of the findings and the process which generated them.

By way of concluding, it is suggested that researchers should summarize the problem studied and present summary tables of the main findings first in any reporting. Second, the author feels it is important to interpret what those findings mean within the context of the study, and to make some attempt to match the findings with other studies which exist of the problem — what is referred to as *integration of research and theoretical perspectives.* Finally, the report should settle on how the actions taken have improved or not improved the problem and pose new lines of research or new proposals for curriculum inquiry. Thus the action researcher has a moral responsibility to report the facts of the inquiry; to say what the project means in terms of its results; and to suggest new avenues for further action.

This model is not without its problems. A good grounded theory does not just emerge before the researcher — he or she needs to make a giant leap forward, with data and imagination. It is the *creative/ imaginative* factor which is left out of all discussions of theory-building, and yet without this there would probably be no new theory. This is why one cannot be a slave to theory and why this author would argue that a naturalistic, analytic mode of induction is preferable to the fixed, experimentalist hypthetico-deductive approach to science. The action research approach which I have sketched is, when rigorously applied, just as 'scientific' and most certainly as empirical as anything worked up under quantitative hypothetico-deductive approaches.

ANALYTIC INDUCTION

One way of analysing theories, data and hyptheses is through what Znaniecki called 'analytic induction' which he developed in direct opposition to the statistical method. Znaniecki (1934) argued that this was the true scientific procedure since it seeks out those cases and instances which are negative and which disprove one's theory or hypothesis. Action researchers have been slow to talk about general causal relationships and causation models, perhaps due to the extremely confounded set of variables and conditions of work facing such inquirers. Ultimately, action researchers can test theory and create their own theories for further testing. Denzin (1970) has outlined the process of analytic induction as follows:

1. A rough definition of the phenomenon to be explained is formulated.
2. A hypothetical explanation of that phenomenon is formulated.
3. One case is studied in the light of the hypothesis with the object of determining whether the hypothesis fits the facts in that case.
4. If the hypothesis does not fit the facts, either the hypothesis is reformulated or the phenomenon to be explained is redefined, so that the case is excluded.
5. Practical certainty may be attained after a small number of cases has been examined, but the discovery of negative cases disproves the explanation and requires a reformulation.
6. This procedure of examining cases, redefining the phenomenon, and reformulating the hypothesis is continued until a universal relationship is established, each negative case calling for a redefinition or a reformulation. (Denzin, 1970:195)

Analytic induction seems to support the logic of the scientific method and tends to support the hypothetico-deductive method pursued by positivist researchers. The basic idea is that of theoretical sampling as distinct from strict statistical sampling. There is no reason why this approach cannot be put to scientific use by action researchers. What this will mean is that one must go out of one's way to look for cases which disprove one's hypotheses and negate the data, as Karl Popper (Popper, 1972) argued. The aim is to establish universal theoretical propositions on the grand-theory scale, when action researchers are really working at the level of 'grounded theory'.

CONSTANT COMPARATIVE METHOD

In this method of analysis a system of inductive coding is combined simultaneously with making comparisons of incidents, events, and data observed. Thus, as data are recorded they are also compared across cases and categories. The strength of the constant comparative method is that analysis proceeds hand in hand with data collection. This method seeks to determine relationships as an inductive process (Glaser and Strauss, 1967). Its major use is in the construction of categories and concepts rather than in mere enumeration.

Enumerative counting

Here the purpose is to search through the data, recording recurrences and incidents that can then be categorized separately for analytic purposes. We might, for example, count the number of questions posed by a teacher during the lesson, or the number of verbal contacts a pupil makes in a full school-day cycle. Frequency distribution diagrams, histograms etc. can be constructed to show percentages and portions of time given over to such behaviour.

Pre-coded behaviour protocols

A separate style of analysis can be conducted through the employment of standardized interaction analysis observation instruments, such as the Flanders or Amidon category systems. Basically, a pre-defined set of categories — ten in the case of the Flanders instrument — is in hand and each time a behaviour occurs (e.g. pupil asks questions, teacher lectures, etc.) the observer records a code — usually a number between one and ten — every three seconds. The important point about protocols is that the initial categories must be sound and valid for the observations covered in the study.

Explanation

One is essentially looking for the meaning in human actions. When one acts one creates meaning. Actions, it should be recounted, have meaning not only for the actors who perform them — the child who jumps ahead in a queue — but also for the researcher who must try to explain the phenomenon of 'queue-jumping'. Explanation goes hand in hand with interpretation, by discussing the action and then signifying the meaning of the action.

Action researchers have a duty to go beyond the mere description of results — to try to explain the significance of their study to their audience. This requires skill in communicating the principal results and *interpreting* the data with a view to theory development; theory rejection; hypothesis reformulation etc. The author is not of the belief that theory construction/refutal is that pressing a task for teacher-researchers, but rather that teacher-researchers will engage in action research to ease difficult situations, to find relief and to increase professional understanding.

CONCLUDING COMMENTS

It is perhaps best, by way of summarizing the thrust of this chapter, to cite the following procedural steps in the analysis of data:

1. After a cycle of data collection, it may be useful to go back and read the general proposal and plan of the study. Here we may find that we need to reformulate our problem definition.
2. Read through any intentional hypotheses and the text of all the case data, including records, field notes, diaries, test data etc. Read through the study in a linear routine. Studies in the action research domain are basically narrative. First, what was/is the problem; second, what plan was developed; third, how was data collected; fourth, how was the data processed and analysed; finally, what has been found out? Offer some ideas for interesting new inquiries that could take up where you have stopped.
3. Keep your audience in mind because reporting in this linear scientific method also helps to induct other neophyte researchers into the canons of research inquiry — the paradigm for work in the field of curriculum inquiry.
4. Keep a balance between the inquiry (which has its roots in the field) and the reporting of the inquiry (which has to do with the process of communication).

In Chapter 6, a number of research techniques for the analysis of action research data have been described. Given that a great deal of analysis is that of dialogue and text/documentary data, then the methods of discourse analysis — such as *episode analysis, content analysis, dilemma analysis,* and broader tools of critical evaluation such as *dialogical evaluation* and *triangulation* — will prove of enormous significance for processing data collected in natural settings.

8 Towards Critical Communities: Networks, Dissemination and the Ethics of Action Research

Not to want to say
not to know what you want to say
not to be able to say what you want to say
and never to stop saying, or hardly ever,
that is the thing to keep in mind
even in the heat of composition . . . .

Samuel Beckett, Molloy

In this final chapter those issues which impinge upon the organization, support, communication and dissemination of the results of practitioner action research will be considered. Additionally, the issue of the 'ethics' or morality of action inquiry work will be undertaken, and some *ethical procedures* and guidelines for researchers will be suggested.

Lawrence Stenhouse wisely remarked that 'the critical problems involved in an effective system of support for schools are those of power and authority' (Stenhouse, 1975:181). We forget this at our peril. The power of the single teacher working alone is quite limited and yet without his or her commitment to inquiry, little in the way of improvement can be hoped for.

This chapter falls into five parts: first, the treatment of *collaborative networks*; second, a discussion of the concept of *critical communities of discourse*; third, the mechanics of supporting and maintaining a *research community or cell*; fourth, the treatment of effective strategies for *dissemination of findings*; and lastly, the *ethics of action research*.

COLLABORATIVE NETWORKS

The collaborative network refers to those individuals and agencies which offer support of a moral, physical or economic nature in sustaining discourse about action inquiry and who seek to interact to achieve an improvement in understanding, practical performance and even the solution of a practical curriculum problem. Collaboration implies much more than cooperation between individuals; it implies a commitment to equality and co-inquiry (Kyle and McCutcheon, 1984:174). Abraham Shumsky (Shumsky 1956; 1958) argued that not only was collaboration essential, but that the action research process was a way of learning, of acquiring new knowledge and one which was instrumental in the building of 'community' and feelings of 'belongingness', as well as an effective mode of inservice education.

Corey (1953:87) hinted at the need for collaborative networks by observing that:

> there is little likelihood that curricular experimentation will occur in school systems unless teachers, administrators and supervisors have an appreciable degree of freedom and willingness to admit and talk about the jobs that trouble them.

One way in which it is possible for teachers and other practitioners to experiment with promising approaches is for them to test their action ideas against the sounding board of others in the profession. Curriculum and educational practice tend to isolate individuals rather than to expedite the flow of information. Such constraints are no longer acceptable. Thus professional discussion is a prerequisite for action research to feed the development of curriculum knowledge.

However, the issue of collaborative work raises serious problems of *second order action research* (Elliott, 1985b). Given that much educational action research takes place within the framework of participating teachers and often an outside 'consultant' or 'facilitator', Elliott (1985b:259) suggests that:

> Facilitators of teacher-based action research need to be constantly deliberating about their own practice and its relationship to the nature of the activity they are trying to facilitate. If they do not engage in this kind of *second order action research* they will succumb to pressures to control teachers' thinking, and thereby distort rather than enable the processes of *first-order action research*.

One hypothesis put forward here is that collaborative communication and discussion will be most productive in settings where the participants know and respect one another. Most people are afraid of failure but to be a professional also means committing oneself to experimentation — which entails a risk of failure. The important thing is to distance ourselves from a sense of *personal failure*. By this I mean that if a promising line of experimentation does not pay off, it is simply an experiment that has failed — not the person behind the experiment. Rocket scientists do not degrade one another because their laboratory experiments fail to produce results the first time they are tested. They treat such experiments as ideas worth testing; they do not rush forward with claims of a grandiose nature until results are confirmed by independent observers and experiments. And so it should be with curriculum researchers.

Basic to this idea of learning in a collaborative and mutually supportive group is the assumption that one learns by being an active rather than passive participant — a player rather than a spectator. This writer has been involved in numerous teacher workshop groups over the years and has noticed a tendency for some teachers to 'hide' within the group, seeking not to expose their lack of skill or knowledge. This is a tendency which must be combatted by seeking to establish conditions whereby all participants are made to feel that their independent and personal contributions have significant value for the group. Members may decide not to join in if the scope and definition of their task is not clearly demarcated. Group members require a project definition of a problem that appeals to their professional experience — they must be given freedom and the power of decision-making to participate effectively.

Yet if curriculum problems are to be solved then there must be *freedom* to experiment with solutions and a work ethic must be cultivated which suggests that it is professional behaviour to experiment with curriculum practice. It seems to this writer that what is needed is a totally new set of expectations about the relationship between practitioners and their working environment which makes them more independent rather than dependent. To learn anything an individual requires time, resources, knowledge and a critical response from others. This proposal is akin to what Illich (1971) described as 'learning webs', or educational networks.

Establishing a core working group

The first thing is to set up a core team, or cell, of participants. The qualifications and subject expertise are less important than the motivation and attitudes of the group members towards tackling an issue. The will to win is crucial and telling in the successfulness of group endeavour, and it is therefore important that the team wants to be involved voluntarily. Two suggestions made by Illich (Illich, 1971:81) will be developed here as they seem to the present writer to represent fruitful ways forward for those who wish to become fully fledged collaborators: the idea of *skill exchanges* and that of *networks of professionals*.

Skill exchanges
The central notion here is that of an exchange or clearing house concept which permits persons with special skills to list these and how they can be contacted. A 'skill model' is one who has special

skills, such as case study reporting, and who is willing to help others acquire his or her skills. We must also recognize that qualifications of a formal kind, such as an EdD degree, do not necessarily allow that person to be a skill model — that is, many skilled individuals do not hold certificates.

Networks

Here the idea is similar to that of a skill exchange but the notion is that the individuals come together as a *collaborative association or network,* with the avowed goal of promoting a critical discourse directed to the improvement of curriculum. A good example of such a *network* is that of the 'Classroom Action Research Network' (CARN), established by John Elliott in the aftermath of the Stenhouse Humanities Curriculum Project (1967–1972) and Elliott's Ford Teaching Project — both of which were based at CARE, the University of East Anglia. It is encouraging to see the adoption of this 'network' principle with the establishment of centres for applied research in education at several US universities — such as George Mason University, through the direction of Hugh Sockett, Louisville, and Ohio University, where George Wood directs the Institute for Democracy in Education, to name but a few. These universities have gone into a partnership with local school districts to solve practical education problems through the collaboration of practitioners and academics.

The concept of the curriculum action research centre as a collaborative network is one which has as its basic idea the search through curriculum inquiry for diverse ways of improving professional practice. Its focus is normally localized, serving the needs of professionals in a given catchment area (though this is not the case with the UK CARN group) and founded upon such principles as:

- that improvement emerges from the professional commitment of all educators;
- that practitioner reflective inquiry counts as significantly as other forms of curriculum research and development;
- that the contemporary educational community is split between researchers, practitioners and administrators and that a *collaborative network* is needed to allow individual educators to escape the shackles of power and authority inherent in their organizational affiliations.

Collaborative centres can do at least three things to improve curriculum. The first is the establishment of skill exchanges and a community network of concerned members. Second, ensuring that the centre operates *democratically*— that is, that the community has *ownership of the network's ideas.* Third, that special curriculum projects can be launched emerging from the ideas of network members. Special *forums* can develop from the network on particular topics. Forums may then cluster around significant curriculum research and development projects. Funding can be reciprocal.

An example of a research and development CARE project might be organized around the general problems of 'The Induction Teacher'. Forums with teacher educators, master teachers, administrators etc. might examine questions such as:

1. How can teacher training programmes establish skills of self-monitoring and evaluation?
2. How can schools best liaise and collaborate with teacher education institutions?
3. What basic knowledge and skills should a pre-service teacher master?

All these questions are a matter for *deliberation* and curriculum research. Not research in the traditional social scientific sense, but practitioner reflection and deliberation. The definition of research taken is that proposed by Stenhouse (Stenhouse, 1983:185): 'research may be broadly defined as systematic inquiry made public'. This suggests rigour and the sharing of inquiry with others in the public domain — the community concerned. There are therefore strong grounds for getting teachers and other practitioners to see themselves as participants in curriculum research. This assertion applies *a fortiori* to all within the community of professional discourse. Given that so much emphasis is placed on learning through discovery and inquiry in schools, a good procedural way into curriculum inquiry is to engage in the activity as a strategy of teaching. *Qua* educator, the teacher will then place intrinsic value upon the sort of qualities he or she models before pupils.

TOWARDS A CRITICAL COMMUNITY OF DISCOURSE

The theme in this section is the critical community of discourse established by professional educators for the purpose of improving their practice. Such a community would be more tightly interacting and more visible than present trends in the education profession permit. As Reid (1978:i) pointed out some dozen years back:

> The problems of the field of Curriculum Studies are becoming, and in my view should become, the problems of the community at large.

It is the present author's sincerely held view that curriculum shall not be improved significantly until there is established a deliberative and inquiry-related stance towards professional practice. Teachers must engage in curriculum inquiry for teaching to develop as a profession. The point here is that teachers' knowledge must, in a sense, become public knowledge.

The essential community here is the *school community,* which includes teachers, administrators, parents, inspectors, teacher educators, and, of course, pupils. This community may be strengthened through collaboration with nearby schools, outside facilitators and others with a genuine educational responsibility. Note that this community is not an exclusive *teacher community.* We are talking primarily about school-based curriculum improvement and not teacher-based curriculum development — a point made by Skilbeck (Skilbeck, 1984). The real purpose of curriculum improvement is practical action fostered by the school will. Curriculum is thus a practical as opposed to a theoretical art.

Teachers have a wide variety of conversations and more serious curriculum talk which shall be referred to here as *discussion.* David Bridges argues that teacher discussions can be broadly classified into three distinctive types, distinguished centrally in terms of their purpose:

> These are: first, discussion with academic or professional colleagues from which he hopes *to learn something*; secondly, discussion with his students through which he hopes *to teach something;* and, thirdly, discussion, for example, with colleagues, students or parents, through which, with the others involved, he hopes *to decide on a course of action* or a policy leading to a course of action. (Bridges, 1975:81)

Bridges has made some very significant points regarding the type of curriculum discussions one ventures into, and the present author believes that it is with the third type of discussion, that which focuses upon *deliberation and decisions about action,* that the group is most concerned. For it is with moral and practical policies that the stuff of curriculum decisions are concerned — whether to implement values clarification as a suitable pedagogy or some other form of values education, to give an example of the sort of practical curriculum policy which is referred to. Teachers are increasingly finding that they have to make just this sort of decision, particularly as school-based curriculum development and deliberation grow as a movement. Bridges' three ideal types can be classified as *acquisitive discussions* (where the teacher learns something), *pedagogical discussions* (where the teacher wishes to teach something), and *deliberative decisions* (where the teacher wishes to decide on action or set policy). These categories should be borne in mind by the collaborative group, especially the chairperson, as participants often hold one type uppermost as they engage in discussion. For example, teacher A wishes to instruct (*pedagogical discussion*) the group about his or her successful experience with a kit of materials, while teacher B is pressing strongly for rejection of this particular kit (*deliberative discussion*). Discussions often break down because participants are confused and at cross-purposes in their intentions. That is, some proceed towards a right or rational discussion, while others seek group consensus, and others yet again, seek triumphal victory, for example in speeches made at a debate hustings.

One starting point for a collaborative group then is to sort out whether they are in business to: (a) have conversations, (b) have discussions, and (c) clarify the type of discussion they are engaged in.

Development of the action research facilitator role

Since teachers and administrators are somewhat over-worked, it is a little idealistic to suppose that they will be able to mount systematic collaborative action research projects in the face of constraints such as lack of time, lack of research methodology skills, etc. What is required at this stage in the development of curriculum action research in order to place it on a routine basis, are specially trained second order action researchers, or 'facilitators'. In all fairness, teachers will not have time to be involved on a serious level, but they could be helped considerably through the services of the facilitator — there are plenty of people around now with skills in action research, curriculum project development etc. to take on this role. What is more, the new partnership between centres for applied research in education, such as CARE at the University of East Anglia and CARD at George Mason University in Virginia, make this a viable strategy and one which would bring a closer working relationship between third level universities, teacher education institutes and schools on the ground — the possibilities are endless.

The role of the educational facilitator would be to move between schools and the centre studying problems, organizing teacher-researcher working parties, and training teachers in the use of research techniques for data collection, analysis etc. There is little reason why a new appointment of teacher/action research officer could not be developed which could be funded partly by the local school district or local education authority, with the proviso that the appointee teach certain specified hours in schools, and be partly funded by the centre for applied research in education or local university education school, where the appointee might give a graduate course in action research procedures.

At the moment many school central office staff are hired as curriculum specialists. Could not this role be redefined to include the important dynamics of curriculum deliberation and action research? When one considers the number of problems which could be solved by just one such facilitator working in one or more schools, the economies would be well justified. The educational action research facilitator would also have a vital role to play in initial teacher education programmes where the work ethic of the teacher as researcher needs to be sown and cultivated.

SUPPORTING AND MAINTAINING A PROJECT

It would appear that among the most significant obstacles facing action research projects are those of school resources, policy, authority, power and methodology. Resources are at stake because action researchers, like other investigators, require time and some hard resources to mount good research and development projects. Educational policy is involved because it sets the agenda of what is or is not possible under the existing rules of engagement. Authority is involved because curriculum derives its claim to expertness and legitimacy from authorities, whether scholars, texts, or appeals to faith. Power is involved because it is linked to authority and the allocation of resources. Methodology is important because one cannot get involved in research unless one is prepared to conduct it in a systematic and rigorous way — here one focuses upon the acquisition of research skills in data collection, analysis and so on.

Factors relating to support for action research

In a national survey of curriculum changes in Irish secondary schools (Crooks and McKernan, 1984; McKernan, 1984), nine sources of support for curriculum improvement were identified. Table 8.1 sets out the results of a survey of what principals of schools deemed the most effective system of supports.

Table 8.1 *Principals' ranking of sources of teacher support (N=505)*

Source	Rank
Principal as support	1
Short INSET course	2
Staff/department meetings	3
Advice of inspectors	4
Provision of educational journals and books	5

Curriculum materials from external sources	6
Teacher release for curriculum planning	7
Inter-school curriculum meetings	8
Teacher release to study at university	9

Source: Crooks and McKernan (1984:72). Respondents consisted of 70 per cent of all high-school principals in the Republic of Ireland.

It is significant that the top four sources of *support* for curriculum improvement can be conceptualized as *deliberative or discursive.* Notwithstanding the perceived importance that principals placed upon themselves by ranking their role the most important factor, second came the need for short inservice courses. Here the principals had in mind short courses of from one to five days which would target a particular need, skill or area of curriculum — e.g. wordprocessing skills — and then have support on site. Third was the support seen to emerge from good solid reflective-deliberative staff meetings as a communal activity. Fourth was the advice and help of inspectors/advisors. This acknowledges the expertise of good journeymen practitioners. Interestingly, principals were not willing to sanction teacher release for curriculum planning meetings, interschool meetings and lastly, teacher release to study for long university courses. With high teacher:pupil ratios principals did not wish to give up teachers' class time.

Action research has been rediscovered and redefined since the early days of Lewin and Corey. At one end of the continuum there are those who believe that action research will radically alter the way in which schools operate by attempting to identify and eradicate problems. It is likely that this perspective will be more widely shared in the coming years, judging by the response to traditional research, development and dissemination styles of problem solving. One neglected topic is the extent to which practitioners gain a foothold on setting educational research policy. When policy makers begin to appreciate that research is an activity that can be fruitfully undertaken by school practitioners, then the type of issues researched and the difference these projects will make to the ultimate effectiveness of teaching and curriculum will become more apparent. At present the research and development agenda is largely determined by successful grant applicants, usually residing in university positions rather than in classrooms. At a minimum, the following premises need to be accepted for educational action research to flourish:

1. Allow practitioners time, resources and training to do research to improve their curriculum.
2. Allow practitioners the primary role of identifying needed areas of inquiry.
3. Provide external assistance wherever required, e.g. consultants.
4. Provide outlets for curriculum action researchers to share their experiences with other practitioners (conferences, associations, newsletters, journal writing, and so on).
5. Provide opportunities for practitioners to meet regularly for discussion.

DISSEMINATION: THE WRITTEN REPORT

One of the most neglected aspects of using and doing curriculum inquiry is *the writing of the project report*. Composition is difficult even for the most experienced field researchers. Yet if a researcher keeps up-to-date notes, diaries, etc. then he or she has a significant amount of material which is already coded and structured in a fashion which lends itself to reporting. Like the research project itself, the written report needs a beginning, middle and an end, as well as a substantive structural plan: What was researched? By whom? How was the inquiry conducted? How were data analysed? What results emerged? But yet, the two events, the *doing of the research* and the *writing of the research report*, are seen as separate professional activities.

One might be the most fastidious of researchers and have immaculate data at one's disposal but may be unable to communicate it through a lack of skill in writing. Writing is an art form and one needs to attend to details of style, technique — reading is perhaps the best training for any writer. Action researchers must become writers too. They must communicate the life of projects and those who live and breathe within them. An action researcher must, like the novelist, have a *voice*, a complex instrument. The novelist Bernard MacLaverty, who has written about his experiences as a teacher in the celebrated novel *Lamb,* has remarked of the 'voice' that 'it is like trying to define one's soul. It is the sum total of his subject matter. It is the way he approaches his subject matter. More specifically, it is the actual voice he takes. Do you want to take it from an "I" voice, or in the third person?' (MacLaverty, 1988).

Writing probably cannot be taught, yet immersion in good studies can improve style and technique. Action researchers, like the best case-study sociologists, need to be at once good story-tellers as well as social scientists. The whole area of teacher as researcher and teacher as writer of action research reports needs much fuller treatment and direction.

One point that should be underlined at this stage is that writing is not the only mode of communicating and disseminating the experience of an action research project. Countless other effective methods exist: television and videotape productions, oral presentations, demonstration sessions, induction days, poster displays/sessions, roundtable discussion formats, radio and audio tape, and lately disc and computer diskettes giving either visual screen images or printed words. Members of action research teams will need to decide what medium best suits the project and its resources. For example, some schools now have cable channels and have home studio production capabilities. A project in this situation could be disseminated through forum discussions, roundtable discussion format or special one-hour documentary-type programmes. Yet the written report does hold a special place in dissemination, possibly due to the strong force of tradition.

For a discussion on the reporting of research see Hopkins (1985). Several good examples of teacher action research studies, mainly of a small-scale kind, are reported in Jon Nixon's *A Teacher's Guide to Action Research,* and Hustler, Cassidy and Cuff's *Action Research in Classrooms and Schools* (Nixon, 1981; Hustler et al., 1986).

Styles of reporting

A report can be written in the *formal style*, for example a director's final report of a curriculum development project to funding agents; or be an academically executed research monograph with its scholarly and often detached perspective. Other examples of formal writing would be the academic PhD thesis, which presents an argument or set of hypotheses and then sets out to establish evidence for these. On the other hand, an action research project can be presented *informally* as a descriptive case study or short, sharp and incisive piece of evaluation reportage.

Importance of titles

Titles should disclose something of the report's focus or thrust. Thus *Chocolate, Cream, Soldiers* lets the reader in on the collusion of an unlikely triumvirate of sponsors, curriculum *cognoscenti* and combatants in the unrest in Northern Ireland, all of which played a role in the Schools Cultural Studies Project. Spradley, a social ethnographer who worked with alcoholics and nomads, gives us a few good working examples in *You Owe Yourself a Drunk: An Ethnography of Urban Nomads* (Spradley, 1970) and *Guests Never Leave Hungry: The Autobiography of James Sewid, a Kwakiutl Indian* (Spradley, 1969). Such titles tell us something of the research before reading page one.

The use of metaphoric devices has become extremely popular in recent years; however, if poorly executed such titles can act as a millstone to a report by being off-putting in nature.

The main body of text

Decide on the topics, headings etc. that you will treat in the report and develop these one at a time, fleshing out the main text by general reference back to field notes and other records. Write up each of these topics in a first draft.

Write the introduction and the conclusion last

Do not begin with the introduction. Write up the introductory part of the report *after* you have written the main text or document. Add the conclusion and write up the abstract (if required) as the final step.

Edit the manuscript

Edit the first rough draft and then get a collaborative colleague to read the document for honest and fair comment and critique. Be sure to select a colleague who can give an informed perspective on the work.

Some exemplars

One strategy for arriving at a finished product is to model the report or paper on a published piece. There are plenty of examples of action research reports in published books and journals. If the report has to be written in a formal style then consult theses and monographs housed in university collections. Conventions must be adhered to and these will have to be carefully noted, depending on the target audience of the report.

Notes on the arrangement of short reports and articles

We do wish to keep a record of our experiments and attempts at action research problem solving. The format followed by many journals places a ready-made model before us:

1. *Statement of problem/nature of the inquiry.* Clearly define the difficulty or practical problem which is the subject of the inquiry. One need not cite every research study bearing upon the investigation, yet relevant citations may prove helpful for the interested reader who wishes to make cross-referenced studies.

   Discuss any hypotheses that were formulated directly as possible research solutions. These need not be stated formally as research and null hypotheses but posited as clear educational hunches or actions.
2. *Subjects of the study, setting and background.* Here it would be helpful to indicate exactly who the subjects of the study are, and

to say something about the objectives of the inquiry and the research setting, possibly with a map; the activities which occur in the setting; important events; the time when these events occur; the key actors involved in the setting; how the researcher interacted with subjects; and the affective dimensions of this action.

3. *Research methods employed in the study.* Describe the research methods by which data were collected — whether questionnaires, interviews, participant observation, dialogue journals, diaries, or whatever. Discuss the research method in detail so that other investigators can repeat the study to check results.

4. *Results.* Describe the major findings of the study. One can use tables to summarize voluminous data but should be sure to refer to table data in the text of the report. Ensure that table headings indicate the nature of the data contained in tables, figures, diagrams etc.

5. *Discussion and conclusions.* Here the researcher can refer to the major conclusions and offer interpretive accounts of the findings and what they mean in the context of the setting and study. One may wish to point to the implications for future practice and cite particularly ripe areas which require further research investigation. Also, this section should indicate whether the action research project was successful or not in reaching a solution of the problem which triggered the study.

6. *List of references/bibliography.* Any studies cited in the report should be listed in full. For example, for journal articles:

McKernan, J. (1988) The countenance of curriculum action research: traditional, collaborative and emancipatory-critical conceptions, *Journal of Curriculum and Supervision,* Vol. 3, No. 3, Spring, pp. 173–200.

and for books:

Dewey, J. (1910) *How We Think.* Boston: D. C. Heath Co.

7. *Acknowledgements.* It is a matter of strict professional courtesy to acknowledge at the end of the report, any individuals or institutions who gave support or assistance in any form during the course of the inquiry.

8. *Addresses and affiliations of author and co-authors.* It is useful to indicate the addresses of the authors so that readers can obtain a copy of the report. For this reason it is wise to produce a number of mimeo or photocopies of the written report. If the study is published by a journal then the publisher will often provide a number of reprints to the author for this purpose. The author(s) may also include a note on his or her own affiliation or rank. For

example, 'Sam Jones is Head Teacher at Hillsbury High School'.

Publication as dissemination of research

There has been some discussion as to whether teacher inquiry is really research at all (Stenhouse, 1981; Hopkins, 1985). Stenhouse has proffered that research 'is systematic and sustained inquiry, planned and self-critical, which is subjected to public criticism and to empirical tests where these are appropriate' (Stenhouse, 1981:113). In Stenhouse's view 'private research' for the eyes of the inquirer alone, would not count as 'research' partly because it does not benefit or profit from public criticism, and partly because Stenhouse viewed research as a community activity. This is, I believe, a crucial point. We must show our experiments to our peers so that both we and they can learn from them. Even among student researchers there has been a lapse in this concept of research as publicly defended work — to wit, the long tradition of the *disputatio*, or the public defence of one's dissertation, long practised in European universities before a university degree is awarded. The doctoral oral examination is a living example of this tradition of research defence before a select group. This is a tradition which the present writer feels should be re-established in universities.

However, publication serves several important functions. First, it allows work to be refined and improved. Secondly, it allows knowledge to be documented and stored in the academy, ensuring also a wide distribution to colleagues around the world.

Dissemination of documents

There are some basic guidelines which may improve the effects of the action research project, and which may be seen as part of the process of dissemination itself. Bradley (1985) argues:

1. Publish enough documents for all possible participants and extra copies for interested administrators, external consultants etc. Ensure that enough copies of a curriculum document are on hand until the next revision cycle of a project.
2. Hold meetings to explain the document. This will aid the reflective process and assist in understanding. Be sure to go through the document with the participants as some may simply regard it as another 'handout'.
3. Attempt to link documents with inservice training. This approach will emphasize the practical and usable notion of action research and help to achieve implementation.

The present writer agrees with the plea for more written documents of teacher/practitioner educational action research, yet it is not good enough simply to write a subjective and anecdotal account. Standards are being set and research must be systematic. At a minimum, there should be a strict adherence to the eight steps outlined in the preceding section. Moreover, the accounts ought to be written not only 'from the head', but also 'from the heart' — meaning, with a passionate concern for actual fact-finding and an equal passion for describing the feelings, beliefs and values challenged by the study. Studies need not be biased towards quantification, despite the fact that quantitative studies still dominate curriculum and educational research. Yet times are changing, and if curriculum action research is to be a respected paradigm then it must be governed by systematic research incorporating rigour in design and reportage.

There is too much research on education today. Examples would be research on the sociology and psychology of education, which only contributes in an incidental way to curriculum and education. Research should only count if it qualifies as research in education, as indicated by the extent to which it improves practice. The most immediate way in which research can improve practice is teacher curriculum action research. In closing, a simple point should be made — teachers must be involved in curriculum inquiry for real improvements in curriculum.

ETHICAL ISSUES AND ACTION RESEARCH

With a few exceptions (APA, 1967; Kemmis and McTaggart, 1988; Kemmis and Robottom, 1981; Hopkins, 1985; and Simons, 1982) there has been a paucity of discussion relating to the ethical issues involved in curriculum inquiry, and action research in particular. This is a volatile state of affairs as a clear code of practice for a profession should surely take account of this issue.

It is crucial for all participants to know what their rights are in research of any kind. Perhaps the best basis is for the participants to be engaged via a contract — this would seem singularly appropriate where curriculum evaluation work is under way. The action researcher must be honest, fair and, of course, truthful at all times. The following are criteria which may function as *principles of procedure* governing action research.

Ethical criteria for action researchers

1. All those affected by an action research study have a right to be informed, consulted and advised about the object of the inquiry.
2. Action research should not proceed unless permission has been obtained from parents, administrators and others concerned.
3. No individual participant will have unilateral rights to veto the

content of any project report.

4. All documentary evidence, such as files, correspondence and suchlike, should not be examined without official permission.
5. Copyright law should always be strictly observed.
6. The researcher is responsible for the confidentiality of the data.
7. Researchers are obliged to keep efficient records of the project and make these available to participants and authorities on demand.
8. The researcher will be accountable to the school community who impact on the project, i.e. other teachers, parents and pupils.
9. The researcher is accountable to report the progress of the project at periodic intervals. This criteria will also help to satisfy the need for ongoing formative evaluation to determine new lines of interest and problem redefinition.
10. Research should never be undertaken which can cause physical or mental harm to any of the subjects concerned, e.g. administering drugs to unknowing participants would count as an extreme example of such a violation.
11. The researcher has a right to report the project fairly.
12. The researcher must make the ethical contractual criteria known to all involved.
13. Researchers have a right to have their name on any publication resulting from the project. This will help answer the delicate ethical question of 'Who gets credit for publications?' That is, whose name will appear on the article or report?

Epilogue

We shall only teach better if we learn intelligently from the experience of shortfall; both in our grasp of the knowledge we offer and our knowledge of how to offer it. That is the case for research as the basis for teaching.

Lawrence Stenhouse (1983:193)

In recent years the action research movement has made a significant contribution to curriculum and to teachers' professional development. The signs are that this movement will continue to grow. The research practitioner strives towards the attainment of critical self-reflection and autonomy in curriculum work. A considerable amount of space has been devoted to the methodology of action research in this book: techniques by which practitioner-researchers understand and interpret their actions and the consequences of human action. Above all else, research is *interpretive*. It is essentially interpretive of what is discussed, or 'said', in curriculum social discourse, and it proclaims to *record action-discourse* so that it may be understood. Action research is both a social activity in that it involves a number of individuals and it is microethnographic in the sense that it focuses upon social action within a small activity space — usually the classroom with its social surround of rituals, customs, and beliefs. What it is that these researchers do is *reflect and record,* in that order. They write down their experiments, thus preserving them for further reflection-on-action.

A warning bell needs to be sounded here in connection with action research theory. Some, but not all, critical theorists have become obsessed with the use and development of grand theory as a principal goal. The god of methodology has become replaced with the god of theory; in this case the critical social philosophy of the Frankfurt School, especially the work of Jurgen Habermas. Practitioners are being asked to 'genuflect'[1] to this paradigm; to use grand theory as a goodness of fit for their idiosyncratic situations. The present writer considers this to be wrong on at least two counts. First, no action research can be liberationist or emancipatory by imposing a grand theory from above; second, the language of Jurgen Habermas, Stephen Kemmis, Wilfred Carr and those who subscribe

1. The author is grateful to John Elliott of the University of East Anglia for this metaphor of 'genuflecting'. It is also Elliott's belief that action research is in danger of being hijacked by grand theorists.

to the new critical social science is alien to teachers, administrators, and dare I say, even those who work in the academy. It is this writer's belief that this school will not attract a wide following of teachers because of its abstract and difficult language; and further that the 'becoming critical' model of Carr and Kemmis is an attempt to 'hijack' the action research movement in order to *take theoretical control*, in much the same way that they see education being controlled by unjust forces. It is a form of 'academic imperialism'. This is simply about power and control of educational inquiry, but need not be the case as some educators (Bigelow, 1990; Wood, 1988) have demonstrated the ability to apply critical theory without using alienating language.

This brings us back to the original point about the inappropriateness of grand theory for good action research. John Elliott, speaking at the 1988 Annual AERA Meeting, expressed his concern about the action research movement being 'hijacked' by the critical social science school and by the current penchant, at least among university educational action researchers, with 'grand theory'. Elliott argues that one might do better to reread the 'middle-range' theories of writers like R. S. Peters, especially *Ethics and Education* (1966), and the complete works of Lawrence Stenhouse. The author's own view is that serious disciples of action research should start not with grand, or even middle-range, theories, but read writers like C. W. Mills' *The Sociological Imagination* (1959) and Barney Glaser and Anselm Strauss' *The Discovery of Grounded Theory* (1967), so that they can make their own models, theories and grand designs.

The message is quite simple — there are research techniques to be learned and mastered which will provide rich data for practitioners to analyse their curriculum problems in their attempts to improve practice. This will call up all of one's reserves of personal courage, for at the end of the analysis one is inquiring into one's effectiveness as a practitioner. Initial and inservice education and training agencies have a masterful role to play in equipping novice and experienced teachers and administrators with the methodological know-how. We must, however, move away from teacher education, which trains classroom managers as technical instructors, and towards a system which permits critical, practical and moral reflection about teaching and learning. This book argues for recognition of the interaction between theory and practice — and not the separation of theory-research from practice.

Engagement in action research will enable practitioners to become better at doing inquiry. It will also help them to become better teachers, for in the process of doing curriculum inquiry they will come to learn more about themselves, their pupils and their problems.

This book has been written for the practitioner who wishes to conduct curriculum inquiry to improve practice. The possibility exists of creating a whole new work ethic of research in the conduct of professional curriculum practice. If research is to be done by anyone it should be those who go to work in schools.

At the risk of sounding idealistic, the author will offer a final proposition by which he will take a stand; it is in the form of an assertion that curriculum will only be improved by researching our teaching — the inspiration is not the author's own, but one which was pivotal to the philosophy of curriculum espoused by the late Lawrence Stenhouse. Stenhouse further believed that knowledge should never be taught as a rhetoric of conclusions, detached from the process of inquiry which generated the knowledge in the original instance. Knowledge, according to this view, is always provisional and subject to modification in the light of experience; and theories and practices founded on research demand a research stance from practitioners. The goal then of the teacher-researcher is to gain the wisdom which he or she does not yet possess through studying his or her own work. That is also the case for curriculum action research. Perhaps it is proper and fitting to leave the last word to Lawrence Stenhouse.

References

Adelman, C. and Walker, R. (1975) Developing pictures for other frames: action research and case study. In Chanan, G. and Delamont, S. (Eds.) *Frontiers of Classroom Research*. Slough, Berks: National Foundation for Educational Research.

Aiken, W. M. (1942) *The Story of the Eight Year Study*. New York: Harper.

Allport, G. W. (1942) *The Use of Personal Documents in Psychological Science*. New York: Social Science Research Council.

American Psychological Association (1967) *Casebook on Ethical Standards of Psychologists*. Washington, DC: American Psychological Association.

Apple, M. (1982) *Education and Power*. Boston: Routledge and Kegan Paul.

Association for Supervision and Curriculum Development (1957) *Research for Curriculum Improvement*. 1957 Yearbook, Washington, DC: ASCD.

Awbrey, M. J. (1989) A teacher's action research study of writing in kindergarten: Accepting the natural expression of children. *Peabody Journal of Education* (Special Issue: The Potential and Practice of Action Research, Part I) 64, (2) Winter, 33–64.

Bain, A. (1879) *Education as a Science*. New York: Appleton.

Bailey, K. D. (1978) *Methods of Social Research*. New York: Free Press.

Bales, R. F. (1950) *Interaction Process Analysis: A Method for the Study of Small Groups*. Reading, Mass: Addison-Wesley.

Ball, S. and Goodson, I. (Eds.) (1985) *Teachers' Lives and Careers*. Lewes, Sussex: Falmer Press.

Barker, R. G. (1963) *The Stream Of Behavior*. New York: Appleton.

Barker, R. G. (1965) Explorations in ecological psychology. *American Psychologist*, 20, 1–14.

Barker, R. G. (1968) *Ecological Psychology*. Stanford, Ca: Stanford University Press.

Barker, R. G. and Wright, H. (1951) *One Boy's Day: A Specimen Record of Behavior*. New York: Harper.

Barker, R. G. and Wright, H. L. (1955) *Midwest and its Children*. New York: Harper.

Barker, R. G., Wright, H. F., Barker, L. S., and Schoggen, M. (1961) *Specimen Records of American and English Children*. Publication No. 1, *Primary Records in Psychology*. Lawrence, Kansas: University of Kansas, Social Science Studies.

Becker, H. S. (1958) Problems of inference and proof in participant observation. *American Sociological Review*, 23:652–660.

Becker, H. S. (1966) Introduction. In Shaw, C. *The Jack-Roller*. Chicago: University of Chicago Press.

Beckett, S. (1976) *Molloy*. London: John Calder.

Berger, J. (1980) *About Looking*. London: Writers and Readers.

Bigelow, W. (1990). Inside the classroom: Social vision and critical pedagogy. *Democracy and Education*. 4, (3), 13–19.

Bissex, G. and Bullock, R. (Eds.) (1987) *Seeing for Ourselves: Case Study Research by Teachers of Writing*. Portsmouth, NH: Heinemann Educational.

Bobbitt, F. W. (1918) *The Curriculum*. Boston: Houghton-Mifflin.

Bogdan, R. C. and Biklen, S. K. (1982) *Qualitative Research for Education: An Introduction to Theory and Methods*. Boston: Allyn and Bacon.

Bonser, S. and Grundy, S. (1988) Reflective deliberation in the formulation of a school curriculum policy. *Journal of Curriculum Studies*, 20, (1), 35–45.

Boone, R. G. (1904) *Science of Education.* New York: Charles Scribner's.

Borg, W. (1981) *Applying Educational Research: A Practical Guide for Teachers.* New York: Longman.

Borg, W. and Gall, M. (1983) *Educational Research: An Introduction.* New York: Longman.

Bradley, L. (1985) *Curriculum Leadership and Development Handbook.* Englewood Cliffs, New Jersey: Prentice Hall.

Brandt, R. M. (1972) *Studying Behavior in Natural Settings.* New York: Holt, Rinehart and Winston.

Brennan, M. and Noffke, S. E. (1988) Reflection in student teaching: the place of data in action research. Paper read at the Annual Meeting of American Educational Research Association, New Orleans, April, 1988.

Bridges, D. (1975) Discussion and decision-making. In Bridges, D. and Scrimshaw, P. (Eds.) *Values And Authority in Schools.* London: Hodder and Stoughton, 81–102.

Brown, R. (1967) Research and consultancy in industrial enterprises. *Sociology,* 1, 33–60.

Buchman, M. (1983) Argument and conversation as discourse models of knowledge use. East Lansing, Michigan: Institute for Research on Teaching, Michigan State University. Occasional Paper No. 68.

Buckingham, R. B. (1926) *Research for Teachers.* New York: Silver Burdett Co.

Burgess, R. G. (Ed.) (1984) *The Research Process in Educational Settings: Ten Case Studies.* London: Falmer Press.

Burgess, R. G. (1985) *Issues in Educational Research: Qualitative Methods.* London: Falmer Press.

Button, L. (1974) *Developmental Group Work with Adolescents.* London: Hodder and Stoughton.

Button, L. (1981) *Group Tutoring for the Form Teacher.* London: Hodder and Stoughton.

Butzow, J. W. and Gabel, D. (1986) Be researchers. *The Science Teacher,* 53 (1):33–37.

Calderhead, J. (1988) *Teachers' Professional Learning.* London: Falmer Press.

Campbell, D. and Fiske, D. (1959) Convergent and discriminant validation by the multi-trait multi-method matrix. *Psychological Bulletin,* 56, 81–105.

Carr, W. (1989) Action research: ten years on. *Journal of Curriculum Studies,* 21,(1) 85–90.

Carr, W. and Kemmis, S. (1986) *Becoming Critical: Education, Knowledge and Action Research.* Lewes, Sussex: Falmer Press.

Carson, T. and Coutre, J. C. (Eds.) (1987) *Collaborative Action Research: Experiences and Reflections.* Improvement of Instruction Series, Monograph No. 18, Edmonton, Alberta: Alberta Teachers' Association.

Castaneda, C. (1970) *The Teachings of Don Juan: A Yaqui Way of Knowledge.* Harmondsworth: Penguin Books.

Cazden, C., Diamondstone, J. and Naso, P. (1988) Relationships between teacher research and researcher research on writing instruction. Paper read at the 1988 Meeting of the American Educational Research Association, New Orleans, 8 April 1988 SIG on Language Development.

Center For New Schools (1972) Strengthening alternative high schools. *Harvard Educational Review,* 42, 313–350.

Center For New Schools (1976) Ethnographic evaluation in education. *Journal of Research and Development in Education,* 9, (4) :3–11.

Chein, I., Cook, S. and Harding, J. (1948) The field of action research. *American Psychologist,* 3, 43–50.

Child, I., Potter, E. and Levine, E. (1946) Children's textbooks and personality development: an exploration in the social psychology of education.

Psychological Monographs, LX, No. 3.

Clark, A. W. (Ed.) (1976) *Experimenting with Organizational Life: The Action Research Approach.* New York: Plenum Press.

Cohen, L. and Manion, L. (1977) *A Guide to Teaching Practice.* London: Methuen.

Collier, J. (1945) United States Indian administration as a laboratory of ethnic relations. *Social Research,* 12, (May).

Connelly, F. M. and Ben-Peretz, M. (1980) Teachers' roles in the using and doing of research and development. *Journal of Curriculum Studies,* 12 (2):95–107.

Connelly, F. M. and Clandinin, J. D. (1988) *Teachers as Curriculum Planners: Narratives of Experience.* New York: Teachers College Press.

Corey, S. (1953) *Action Research to Improve School Practices.* New York: Columbia University, Teachers College Press.

Corey, S. (1954) Action research in education. *Journal of Educational Research,* 47, January:375–380.

Cowie, H. and Rudduck, J. (1989) *Learning Together — Working Together Series.* Vol 1, *Cooperative Group Work: An Overview,* and Vol 2, *School and Classroom Studies.* Wetherby, West Yorkshire: BP Educational Service.

Crooks, T. and McKernan, J. (1984) *The Challenge of Change: Curriculum Development in Irish Post-Primary Schools, 1970–1984.* Dublin: Institute of Public Administration.

Davis, E. (1981) *Teachers As Evaluators.* Sydney: George Allen and Unwin.

Denzin, N. (1970) *The Research Act in Sociology.* London: Butterworths.

Denzin, N. (1978) *The Research Act: A Theoretical Introduction to Sociological Methods.* 2nd Edn. New York: McGraw-Hill.

Dewey, J. (1910) *How We Think.* Boston: D.C. Heath.

Dewey, J. (1929) *The Sources of a Science of Education.* New York: Horace Liveright.

Dewey, J. (1938) *Logic: The Theory of Inquiry.* New York: Henry Holt.

Ebbutt, D. (1983a) Educational action research: Some general concerns and specific quibbles. Cambridge Institute of Education. (Mimeo).

Ebbutt, D. (1983b) Teachers as researchers: How four teachers co-ordinate the process of research in their respective schools. London: Schools Council Working Paper No. 10 TIQL Project.

Ebbutt, D. and Elliott, J. (Eds.) (1985) *Issues in Teaching for Understanding.* Layerthorpe, York: Longmans. Schools Curriculum Development Committee, Schools Council Programme 2.

Eisner, E. (1980) *The Educational Imagination.* New York: Macmillan.

Elliott, J. (1977) Developing hypotheses about classrooms from teachers' practical constructs: an account of the Ford Teaching Project. *Interchange,* 7, (2): 2–20.

Elliott, J. (1978a) What is action research in schools? *Journal of Curriculum Studies* 10, (4): 355–357.

Elliott, J. (1978b) Classroom accountability and the self-monitoring teacher. In Harlen, W. (Ed.) *Evaluation And The Teacher's Role.* pp. 47–90.

Elliott, J. (1980) Implications of classroom research for professional development. In Hoyle, E. and Megarry, J. (Eds.) *Professional Development of Teachers: World Yearbook of Education, 1980.* London: Kogan Page, pp. 308–324.

Elliott, J. (1981) Action research: a framework for self-evaluation in schools. Working Paper No. 1, Schools Council Programme 2, Teacher-Pupil Interaction and the Quality of Learning Project. Cambridge: Cambridge Institute of Education.

Elliott, J. (1983) A curriculum for the study of human affairs: the contribution of Lawrence Stenhouse. *Journal of Curriculum Studies,* 15 (2):108–109.

Elliott, J. (1985a) Educational action research. In Nisbet, J. et al. *World Yearbook of Education, 1985.* London: Kogan Page, pp. 231–250.

Elliott, J. (1985b) Facilitating action research in schools: some dilemmas. In Burgess, R.G. (Ed.) *Field Methods in the Study of Education.* Lewes, Sussex: Falmer Press, pp. 235–262.

Elliott, J. (1987) Educational theory, practical philosophy and action research. *British Journal of Educational Studies,* Vol. XXXV, No. 2, (June 1987): 149–169.

Elliott, J. (1988) Teachers as researchers: implications for supervision and teacher education. Paper read at the 1988 Meeting of the American Educational Research Association Conference, New Orleans.

Elliott, J. (1989) Academics and action research: the training workshop as an exercise in ideological deconstruction. Paper presented at the 1989 Meeting of the American Educational Research Association, Division B, 30 March, San Francisco, California.

Elliott, J. and Adelman, C. (1973) Reflecting where the action is: the design of the Ford Teaching Project. *Education for Teaching,* 92, pp. 8–20.

Elliott, J. and Adelman, C. (1976) Innovation at the classroom level: the Ford Teaching Project. Course CE023 Milton Keynes: Open University Press.

Elliott, J. and Ebbutt, D. (Eds.) (1986) *Case Studies in Teaching for Understanding.* Cambridge: Cambridge Institute of Education.

Elliott, J. and Partington, D. (1975) Three points of view in the classroom. Ford Teaching Project Document. Cambridge: Cambridge Institute of Education.

Erickson, F. and Mohatt, G. (1982) Cultural organization of participant structures in two classrooms of Indian students. In Spindler, G. (Ed.) *Doing the Ethnography of Schooling: Educational Anthropology in Action.* New York: Holt, Rinehart and Winston.

Farley, J. (1985) Topics in dialogue journals of mildly retarded students. *Dialogue,* Vol. II (4) May: 2–3.

Flanders, N. (1970) *Analysing Teaching Behavior.* Reading, Mass.: Addison-Wesley.

Florio-Ruane, S. (1986) Conversation and narrative in collaborative research. In Witherall, C. S., Noddings, N. and Duran, A. (Eds.) *Lives in Narrative: The Use of Subjective Accounts in Educational Research and Practice.* New York: Teachers College Press.

Freire, P. (1973) *Education for Critical Consciousness.* Translated from Portuguese by Ramos Myra. New York: Continuum.

Freire, P. and Faundez, A., (1989) *Learning To Question: A Pedagogy of Liberation.* New York: Continuum (Distributed by Harper and Row).

Freilich, M. (Ed.) (1970) *Marginal Natives: Anthropologists At Work.* New York: Harper and Row.

Fuchs, E. (1969) *Teachers Talk: Views from Inside City Schools.* New York: Free Press.

Gadamer, H. G. (1984) *Reason in the Age of Science.* Cambridge, Mass.: MIT Press.

Gaden, G. (1988) Professional attitudes. *Irish Educational Studies,* Vol. 7, No. 1, Spring, pp. 27–40.

Galton, M. (1978) *British Mirrors.* Leicester: University of Leicester, School of Education.

Geertz, C. (1973) *The Interpretation of Cultures.* New York: Basic Books.

Giroux, H. and McLaren, P. (1987) Teacher education as a counter public sphere: notes towards a re-definition. In T. S. Popkewitz (Ed.) *Critical Studies in Teacher Education,* Lewes: Falmer Press, 266–297.

Glaser, B. and Strauss, A. (1967) *The Discovery of Grounded Theory: Strategies for Qualitative Research.* Chicago: Aldine.

Glasser, W. (1969) *Schools Without Failure.* New York: Harper and Row.

Glatthorn, A. A. (1977) *Handbook for Self Appraisal and Collegial Development.* Philadelphia: Graduate School of Education, University of Pennsylvania (Mimeo).

Glatthorn, A. A. (1985a) Case study: an overview of one kind of research. Philadelphia, Pa.: Graduate School of Education, University of Pennsylvania (Mimeo).

References

Glatthorn, A. A. (1985b) Personal time analysis. Philadelphia, Pa: University of Pennsylvania, Graduate School of Education (Mimeo).

Goetz, J. L. and LeCompte, M. D. (1984) *Ethnography and Qualitative Design in Educational Research.* New York: Academic Press.

Gold, R. (1958) Roles in sociological field observations. *Social Forces,* 36, March, 217–223.

Goodson, I. (1981) Life histories and the study of schooling. *Interchange,* Ontario, 11, (4).

Goodson, I. (1983) The use of life histories in the study of teaching. In Hammersley, M. (Ed.) *The Ethnography of Schooling.* Driffield: Nafferton.

Goswami, D. and Stillman, P. (Eds.) (1987) *Reclaiming the Classroom: Teacher Research as an Agency for Change.* Portsmouth, NH: Boynton Cook.

Gregory, R. (1988) *Action Research in the Secondary School.* London: Routledge, Chapman and Hall.

Griffin, G., Lieberman, A. and Jacullo-Noto, J. (1983) *Executive Summary of the Final Report on Interactive Research and Development on Schools.* Austin, Texas, University of Texas, Research and Development Center for Teacher Education.

Gronlund, N. E. (1981) *Measurement and Evaluation in Teaching.* 4th Edn. New York: Macmillan.

Habermas, J. (1972) *Knowledge and Human Interests.* London: Heinemann.

Habermas, J. (1976) *Communication and the Evolution of Society.* Boston: Beacon Press.

Hagedorn, H. (1984) *A Working Manual of Simple Program Evaluation Techniques for Community Mental Health Centers.* Washington, DC: Government Printing Office.

Halsey, A. H. (1972) *Educational Priority* Volume I: *Educational Priority Area Problems and Policies.* London: HMSO.

Hammersley, M. and Atkinson, P. (1983) *Ethnography: Principles and Practice.* London: Tavistock Publications.

Hargreaves, D. H. (1967) *Social Relations in a Secondary School.* London: Routledge and Kegan Paul.

Hawkins, S. (1975) Tape-record your teaching: a step-by-step approach. *Learning Resources* 2, (2) April.

Henry, J. (1963) *Culture Against Man.* New York: Random House.

Herron, D. (1983) The Work of the National School Principal: A Diary Method of Study of Dublin Principals. Unpublished Master of Education Thesis, Education Department, University College Dublin, Ireland.

Hodgkinson, H. L. (1957) Action research — a critique. *Journal of Educational Sociology,* 31, December, (4):137–153.

Holly, M. L. (1984) *Keeping a Personal-Professional Journal.* Geelong, Victoria: Deakin University Press.

Holly, M. L. (1989) Teachers' reflective writings. *Cambridge Journal of Education* 19, (1).

Holmes Group (1986) *Tomorrow's Teachers.* East Lansing, Michigan: Michigan State University.

Holsti, O. R. (1969) *Content Analysis for the Social Sciences and Humanities.* Reading, Mass: Addison-Wesley.

Hook, C. (1985) *Studying Classrooms.* Geelong, Victoria: Deakin University Press.

Hopkins, C. and Antes, R. (1985) *Classroom Measurement and Evaluation.* Itasca, Illinois: Peacock Publishing Co.

Hopkins, D. (1985) *A Teacher's Guide to Classroom Research.* Philadelphia, Pa: Open University Press.

Hovda, R. and Kyle, D. (1984) Action research: a professional possibility. *Middle School Journal* (May): 21–23.

Hoyle, E. (1972) Creativity in the School. Unpublished paper, OECD Workshop, Estoril, Portugal.

Hoyle, E. (1984). The professionalization of teachers: a paradox. In Gordon, P. (Ed.) *Is Teaching A Profession?* Bedford Way Papers 15, London: Institute of Education, 1983, pp. 44–54.

Huling, L., Trang, M. and Correll, I. (1981) Interactive research and development: a promising strategy for teacher education. *Journal of Teacher Education* 32, (6) November–December: 13–14.

Hustler, D., Cassidy, A. and Cuff, E. (Eds.) (1986) *Action Research in Classrooms and Schools.* London: Allen and Unwin.

Illich, I. (1971). *Deschooling Society.* New York: Harper and Row.

Jackson, P. (1968) *Life in Classrooms.* New York: Holt, Rinehart and Winston.

Janesick, V. (1983) Using a journal to develop reflection and evaluation options in the classroom. Paper read at the 1987 American Educational Research Association Meeting, Montreal, Canada.

Jaques, E. (1952) *The Changing Culture of a Factory.* New York: Dryden Press.

Jenkins, D. (1980) An adversary's account of SAFARI's ethics of case study. In Simon's H. (Ed.) *Towards a Science of the Singular.* Norwich: University of East Anglia. Occasional Publication No. 10.

Jenkins, D. (1984) Chocolate cream soldiers: sponsorship, ethnography and sectarianism. Chapter 10 In Burgess, R.G. (Ed.) *The Research Process in Educational Settings: Ten Case Studies.* London: Falmer Press.

Jenkins, D., O'Connor, S., Kemmis, S., Anderson, T., and Breslin, A. (1980) *Chocolate Cream Soldiers.* Final Evaluation Report of the Rowntree Schools' Cultural Studies Project. Coleraine, Northern Ireland: Education Centre, Ulster University.

Jenkins, F., Kent, D.C., Sims, V.M., and Waters, E.A. (1946) The Southern Study: Cooperative Study for the Improvement of Education: A Staff Report of the Southern Association Study in Secondary Schools. *Southern Association Quarterly* X, (February–August).

Kemmis, S. (1983) Action research. In Husen T. and Postlethwaite T. (Eds.) *International Encyclopedia of Education: Research and Studies* Oxford: Pergamon.

Kemmis, S. and McTaggart, R. (Eds.) (1982) *The Action Research Reader.* Geelong, Victoria: Deakin University Press.

Kemmis, S and McTaggart, R. (Eds.) (1988) *The Action Research Planner.* 3rd Edn. Geelong, Victoria: Deakin University Press.

Kemmis, S. and Robottom, I. (1981) Principles of procedure in curriculum evaluation. *Journal of Curriculum Studies,* 13, (2).

Kerkman, D. H. (1964) *Behavior Setting at School in Communities Differing in Size.* Doctoral Dissertation, University of Kansas, Ann Arbor, Michigan: University Microfilms No. 65–587.

Kerlinger, F. N. (1986) *Foundation of Behavioral Research.* 3rd Edn. New York: Holt, Rinehart and Winston (1st Edn, 1964).

King, A. and Brownell, J. A. (1966) *The Curriculum and the Disciplines of Knowledge.* New York: John Wiley.

Kinsey, A. C., Pomeroy, W. B., Martin, C. E. and Gebhard, P. H. (1953) *Sexual Behavior in the Human Female.* Philadelphia: W.B. Saunders.

Kreeft, J. (1984) Dialogue writing — bridge from talk to essay writing. *Language Arts,* 61 (2):141–150.

Kyle, D. and McCutcheon, G. (1984) Collaborative research: development and issues. *Journal of Curriculum Studies,* 16 (April–June):173–179.

Lang, K. and Lang, G. (1960) Decisions for Christ: Billy Graham in New York City. In M. Stein, A.J. Vidich, and D.M. White (Eds.) *Identity and Anxiety.* Glencoe, Ill.: Free Press.

References

Lazarsfeld, P. and Rietz, G. G. (1975) *An Introduction to Applied Sociology.* New York: Elsevier.

LeCompte, M. (1969) The Dilemmas of Inner-City School Reform: The Woodlawn Experimental School Project. Unpublished MA thesis, Education and Social Order, Chicago: University of Chicago.

Lewin, K. (1946) Action research and minority problems. *Journal of Social Issues,* 2:34–46.

Lewin, K. (1947a) Group decision and social change. In T. Newcomb and E. Hartley (Eds.) *Readings in Social Psychology.* New York: Henry Holt, pp. 330–344.

Lewin, K. (1947b) Frontiers in group dynamics: II. Channels of group life; social planning and action research. *Human Relations,* II:142–153.

Lewin, K. (1948) *Resolving Social Conflicts.* New York: Harper.

Lieberman, A. and Miller, L. (1984) School improvement: themes and variations. *Teachers College Record,* 86, (1) (Fall):4–19.

Lippitt , R. and Radke, M. (1946) New trends in the investigation of prejudice. *Annals of the American Academy of Political and Social Science,* Vol. 244: 167–176.

Lomax, P. (Ed.) (1989) *The Management of Change: Increasing School Effectiveness and Facilitating Staff Development Through Action Research.* BERA Dialogues No. 1, Clevedon: Multilingual Matters Ltd.

McCall, G. J. and Simmons, J. L. (Eds.) (1969) *Issues in Participant Observation: A Text and Reader.* Reading, Mass: Addison-Wesley.

MacLaverty, B. (1988) Interview in *Sunday Tribune,* 25 September 1988, Dublin: Sunday Tribune Ltd.

McKernan, J. (1973) Some Social Factors Affecting the Educational Participation and Attainment of Itinerant Children in the Galway City Primary Schools. Unpublished MA thesis, Galway: Education Department, University College Galway, Ireland.

McKernan, J. (1978) Teaching Controversial Issues: Beliefs, Attitudes and Values as Social-Psychological Indicators in some Northern Ireland Secondary Schools. Unpublished PhD thesis. Coleraine: Northern Ireland, Education Centre, Ulster University.

McKernan, J. (1982a) Constraints on the handling of controversial issues in Northern Ireland secondary schools. *British Educational Research Journal,* 8 (1):57–71.

McKernan, J. (1982b) Value systems and race relations in Northern Ireland and America. *Ethnic and Racial Studies,* 5 (2) April:156–174.

McKernan, J. (1984) Curriculum development in the Republic of Ireland. *Journal of Curriculum Studies,* 16,(3).

McKernan, J. (1987) Action research and curriculum development. *Peabody Journal of Education,* 64, (2), Winter. The Potential and Practice of Action Research, Part 1, 6–19.

McKernan, J. (1988a) The countenance of curriculum action research: traditional, collaborative and critical-emancipatory conceptions, *Journal of Curriculum and Supervision,* 3, (3) Spring:173–200.

McKernan, J. (1988b) Teacher as researcher: paradigm and praxis. *Contemporary Education,* Vol. LIX, (3) Spring 1988, 154–158.

McKernan, J. (1988c) In defense of Education for Living in post-primary curriculum. *Oideas,* Journal of the Government Department of Education (Ireland), 32, Spring, 1988, pp. 65–83.

McKernan, J. (1989) Varieties of curriculum action research: constraints and typologies in Anglo-Irish and American projects. Paper presented at the 1989 Annual Meeting of the American Educational Research Association, April, San Francisco, CA. Division B, International Symposium on Curriculum Action Research — Teacher as Researcher.

McKernan, J. (1991) Action inquiry: planned enactment. In Short, Edmund (Ed.) *Forms Of Curriculum Inquiry.* Albany, New York: State University of New York Press (in Press).

McKernan, J, et al., (1985) *Learning for Life: Tutor's Guide.* Dublin: Gill and Macmillan.

McTaggart, R., Kemmis, S., Fitzpatrick, M., Henry, C., Dawkins, S. and Kelly, M. (1982) *The Action Research Planner.* 2nd Edn. Geelong, Victoria: Deakin U. Press.

Marrow, A. (1969) *The Practical Theorist: The Life and Work of Kurt Lewin.* New York: Basic Books.

Marsh, N., et al. (1984) Using action research to design a management development scheme. *Journal of Management Development,* 3, (2): 56–65.

Miller, J. (1990) *Creating Spaces and Finding Voices: Teachers Collaborating for Empowerment.* Albany, NY: State University of New York Press.

Mills, C. W. (1959) *The Sociological Imagination.* Oxford: Oxford University Press.

Mohr, M. and Maclean, M. (1987) *Working Together: A Guide for Teacher Researchers.* Urbana, Ill.: National Council for Teachers of English.

Moreno, J. L. (1934) *Who Shall Survive?* Nervous and Mental Disease Monograph. No. 58, Washington, DC.

Mulryan, C. (1984) Effective communication of mathematics at primary level: focus on the textbooks, *Irish Educational Studies,* (2):62–81.

Munby, H. (1986) Metaphor in the thinking of teachers:an exploratory study, *Journal of Curriculum Studies,* 18:197–209.

Nixon, J. (Ed.) (1981) *A Teacher's Guide to Action Research: Evaluation, Enquiry and Development in the Classroom.* London: Grant McIntyre.

Noffke, S. E. and Brennan, M. (1988) Action research and reflective student teaching. Paper presented at the Annual Meeting of the Association of Teacher Educators, San Diego, February 1988.

Noffke, S. and Zeichner, K. (1987) Action research and teacher thinking: the first phase of the action research on action research project at the University of Wisconsin-Madison. Paper read at the 1987 Meeting of the American Educational Research Association. Washington, DC.

Oakeshott, M. (1962) *Rationalism and Politics.* London: Methuen.

Oja, S. N. (1983) *Final Report: A Two Year Study of Teacher Development in Relation to Collaborative Action Research in Schools.* Durham, New Hampshire: University of New Hampshire, Collaborative Action Research Project Office.

Oja, S. N., and Smulyan, L. (1989) *Collaborative Action Research: A Developmental Process.* Philadelphia: Falmer Press.

Osborn, A. (1953) *Applied Imagination: Principles and Procedures of Creative thinking.* New York: Scribner.

Osborn, A. F. (1963) *Applied Imagination.* New York: Charles Scribner's.

Parlett, M. and Hamilton, D. (1972) Evaluation as illumination: a new approach to the study of innovatory programmes. Occasional Paper No. 9, Centre for Research in the Educational Sciences, Edinburgh: Edinburgh University, Scotland.

Perl, S. and Wilson, N. (1986) *Through Teacher's Eyes: Portraits of Writing Teachers At Work.* Portsmouth, NH: Heinemann.

Peters, R. S. (1966) *Ethics and Education.* London: George Allen and Unwin.

Piaget, J. (1926) *The Language and Thought of the Child.* New York: Harcourt, Brace and World.

Polyani, M. (1973) *Personal Knowledge.* London: Routledge and Kegan Paul.

Popper, K. (1972) *The Open Society and its Enemies.* London: Routledge and Kegan Paul.

Postman, N. and Weingartner, C. (1971) *Teaching a Subversive Activity.* Harmondsworth: Penguin Books.

References

Progoff, I. (1975) *At a Journal Workshop*. New York: Dialogue House.

Rainey, B. G. (1973) Action research: a valuable professional activity for the teacher. *Clearing House*, 47, (6), (Feb):371–375.

Rapoport, R. N. (1970) Three dilemmas in action research. *Human Relations*, 23, (6):499.

Reid, W. A. (1978) *Thinking About the Curriculum: The Nature and Treatment of Curriculum Problems*. London: Routledge and Kegan Paul.

Reid, W. A. and Walker, D. F. (1975) *Case Studies in Curriculum Change*. London: Routledge and Kegan Paul.

Roby, T. W. (1985) Habits impeding deliberation, *Journal of Curriculum Studies*, 17 (1):17–35.

Rokeach, M. (1960). *The Open and Closed Mind*. New York: Basic Books.

Rokeach, M. (1973). *The Nature of Human Values*. New York: The Free Press.

Ross, D. D. (1984) A practical model for conducting action research in public school settings. *Contemporary Education*, 55, (2):113–116.

Royal Anthropological Institute of Great Britain and Ireland (1951) *Notes and Queries on Anthropology*. 6th Edn. London: Routledge and Kegan Paul.

Rudduck, J. (1978) *Learning through Small Group Discussion*. London: Society for Research in Higher Education.

Rudduck, J. (Ed.) (1979) *Learning to Teach through Discussion*. Norwich: Centre for Applied Research in Education, University of East Anglia.

Rudduck, J. (1984) A study in the dissemination of action research. In Burgess, R. G. (Ed.) *The Research Process in Educational Settings: Ten Case Studies*, Lewes, Sussex: Falmer Press, pp. 187–210.

Rudduck, J. (1989) Critical thinking and practitioner research: have they a place in initial teacher training? Division of Education, Sheffield University. Paper presented at the 30 March Meeting of the American Educational Research Association, San Francisco, Ca.

Rudduck, J. and Hopkins, D. (Eds.) (1985) *Research as a Basis for Teaching*. London: Heinemann.

Sanford, N. (1970) Whatever happened to action research? *Journal of Social Issues*, 26 (4): 3–23.

Sarason, S. (1971) *The Culture of the School and the Problem of Change*. Boston: Yale University Press.

Schaefer, R. (1967) *The School as a Center of Inquiry*. New York: Harper and Row.

Schatzman, L. and Strauss, A. (1973) *Field Research: Strategies for a Natural Sociology*. Englewood Cliffs, New Jersey: Prentice Hall.

Schon, D. (1983) *The Reflective Practitioner: How Professionals Think in Action*. New York: Basic Books.

Schon, D. (1987) *Educating the Reflective Practitioner*. San Francisco: Jossey Bass.

Schools Council/Nuffield Humanities Project (1970) *The Humanities Curriculum Project: An Introduction*. London: Heinemann.

Schubert, W. H. (1986) *Curriculum: Perspective, Paradigm and Possibility*. New York: Macmillan Publishing Co.

Schwab, J. (1969) The practical: a language for curriculum. *School Review 78*.

Schwab, J. (1971) The practical: arts of electic. *School Review*, 79, 493–542.

Schwab, J (1973). The practical 3: translation into curriculum. *School Review*, 81, 501–522.

Schwab, J (1983). The practical 4: something for curriculum professors to do. *Curriculum Inquiry*, 13, (3): 239–265.

Selander, S. (1987) *Perspectives on Action Research*. Stockholm: Stockholm Institute of Education, Department of Educational Research, Reports on Education and Psychology No 1.

Selltiz, C., Jahoda, M., Deutsch, M. and Cook, S. (1959) *Research Methods in Social Relations*. New York: Holt, Rinehart and Winston.

Shaw, C. (1931) *The Natural History of a Delinquent Career.* Chicago: University of Chicago Press.

Shaw, C. (1938) *Brothers in Crime.* Chicago: University of Chicago Press.

Short, E. C. (1987) Curriculum research in retrospect. Paper read at the 1987 Meeting of the American Educational Research Association, Society for the Study of Curriculum History, Washington DC, April.

Short, E. C. (Ed.) (1991) *Forms of Curriculum Inquiry.* Albany, New York: State University of New York Press (in press).

Shumsky, A. (1956) Cooperation in action research: a rationale. *Journal of Educational Sociology,* 30, (1):180–185.

Shumsky, A. (1958) *The Action Research Way of Learning: An Approach to Inservice Education.* New York: Bureau of Publications, Columbia University, Teachers College.

Simon, A. and Boyer, E. (Eds.) (1975) *Mirrors for Behavior: An Anthology of Classroom Observation Instruments.* Philadelphia: Research for Better Schools.

Simon, S., Howe, L. and Kirschenbaum, H. (1972) *Values Clarification: A Handbook of Practical Strategies for Teachers and Students.* New York: Hart Co.

Simons, H. (1982) Suggestions for a school self-evaluation based on democratic principles. In McCormick, R. (Ed.) *Calling Education to Account.* London: Heinemann.

Simons, H. (1980) *Towards a Science of the Singular.* Norwich: University of East Anglia, Centre for Applied Research in Education.

Simons, H. (1987) *Getting to Know Schools in a Democracy.* London: Falmer Press. Social Research and Educational Studies Series: 5.

Skilbeck, M. (1984) *School Based Curriculum Development.* London: Harper.

Smith, B. O., Meux, M., Coombs, J., Nuthall, G. and Precians, R. (1967) *A Study of the Strategies of Teaching.* Urbana, Illinois: Bureau of Educational Research, University of Illinois, College of Education.

Smith, B. O., Meux., M. et al. (1970) *A Study of the Logic of Teaching.* Urbana, Illinois: University of Illinois Press.

Smith. L. and Geoffrey, W. (1968) *The Complexities of an Urban Classroom.* New York: Holt, Rinehart and Winston.

Sockett, H. T. (1983) Toward a professional code in teaching. In Gordon, P., Perkin, H., Sockett, H. and Hoyle, E. (Eds.) (1983) *Is Teaching a Profession?* Bedford Way Papers 15. London: Institute of Education, 26–43.

Sockett, H. T. (1984). The educational agenda: a view of the future. *Irish Educational Studies,* 4, (2): 1–20.

Sockett, H. T. (1988) Research, practice and professional aspiration. *Journal of Curriculum Studies,* 20, (6).

Sockett, H. T. (1989) Practical professionalism. In Carr, W. (Ed.) *New Directions in Theory and Practice.* Lewes, Sussex: Falmer.

Sontag, S. (1977) *On Photography.* New York: Strauss and Giroux.

Spradley, J. P. (1969) *Guests Never Leave Hungry: The Autobiography of James Sewid, a Kwakiutl Indian.* New Haven, Conn: Yale University Press.

Spradley, J. P. (1970) *You Owe Yourself a Drunk: An Ethnography of Urban Nomads.* Boston: Little and Brown.

Spradley, J. P. (1979) *The Ethnographic Interview.* New York: Holt, Rinehart and Winston.

Spradley, J. P. (1980) *Participant Observation.* New York: Holt, Rinehart and Winston.

Spradley, J. P. and McCurdy, D. (Eds.) (1972) *The Cultural Experience: Ethnography in Complex Society.* Chicago: Science Research Associates.

Stake, R. (1967) The countenance of educational evaluation. *Teachers College Record,* 68, April, 523–540.

Stake, R. (1985) Case study. Chapter 20 in Nisbet, J., et al. (Eds.) *World Yearbook Of Education 1985: Research, Policy and Practice.* London: Kogan Page, 277–285.

Staton, J. (1980) Writing and counselling: using a dialogue journal. *Language Arts,* 57, (5):514–518.

Staton, J., Kreeft, J. and Shelley, G. (Eds.) (1985) *Dialogue,* II, (4). Washington, DC: Center for Applied Linguistics.

Staton, J., Shuy, R.W., Peyton, J. and Reed, L. (1988) *Communication: Classroom, Linguistic, Social and Cognitive Views.* Norwood, NJ: Ablex.

Stenhouse, L. (1967) *Culture and Education.* London: Nelson.

Stenhouse, L. (1971) The Humanities Curriculum Project: the rationale. *Theory Into Practice,* X, (3) June, 154–162.

Stenhouse, L. (1972) Teaching through small group discussion: formality, rules and authority. *Cambridge Journal of Education,* 2 (1):18–24.

Stenhouse, L. (1975) *An Introduction to Curriculum Research and Development.* London: Heinemann Educational.

Stenhouse, L. (1977) Exemplary case studies: towards a descriptive educational research tradition grounded in evidence. Research Proposal submitted to Social Science Research Council, UK.

Stenhouse, L. (1978). Case study and case records: towards a contemporary history of education. *British Educational Research Journal,* 4 (2):21–39.

Stenhouse, L. (1981) What counts as research? *British Journal of Educational Studies,* XXIX, (2) (June):113.

Stenhouse, L. (1983) *Authority, Education and Emancipation.* London: Heinemann.

Stenhouse, L., Verma, G., Wild, R., Nixon, J., et al. (1982) *Problems and Effects of Teaching about Race Relations.* London: Routledge and Kegan Paul.

Taba, H. (1962) *Curriculum Development: Theory and Practice.* New York: Harcourt, Brace and World.

Taba, H., et al. (1949) *Curriculum in Intergroup Relations: Secondary School.* Washington, DC: American Council on Education.

Taba, H., Brady, E. and Robinson, J. (1952) *Intergroup Education in Public Schools.* Washington, DC: American Council on Education.

Taba, H. and Noel, E. (1957) *Action Research: A Case Study.* Washington: Association for Supervision and Curriculum Development NEA.

Thomas, W. I. and Znaniecki, F. (1927) *The Polish Peasant in Europe and America: Monograph of an Immigrant Group.* New York: Alfred Knopf.

Thomson, J. and Smith, A. (1877) *Street Life in London.* London: Sampson, Low, Murston, Searle and Rurington.

Thorndike, R. L. and Hagen, E. (1969) *Measurement and Evaluation in Psychology and Education.* New York: John Wiley.

Tikunoff, W. J., Ward, B. and Griffin, G. (1979) *Interactive Research and Development on Teaching Study: Final Report.* San Francisco, Ca: Far West Laboratory for Educational Research and Development.

Toffler, A. (1971) *Future Shock.* London: Pan Books.

Trow, M. (1957) Comment on participant observation and interviewing: a comparison. *Human Organization,* 16:33–35.

Verduin, J. (1967) *Cooperative Curriculum Improvement.* Englewood Cliffs, NJ: Prentice Hall.

Walker, D. F. (1971) A naturalistic model for curriculum development. *School Review,* 80 , (1):51–69.

Walker, R. (1985) *Doing Research: A Handbook for Teachers.* London: Methuen.

Walker, R. and Adelman, C. (1972) *Towards a Sociography of Classrooms.* Final Report, Social Science Research Council Grant HR-996-1: The long-term observation of classroom events using stop-frame cinematography.

Walker, R. and Adelman, C. (1975) *A Guide to Classroom Observation.* London: Methuen.

Walker, R. and Weidel, J. (1985) Using photographs in a discipline of words. In

Burgess, R. G. (Ed.) *Field Methods in the Study of Education.* Lewes: East Sussex, Falmer Press, 191–216.

Wallace, M. (1987) A historical review of action research: some implications for the education of teachers in their managerial role. *Journal of Education For Teaching,* 13, (2):97–115.

Wann, K. D. (1950) *Teacher Participation in Action Research Directed Toward Curriculum Change.* New York: Teachers College, Columbia University, Bureau of Publications.

Wann, K. D. (1952) Teachers as researchers. *Educational Leadership,* 9, (May):489–495.

Webb, E., Campbell, D., Schwartz, R. and Sechrest, L. (1966) *Unobtrusive Measures: Non-Reactive Research in the Social Sciences.* Chicago: Rand McNally.

Webb, S. and Webb, B. (1932) *Methods of Social Study.* London: Longmans, Green and Co.

Weinstein, D. F. (1986) *Administrator's Guide to Curriculum Mapping: A Step by Step Manual.* Englewood Cliffs, NJ: Prentice Hall.

Whyte, W. F. and Hamilton, E. L. (1964) *Action Research for Management: A Case Report on Research and Action in Industry.* Homewood, Illinois: Dorsey Press.

Willems, E. P. and Rausch, H. L. (Eds.) (1969) *Naturalistic Viewpoints in Psychological Research.* New York: Holt, Rinehart and Winston.

Winter, R. (1982) Dilemma analysis. *Cambridge Journal of Education,* 12, (3) Michaelmas Term, 1982.

Winter, R. (1987) *Action Research and the Nature of Social Inquiry: Professional Innovation and Educational Work.* Avebury, Aldershot: Gower Publishing Co.

Winter, R. (1989) *Learning from Experience: Principles and Practice in Action-Research.* Lewes, Sussex: Falmer Press.

Wolcott, H. (1973). *The Man in the Principal's Office: An Ethnography.* New York: Holt, Rinehart and Winston.

Wood, G. (1988) Education for democratic empowerment: educating democratic educators. *Educational Foundations* 2, (3), 37–55.

Woods, P. (1986) *Inside Schools: Ethnography in Schools.* London: Routledge Education Series.

Wright, H. F. (1967) *Recording and Analysing Child Behavior.* New York: Harper and Row.

Zeichner, K. and Liston, D. P. (1987) Teaching student teachers to reflect. *Harvard Educational Review,* 57, (1), February:1–22.

Zelditch, M. (1962) Some methodological problems of field studies. *American Journal of Sociology,* 67:566–576.

Znaniecki, F. (1934) *The Method of Sociology.* New York: Farrar and Rinehart.

Zuber-Skerritt, O. (Ed.) (1991) *Proceedings of the First World Congress on Action Research, Action Learning and Process Management.* Brisbane, Queensland: Griffith University (forthcoming).

Author Index

Adelman, C. 11, 21, 23, 42, 100, 106, 188–9, 192, 200, 211
Aiken, W.M. 9
Allport, G.W. 84, 152
American Psychological Association 249
Antes, R. 108
Apple, M. 36
Aristotle 21
Atkinson, P. 93
Awbrey, M.J. 93

Bailey, K.D. 62
Bain, A. 8
Bales, R.F. 115, 118
Ball, S. 139
Barker, R.G. 7, 60, 93, 97, 99
Becker, H.S. 60, 76, 137, 139, 225–6
Beckett, S. 235
Ben-Peretz, M. 12
Berger, J. 102
Bigelow, W. 252
Biklen, S.K. 4, 15, 93, 101, 225
Bobbitt, F. 46
Bogdan, R.C. 4, 15, 93, 101, 225
Bonser, S. 22, 46
Boone, R.G. 8
Borg, W. 225
Boyer, E. 61, 115–16, 164
Bradley, L. 248
Brady, E. 10
Brandt, R.M. 67, 150
Brennan, M. 46
Bridges, D. 240
Brown, R. 17
Brownell, J.A. 44
Buchman, M. 210
Buckingham, R.B. 8, 44
Bullock, R. 43, 93
Burgess, R.G. 79, 207
Button, L. 182
Butzow, J.W. 12

Calderhead, J. 47
Campbell, D. 189
Carr, W. 4, 6, 11, 14, 24–6, 31, 215, 251
Carson, T. 12
Cassidy, A. 71, 246
Casteneda, C. 62
Cazden, C. 92
Center for New Schools 75
Chein, I. 8
Child, I. 148
Clandinin, J. 42
Clark, A.W. 3
Cohen, L. 200
Collier, J. 8
Connelly, F.M. 12, 42
Cook, S. 8
Corey, S.M. 8–10, 16, 31, 41, 236
Correll, I. 12
Coutre, J. 12
Cowie, H. 324
Crooks, T.A. 242
Cuff, E. 71, 246

Davis, E. 216
Denzin, N. 76, 93, 132, 136, 189, 192–3, 232
Dewey, J. 8, 16, 19, 31, 41, 44, 47, 170, 223

Ebbutt, D. 23, 25, 42, 75, 79
Eisner, E. 6, 207
Elliott, J. 3, 6, 11–12, 21–3, 30–33, 41–2, 44, 72, 75, 79, 105, 126, 142, 146, 188–92, 201, 211, 213, 236, 238, 252
Erickson, F. 61

Farley, J. 91
Fiske, D. 189
Flanders, N. 59, 115, 116–18, 164
Florio-Ruane, S. 210
Foucault, M. 43

Frank, A. 85
Frielich, M. 132
Friere, P. 14, 31

Gabel, D. 12
Gadamer, H.G. 6, 32
Gaden, G. 49
Gall, M. 225
Galton, M. 61, 115
Geertz, C. 59, 80
Geoffrey, W. 15, 59, 61, 93, 118
Gilbert, W.S. 142
Giroux, H. 46, 49
Glaser, B. 53, 73, 77, 148, 225–6, 228
Glasser, W. 182
Glatthorn, A.A. 76, 153, 155, 196–7
Goetz, J.L. 15, 63, 76, 93, 97, 132, 137, 140, 225
Gold, R. 62
Goodson, I. 137, 139
Goswamii, D. 43, 93
Gregory, R. 16
Griffin, G. 11–12
Gronlund, N. 68, 119, 121, 156
Grundy, S. 22, 46

Habermas, J. 6, 14, 25, 31, 43, 211, 213, 251
Hagedorn, H. 132
Hagen, E. 156
Halsey, A.H. 4
Hammersley, M. 93
Hamilton, D. 14, 93, 153, 192, 207
Hamilton, E.L. 10
Harding, J. 8
Hargreaves, D.H. 93
Heidegger, M. 43
Henry, J. 15, 93
Herr, M. 85
Herron, D. 111, 113
Hodgkinson, H.L. 10
Holly, M.L. 88
Holmes Group 47
Hook, C. 42, 84, 119, 126, 225
Hopkins, C. 108
Hopkins, D. 11–12, 15, 42, 156, 225–6, 246, 248
Hovda, R. 12
Howe, L. 182

Hoyle, E. 47, 52
Huling, L. 12
Hustler, D. 42–3, 71, 246

Illich, I. 49, 237

Jacullo-Noto, S. 12
Janesick, V. 88
Jaques, E. 10
Jenkins, D. 84, 207–9
Jenkins, F. 9

Kemmis, S. 4, 6, 11, 14, 24–6, 31, 42, 111, 126, 207, 215, 249, 251
Kerkman, D.H. 106
Kerlinger, F.N. 119, 148, 156
King, A. 44
Kinsey, A.C. 140
Kirschenbaum, H. 162
Kreeft, J. 86–7, 90
Kyle, D. 12, 236

Lang, K. 65
Lazarsfeld, P. 9, 16
LeCompte, M. 15, 63, 76, 93, 97, 132, 137, 140, 225
Lewin, K. 3, 8–10, 16–19, 31, 210
Lieberman, A. 11–12
Likert, R. 16
Lippitt, R. 8, 16, 19–20
Liston, D. 46–7
Locke, J. 189
Lomax, P. 42–3

MacDonald, B. 6
MacLaverty, B. 244
Maclean, M. 43, 93
McCurdy, D. 76
McCutcheon, G. 236
McKernan, J. 3, 8, 11, 29, 31, 36, 44, 88, 94, 97, 99, 140, 146–7, 153, 162, 165, 208, 228–30, 242–3, 247
McTaggart, R. 24–7, 42, 111, 126, 249
Manion, L. 200
Marrow, A. 9–10, 16, 19
Marsh, N. 3
Mead, M. 16
Miller, J. 93

Miller, L. 11
Mills, C.W. 252
Mohatt, G. 61
Mohr, M. 43, 93
Moreno, J.L. 156
Mulryan, C. 148–9
Munby, H. 47

Nixon, J. 11, 42, 138, 245
Noel, E. 16, 18–19
Noffke, S. 46

Oakeshott, M. 21
Oia, S.N. 12
Osborn, A.F. 169
Parlett, M. 14, 93, 153, 192, 207
Partington, D. 189
Perl, S. 93
Peters, R.S. 21, 188
Piaget, J. 68
Polyani, M. 49
Popper, K. 232
Postman, N. 177
Progoff, I. 87

Radke, M. 8, 16, 19–20
Rapoport, R.N. 4
Rausch, H.L. 93
Reid, W. 6, 21–2, 79, 239
Reitz, G.G. 9
Robottom, I. 249
Robinson, J. 10
Roby, T.W. 22
Rokeach, M. 125
Ross, D. 12
Royal Anthropological Institute of
    Great Britain and Ireland 93
Rudduck, J. 12, 41, 43, 46, 75, 82,
    179, 182, 188

Sanford, N. 10
Sarason, S. 7
Schaefer, R. 41
Schatzman, L. 73, 94, 132, 225
Schon, D. 22, 34, 47, 210
Schools Council (UK) 183
Schubert, W.H. 16, 22, 46
Schwab, J. 6, 21–22
Scriven, M. 17
Selander, S. 3, 43

Selltiz, C. 68
Shaw, C. 138
Short, E.C. 13–14
Shumsky, A. 236
Simon, A. 61, 115–16, 164
Simon, S. 182
Simons, H. 75, 249
Skilbeck, M. 21, 166, 208, 240
Smith, A. 100
Smith, B.O. 162, 164
Smith, L. 15, 59, 61, 118, 164
Smulyan, L. 12
Sockett, H.T. 39, 48, 56
Sontag, S. 101
Spradley, J.P. 76, 132, 245
Stake, R. 6, 74, 78, 81, 84
Staton, J. 89–90, 92
Stenhouse, L. 4, 6, 11, 21, 31–2,
    35, 41–4, 47–8, 75, 83, 116, 124,
    183, 188, 195, 235, 238–9, 248,
    251–2
Stillman, P. 43, 93
Strauss, A. 53, 73, 77, 94, 132,
    148, 225–6, 228, 252

Taba, H. 9–10, 16, 18–19, 31
Thomas, W.I. 138, 152
Thompson, J. 100
Thorndike, R.L. 156
Tikunoff, W.J. 11
Toffler, A. 49
Trow, M. 192

Verduin, J. 10

Walker, D.F. 22
Walker, R. 11, 22, 42, 79, 100–
    101, 105–106, 111, 126, 192,
    200
Wallace, M. 3, 8, 10
Ward, B. 11
Webb, B. 9
Webb, E. 7, 99, 138, 140, 189, 193,
    225
Webb, S. 9
Weidel, J. 101
Weingartner, C. 177
Weinstein, D.F. 148
Whyte, W.F. 10
Willems, E.P. 93

Index

Wilson, N. 93
Winter, R. 11, 42–3, 142–4, 146, 223
Wolcott, H. 15, 137–8
Wood, G. 238, 252
Woods, P. 15, 225

Wright, H. 60, 93, 97–8

Zeichner, K. 46–7
Zelditch, M. 132
Znaniecki, K. 138, 152, 232
Zuber-Skerritt, O. 11

Subject Index

Action inquiry seminar 165–8
  procedures 166
action research
  aims of 3–4
  characteristics of 30–31
  constraints on 44–5
  countenance of 31–3
  definitions of 4–5
  historical evolution 8–11
  methodology of 57–200
  models of 15–27
  premisses for 244
  rationale for 4–8
aide memoire 25–67 *see also*
  school & classroom observation
Alberta Teachers Association 12
analysis of action research data
  223–34
  stages of 226
analytic induction 232
analytic memos 72–4
anecdotal records 60, 67–70
  procedures 68–70
applied research 54
archival records 138–9
attitude scales 124–6
  procedures 124–5
audio-tape slide records 106–7
autonomy of
  inquiry 61
  practitioner 61–3

brainstorming 168–71
  definition of 168
  procedures in 170–71
  rules for 169
British Educational Research
  Association 41

Cambridge Institute of
  Education 23
Career history technique 136–9
  see also life history

caring 52
case data 82–4
case records 82–4
case study
  definition of 74
  methodology 75–82
  value of 81–2
case work
  stages in 79–81
Centre for Applied Research in
  Education (UK) 6, 23, 41
checklists 60, 108–11
  data 109
  definition 108
classroom action research network
  (CARN) 11, 41–2, 238
classroom observation 65–7
code of practice 39, 215
coding 227–8
collaboration 12, 235–9
collaborative action research for
  professional development 11–
  13, 235
collaborative networks 235
collegial review 196–9
community of discourse 40, 43,
  239–41
conceptual sampling 228
constant comparative method
  233–4
constraints
  on action research 44
  international survey 44–5
constraints analysis 146–7
content analysis 148–9
Corey-era 10–11
countenance of action research
  31–33
critical action research 4, 14, 24–
  27
critical communities 235, 239–41
critical methods 189–220
critical theory 14, 251–2

critical trialling 216–20
cultural studies 71, 88
curriculum
  concept 4, 11
  definition of 239
  research 11–12
curriculum criticism 206–10
curriculum development 35
cycles of inquiry 227–32
  editing 227
  interpretation 230
  mapping 229
  reporting 231
Deakin action research model 24–7
Deakin University 24, 42
deliberation 14
  and small working groups 179–83
dialogue 33
dialogue journal 60, 89–93
  example of 90–92
  procedures 90
diary method *see also* journal 60, 84–8
  pupil diaries 86–7
  types 85
dilemma analysis 142–6
  case example 144–6
  procedures 143–4
discourse 27, 33, 251
discourse evaluation 210–15
  procedures 212–13
discussion 171
  dyadic 175
  Socratic 175
dissemination of action research 244–9
document analysis 150–53
dyadic discussion 175

Ebbutt's model of action research 23, 25
editing 227, 246
education
  as profession 47–9
  science of 8
educational research 36
eight-year study 9
Elliott's model of action research 22–4

emancipatory action research 15, 24–7, 211
  epilogue 251–3
  episode analysis 162–5
  ethical criteria 249–50
  ethical issues 249–50
  ethnography 64, 210
  evaluation 14
  evaluative methods 189–220
  experimentalism 8–9

facilitator role in action research 241–2
fidelity analysis 214
field notes 93–7
  types 94–5
field studies 59–60
Flanders' Interaction Analysis Category System (FIAC) 115–18
Ford Teaching Project 6, 11, 21, 23, 238
Frankfurt School 6, 251

genuflecting 251
George Mason University 241
grounded theory 53
group discussion 171–5
  role of chairperson 173–4
group dynamics 9–10

handlung (action) 9
Human Relations, Journal of 10
Humanities Curriculum Project (UK) 6, 11, 21, 23, 238

illuminative evaluation 14
interaction analysis
  protocols 115–18
  critique of 117–18
interactive research and development 11–12
intergroup education 18
interview technique 129–32
  key informant interview 132–4

Journal 60, 84–8
see also diary

Kemmis model of action research 26

see also Deakin action research model 24–7
key informant interview 132–4

lecture feedback 199–200
lesson profiling 200–202
Lewin's model of action research 17–18
liberation pedagogy 14
life history technique 136–9
   types of 138
   see also career history
Lippitt–Radke action research procedure 19–20
   literary criticism 207
   logs–personal action 114–16

Massachusetts Institute of Technoogy (MIT) 10, 22
McKernan's model of action research 27–30
methodology of action research 57–200

narrative methods 59–60, 65–107
National Association for Race Relations Teaching and Action Research (UK) 11
National Science Teachers Association (USA) 12
Naturalistic perspective 6–7
naturalistic field research 6, 7
networks 236, 238
neutral chairperson technique 11, 58, 183–8
   role of chairperson 185–6
non-observational techniques 124
non-participant observation 61–2

observation 59
   advantages of 61
   non-participant 61–2
   participant 61, 63–5
   structured 60–61
observational roles 62–63

participant observation 61–5
   defined 63

guidelines for 64–5
Personal action logs 111–14
personal knowledge 49
personal time analysis technique 153–5
photography technique 100–102
   types of photographs 101
physical traces technique 140–41
   guidelines 140
positivism 31
practical action research 20–22
practical activity 21
problem survey technique 175–9
professional
   restricted 47
   extended 47–8
professional development schools 12
professionalization defined 48
professionalism
   criteria for 50–53
   defined 48
projective techniques 134–6
public records 138
pupil evaluation instrument 205–6

quadrangulation technique 192–6
   nature of 193
   procedures for 194–5
qualitative methods 7, 12–13
questionnaire technique 126–9

rating scale techniques 61, 119–23
   category ratings 119
   graphic ratings 120
   numerical ratings 120
   pictorial ratings 121
   self-ratings 122–3
rationale for action research 5–7
reflective
   teacher 53
   practitioner 46–7
   spiral 26
research
   -based practice 43
   classroom 55
   defined 4

fundamental 3
traditional 3
Research Center for Group
  Dynamics 10

school as centre for inquiry 36–8
Schools Cultural Studies Project
  (SCSP) 71, 88
science in education movement 8
scientific action research 15, 20
scientific method 8
second order action research
  241–2 *see also* facilitator
self-autonomy 52
self-report techniques 124–41
seminar technique 165–8 *see also*
  action inquiry seminar
service 51
shadow study 97 *see also*
  specimen record; stream-of-
  behaviour-chronicles
shareability 33
short action research report
  technique 70–72
skill exchanges 237–8
small working groups technique
  179–83
sociometric analysis 156–61
Socratic discussion group 175
Southern Study 9
specimen records technique 97–
  100
  defined 97 *see also* stream-of-
  behaviour chronicles; shadow
  study
stream-of behaviour chronicles
  97–100 *see also* specimen
  records; shadow study
student course evaluation
  technique 202–6
  support for projects 242
  survey techniques 124–41

Taba's model of action research

18–19
Tavistock Institute of Human
  Relations (UK) 10
teacher
  autonomy 55
  as investigator 46
  as reflective practitioner 46–47
  as reflective professional 47
  as researcher 5–6, 11, 33,
    35–56
  professionalism 48–9
teacher Pupil Interaction and
  Quality of Learning Programme
  (TIQL) 42
teaching as a profession 48, 50–53
theoretical knowledge 49
time as a constraint on action
  research 30, 37
time process model of action
  research 27–30
transcontinental ideological
  curriculum divide 56
triangulation technique 23, 189–
  93
type I models of action research
  16–20
type II models of action research
  20–23
type III models of action research
  24–7
typologies of action research 15–
  27

understanding 32, 41, 211–12
University of East Anglia 23, 41,
  238, 241
University of Ulster, Northern
  Ireland 74

video tape recording 102–6
  procedures 103–4

zygonet 41